My main objective has been to combine legal accurac ........ to all students, so I hope you will find this book both stimulating and helpful. Fully updated with recent cases and laws it is written in a lively, clear and accessible way and is designed to help students of all learning styles to understand the subject.

Although aimed at A-Level the books provide a good base for 1st Year LLB, ILEX and other courses, and can be used as self-study guides.

Each Chapter contains **examples** to help you see how the law relates to real life situations; **tasks** and **self-test questions**, to help you check your understanding, as well as **examination tips** and **application practice** to help you prepare for problem questions. Where applicable the books also contain **tips and guidance on evaluating** the law to help with essay questions. **Summaries** and **diagrams** help to make the law clear and the **'must-know' cases are highlighted**. Answers are given for the tasks and self-test questions either in the book or on my website at www.drsr.org

The 'the law explained' series offers a more in-depth coverage of individual areas with additional tasks, examples and examination practice. This means you can pick those topics for which you need more guidance (all the answers are included in the book).

**For a range of free interactive exercises please go to www.drsr.org and click on 'Free Exercises' to see what's available.**

### Other books by Sally Russell

As new books may be available by the time you read this I have not listed my other books by title. They currently include crime and tort at AS level, crime, tort and concepts of law for both the AQA and OCR examination board at A2 level and various books in 'the law explained' series. For the most up to date list of what is available please check my author's page on Amazon or visit my website at www.drsr.org. All my books are available in both Kindle and paperback format.

### About the author

Sally Russell was formerly head of law at a sixth-form college, a senior examiner for AQA and tort advisor for the Institute of Legal Executive Tutorial College. She has written various materials for both teachers and students, for Pearson Education, Hodder education and the National Extension College. She is also a regular contributor to the A-Level Law Review. For more information visit www.drsr.org

# Table of contents

This book covers OCR A2 Unit G153: Criminal Law and Unit G154: Criminal Law Special Study Unit and is divided into seven study blocks. The chapters within each study block contain the main points of law with case examples, food for thought' boxes with key criticisms, and examination tips. There are also tasks and self-test questions, designed to help you check your understanding. Tasks will sometimes ask you to jot down a few thoughts for use in an essay question, so keep these for revision. For answers to the tasks and self-test questions, please go to my website at www.drsr.org and click the button 'Answers to tasks'. For a range of **free interactive exercises**, click on 'Free Exercises' and then the OCR book.

The book has been designed to match the OCR syllabus for A2, but also provides a sound base for 1st Year LLB, ILEX and other courses.

Criminal cases are usually in the form *R v the defendant*. It is quite acceptable just to use the name so if the case is **R v Miller** I have called it **Miller**. If another form is used e.g., **DPP v Miller** then I have used the full title.

Civil cases are between the *claimant* and the *defendant*, however you will still see the use of the word *'plaintiff'* in quotes from older cases heard before 1999. Other than in quotes, I have used the word claimant throughout the book.

A final point: if you are confused by a case, or you see cases which conflict, don't despair. Just say to yourself, 'I can use that in an essay question when asked for a critique of the law'. If there is confusion or uncertainty then there will be a valid case for arguing that the law is not fully satisfactory or does not achieve justice.

**The examination**

Since 2014 there is only one examination session, in June. The substantive law paper (Unit G153) is a two-hour examination worth 120 marks. It contains **three** sections. You must answer one question from Section A (out of 3 essay questions), one from Section B (out of 3 problem questions), and one from Section C (out of 2 'dilemma' questions,). The essays will require an evaluation of the law. They are often in the form of a comment which you are asked to discuss critically. The problem questions require you to apply the law to a given scenario. The dilemma questions are aimed at testing your reasoning skills and ask you to evaluate the accuracy of some given statements as they apply to the facts of a scenario. An example of each type of question, together examination guidance, is provided at the end of the criminal law section. Note that both Sections A and B are 50 marks each, whereas Section C is only 20 marks. Be sure to plan your time accordingly.

What you need for problem and dilemma questions and what you need for essays cannot be divided completely but there is a difference. For each, it is important to know and understand cases well. Problem questions require you to use the current legal tests, which come from cases. Some crimes (including murder) are common law offences so *all* the law comes from cases, and even if the law comes from a statute, that statute has to be *interpreted* by judges. **Key cases** are used to highlight those which are particularly important. You can then apply only the law that is both current and relevant to the given facts – if you ask a solicitor for advice, they won't tell you everything they know, they will pick out the law that suits your case. You have to do the same in a problem question. Don't write down everything you know just to prove that you have learnt it. Being selective is a skill in itself and will be credited. Use the *examination pointers* and **key cases**, plus the *diagrams* or *summaries* at the end of each chapter as a guide for problem questions. An answer to a problem scenario should be rounded off with a conclusion as to liability. So the best approach is to identify the appropriate area of law, apply the relevant rules, consider whether a defence is available and conclude along the lines of "D could therefore be guilty of..., but may be successful in pleading the defence of ..."

The essay questions require more discussion and evaluation of the law. The **Food for Thought** sections are designed to help with this, and a summary including **key criticisms** is found at the end of each Study Block. I have included an example essay question in the summary for each Study Block to give you an idea of the type of thing you will get.

The dilemma questions require you to analyse legal material, identify the particular issues, and apply the appropriate legal rules and principles to a short scenario. You can get full marks without cases and/or statutory provisions but if you do use any you will need to be selective, using only those that are relevant to the specific issue raised by the given statements.

The Special Study Unit (Unit G154) requires you to relate the law that you have learnt on a particular area (the substantive law) to how the law has developed through precedent, statutory interpretation and the proposals of the Law Commission. The 'Food for Thought' boxes are designed to help with this, as well as the summaries including key criticisms at the end of each Study Block. A brief guide to connecting the substantive law to the development is also given in these summaries. This is merely a taster to get you thinking about the Special Study Unit as you go along. The areas of law-covered in this Unit change each year so Study Chapter 22 contains a general guide on how to approach this paper, along with further examination guidance and practice. More information on the specific content each year, along with examination papers and mark schemes, are available on the OCR website www.ocr.org.uk

## Assessment objectives and levels

For both G153 and G154 there are three assessment objectives which the examiners will follow when marking. In brief these are:

> *A01 – Knowledge and understanding of legal rules and principles – 38% of the overall mark*

> *A02 – Ability to analyse and evaluate legal rules and principles – 53% of the overall mark*

> *A03 – Ability to produce a logical and coherent argument in a clear and precise way – 9% of the overall mark*

To reach Level 5 (the top level) you should show:

> *A01 – A wide-ranging and accurate knowledge with clear understanding of the relevant concepts and principles, with reference to relevant cases and statute law*

> *A02 – An ability to identify and evaluate particular criticisms of the law, including current debate and proposals for reform where appropriate. A high level of ability to develop arguments or apply points of law accurately and pertinently to a given factual situation, and reach a logical conclusion*

> *A03 – A logical and coherent approach, this mark depends on the above two so the higher the A01 and A02 mark, the higher the A03.*

## Examination tip

When studying precedent you learnt that the important part of a case is the *ratio decidendi*, the reasoning behind the judge's decision. As you read a case, think about this and look for the legal principle. Learn to summarise the facts in a few words. This can be valuable when it comes to exams and time is short. Never be tempted to write all you know about an area, you will not be credited for irrelevant stuff even if it is correct.

It is important to:

*explain a case briefly but show that you understand the principle*

*show that you understand the law well enough to be selective*

**DO BOTH!**

**Chapter 1:** *Actus reus*: Acts, omissions and causation

**Chapter 2:** *Mens rea*

**Chapter 3:** Strict liability

In order to establish liability in criminal law the prosecution must prove, beyond reasonable doubt, all the components which are contained in the definition of the particular offence. That definition may come from a statute or from the common law.

Most offences are made up of two elements, known by the Latin terms *actus reus* and *mens rea*. The prosecution must prove that the accused committed the criminal act (*actus reus*) with the necessary state of mind (*mens rea*).

The first two Chapters will provide you with a firm foundation on which to build when you come to particular offences. For example, in murder and manslaughter, D must have caused death, and causation is part of the *actus reus* of many crimes. *Mens rea* is also important because this element of the crime is the difference between murder and manslaughter. When you come to the chapters on murder and manslaughter, you will be familiar with many of the cases because they have been used to illustrate the first two chapters.

**Example**

Jane picks up a knife and stabs Jenny, who dies. Jane has the *actus reus* of murder as her act has caused Jenny's death. She also has the *mens rea* because she intended to kill, or at least seriously harm, her. If she did not intend to kill or seriously injure Jenny should would not be guilty of murder but of manslaughter.

A few offences do not require *mens rea* to be proved. These are called strict liability offences and are dealt with in Chapter 3.

> *"... there was gross and criminal negligence, as the man was paid to keep the gate shut and protect the public ... a man might incur criminal liability from a duty arising out of a contract".*
>
> *Wright J*

By the end of this Chapter, you should be able to:

**Explain actus reus in relation to acts, omissions and circumstances**

**Explain how actus reus may involve consequences**

**Illustrate how causation is proved by reference to cases**

**Identify possible criticisms**

## What makes an action criminal?

As noted above, the prosecution must prove D committed the criminal act (*actus reus*) with the necessary state of mind (*mens rea*). Only when both are present is there a crime (except for strict liability crimes, discussed in Chapter 3). *Mens rea* involves the state of mind of D at the time of the offence and we will deal with this in Chapter 2. First, we will look at *actus reus* which involves everything else, i.e., all the different elements of a crime except the mental element.

## Example

Murder is the unlawful killing of a human being with intent. The mental element is the intent, everything else is part of the *actus reus* so the prosecution need to show the act was unlawful, there was a death (killing means someone dies) and it was of a human being.

Although in simple terms *actus reus* means a guilty act or wrongful conduct, there is more to it than this. It may include:

**conduct (an act or omission which is voluntary)**

**circumstances**

**a consequence (which is caused by D's conduct)**

In my example the conduct is the act of killing, the circumstances are that it is unlawful and of a human being, and the consequence is the death which must have been caused by D's actions.

It is very important to identify each element of the *actus reus* of a crime because there can be no crime unless the *actus reus* is complete. This does not necessarily mean D will be acquitted. If part of the *actus reus* of an offence is not proved then *that* offence is not committed, but there may well be a connected offence or an attempt.

## Conduct

As a rule, the conduct must be voluntary. This is seen in **Leicester V Pearson 1952** where a car driver was prosecuted for failing to give precedence to a pedestrian on a zebra crossing. It was shown that his car had been pushed onto it by another car hitting him from behind. He was acquitted. He had not acted voluntarily. (Another example of involuntary acts will be looked at under General Defences: automatism.)

Conduct can consist of an act, an omission, or a state of affairs. An **act** is usually straight forward, e.g., hitting someone. An **omission** is a failure to act. In criminal law, this will not usually make you guilty unless you have a duty to act in the first place. An example is failing to look after your child. A **state of affairs** is where you can commit an offence by just being in a certain state, e.g., 'being *drunk* in charge of a motor vehicle'.

### Act or omission?

In **Fagan v Metropolitan Police Commissioner 1969**, D accidentally drove onto a policeman's foot whilst parking. He didn't move his car when asked; in fact, he used some fairly colourful language which I will not repeat here. He was promptly arrested for, and convicted of, assaulting a police officer in the execution of his duty. He argued that there was no *mens rea* at the time of the act (driving onto his foot) and that the refusal to move was only an omission, not an act. The court held that there was a *continuing act* which started with the driving onto the policeman's foot and continued up to the refusal to move. Thus, not moving when asked to was part of the original act rather than an omission. At this time, he did have *mens rea*. This is one way in which a judge can interpret the law to suit the case. Having decided that this type of assault could not be committed by omission, the CA used the idea of a continuing act to overcome the problem. This case also reaffirms the point that *actus reus* and *mens rea* must be contemporaneous (i.e., coincide or happen at the same time).

A case illustrating the distinction between an act and an omission is **Airedale NHS Trust v Bland 1993**. Tony Bland, who was 17, had been badly injured in the Hillsborough football stadium disaster. He was in what is called a persistent vegetative state and had no hope of recovery. The family and doctors wanted to turn off the life support machine. The HL confirmed a court order allowing this. They drew a distinction between a positive act that killed (such as administering a lethal injection) which could never be lawful, and an omission to act which allowed someone to die (e.g., not providing life-saving treatment).

The cases of **Diane Pretty** and **Ms B** in **2002** also illustrate this distinction. In the first, Mrs Pretty wanted her husband to help her commit suicide and took her case to the HL and then the European Court of Human Rights. She wanted a court order that he would not be prosecuted for assisting her suicide. She failed, as this would be a positive act. In the latter case, Ms B wanted treatment discontinued and succeeded in obtaining a court order to allow this, even though it meant she would die.

So, there is generally no criminal liability for *not* doing something. However, exceptions occur when there is a duty to act.

### Omissions as actus reus in duty situations

A duty can occur when:

**Parliament has expressly provided for it by statute**

**there is a contractual duty**

**a relationship of responsibility gives rise to a common law duty**

**D has created a dangerous situation.**

In these cases, an omission to act is enough.

### Example

You see someone drowning and are a good swimmer but you leave them to die. You are not guilty of any crime. However, as I said above there are exceptions. I will come back to this as we look at the exceptions.

### Statutory duty to act

An example is the **Road Traffic Act 1988,** which makes it an offence for a driver involved in a road accident to fail to stop and give a name and address when asked, or to fail to report the accident to the police. There is a duty to stop, and to report the accident, so failing to do so (an omission) is part of the *actus reus* of each of these offences.

### Contractual duty to act

In **Pittwood 1902**, D was employed as a gate-keeper by a railway company. His job was to keep the gate at the crossing shut whenever a train passed. One day he forgot to close the gate. A hay cart crossed the track and was hit by an oncoming train. One person was killed and another seriously injured. D was under a contractual duty of employment to keep the gates to the crossing shut and to safeguard people using the crossing. His failure to act was in breach of his contractual duty and so amounted to the *actus reus* of manslaughter. The quote at the beginning came from this case.

*In my example, if you were a lifeguard you would have a contractual duty to act so could be liable.*

Similar to this is a duty where you hold a public office. Thus in **Dytham 1979** a policeman who failed to act when he saw D kicking someone to death was liable. Here though, he was not guilty of homicide, only of misconduct in a public office.

### Relationship of responsibility

In **Stone and Dobinson 1977**, a couple had a relative (Fanny) come and live with them. She was anorexic, and often took to her bed for days at a time, refusing food and any other form of assistance. Her condition seriously deteriorated and after inadequate efforts to obtain medical assistance, she was found dead in her bed. The court held that Stone and Dobinson had undertaken the duty of caring for her and they had been grossly negligent in their failure to fulfil their duty. This failure had caused Fanny's death and so they were guilty of manslaughter.

*In my example, if you were the parent of the swimmer or if you had taken on responsibility for the swimmer, as with Dobinson, you would have a duty to act, so could be liable.*

### Creating a dangerous situation

In **Miller 1983**, D was squatting in an unoccupied house. One night he fell asleep whilst smoking. When he awoke he realised he'd set fire to the mattress but did nothing to extinguish it, he merely moved to another room. The house caught fire and damage was caused. He was convicted of arson under s1 **Criminal Damage Act 1971**. The HL upheld his conviction on the basis that if a defendant has unintentionally caused an event, and then realises what has happened, he has a duty to take appropriate action.

*In my example, if you pushed them in, you created the dangerous situation so have a duty to take appropriate action. Again, you could be liable.*

### Task

Compare **Fagan** and **Miller**. Could Miller have been found guilty on the 'continuing act' theory?

## State of affairs

A few crimes can be committed without any apparent voluntary act by the accused. In **Larsonneur 1933**, a Frenchwoman was deported against her will from Ireland and brought to England by the police. She was convicted under the **Aliens Order 1920** of being found in the UK without permission. The state of affairs amounting to the *actus reus* was 'being found', so as soon as she landed in the UK without the required permission she committed the offence. This law has since been repealed but a similar situation is seen in **Winzar v Chief Constable of Kent 1983**. A drunk was told to leave a hospital and refused. He was removed by the police who put him in their car, which was parked on the highway. The police then arrested him for being found drunk on the highway, for which he was later convicted. The state of 'being found' was again enough. So we can see that 'state of affairs' crimes can occur where something which is normally legal may not be so in certain circumstances. Being drunk is legal, but being drunk 'on the highway' or drunk 'in charge of a motor vehicle', (a state of affairs) is not.

### Food for Thought

Think about whether there should be liability for omissions. Use the above cases to support your arguments. There is no 'right' answer. It can be argued that there is a moral duty to act if it will save a life, consider whether there should also be a legal duty. Do you think the court made the right decision in the Tony Bland case? It can be said that turning off the machine was an act, but the court viewed it as an omission. On the other hand in **Fagan** it could be said there was only an omission but the court found a 'continuing act'. Do you think judges have too much discretion, e.g., to distinguish precedents? Is it better to have certainty in the law or to ensure justice is done in a particular case?

Also the 'state of affairs' cases can be criticised. One of the arguments for imposing liability without having to prove fault is that it saves lengthy investigations and court time, but is it fair to D? Should someone be convicted just for being in the wrong place at the wrong time as in **Winzar** and **Larsonneur**? Compare these cases to **Leicester V Pearson 1952**.

### Circumstances

Many crimes are committed only if the conduct is carried out in particular circumstances. The *actus reus* of theft is the appropriation (taking) of property belonging to another. 'Appropriation' is the conduct, that it is 'property' and 'belongs to another' are both circumstances. *All* these must be proved or it is not theft. Many of the offences against the person have the word 'unlawful' in their definition. This means, for example, that If D acted in self-defence then in these circumstances the act is not unlawful, so the *actus reus* is not satisfied.

### Task

Make a separate folder for the more detailed material you need for essays. As you read cases start to question what is satisfactory – or not – about the law and add your thoughts to the folder. Look out for articles from newspapers or law journals on any of the issues you are discussing. Cut them out and put them in the folder, adding a few of your own comments.

## Consequences and causation

Crimes where a particular consequence is part of the *actus reus* are called **result crimes**. Murder is an example. For a murder conviction death must result from D's act. Homicide is the unlawful killing of a human being. The *actus reus* involves not just killing (conduct) but also that it is unlawful and of a human being (circumstances) and that death occurs (the consequence).

*Note that the difference between murder and manslaughter is the mens rea not the actus reus and the word homicide applies to both.*

As well as the consequence itself, it must be proved that D's act *caused* this consequence. Causation is an important issue in many crimes.

Many of the cases on causation involve a homicide because it is a result crime. As causation is also relevant to other crimes it is dealt with here rather than with a particular offence, but you will see many of these cases again when we deal with the specific offences. The prosecution must prove causation both **factually** and **legally**.

### Factual causation: sine qua non

Factual causation is traditionally referred to as the *'sine qua non'* rule. This phrase is defined in Chambers as 'an indispensable condition'. It means D's action must be a *'sine qua non'* or an 'indispensable condition' of the result. More simply put, the result would not have occurred without D's action. It is more commonly called the 'but for' test. The prosecution must show that 'but for' D's conduct, the victim would not have died (or been injured).

### Key case

In **White 1910**, D put cyanide in a drink intending to kill his mother, who was found dead shortly afterwards with the drink 3 parts full. In fact, the mother had died of a heart attack unconnected with the poison. The son was found not guilty of murder. He had the *mens rea* (he intended to kill her) but not the *actus reus* (his act didn't cause her death). He didn't get away with it altogether though; he was guilty of attempted murder.

**White** illustrates the situation where D's act has *not* factually caused death. Any of the following cases on legal causation could also be used for illustrating causation in fact. As you read them, ask the question 'but for D's act would the victim have died/been injured?' If the answer is 'no' then causation in fact is shown. Causation in fact can be very wide.

### Example

I ask a college student to stay on for half an hour to finish a project. She therefore misses her bus and walks home. On the way she is attacked and injured. It can be argued that 'but for' my asking her to stay late she would not have been attacked and so I should be liable for her injury. To avoid such a wide liability the courts have built up some rules on how far someone should be liable for the consequences of their actions. This is causation in law.

### Legal causation: chain of causation

This is based on what is called the 'chain of causation'. It means proving an unbroken link, or chain, between D's action and the end result, for example death in homicide cases. When something has occurred after D's original act, then it may be argued that the chain of causation is broken. We will look at some cases to explain how this works, but in summary; the chain of causation will not be broken if:

**D's action makes a 'significant' contribution to the result (Smith/Cheshire)**

**any intervening act was foreseeable (Roberts)**

**the victim has a particular weakness and the result would not have occurred in a normal person. This is known as the 'thin skull' rule (Blaue)**

In my example, I will argue that the chain has been broken by the attacker. I did not make a significant contribution to the harm, and the attack was not foreseeable. I have not legally caused the injuries.

## Task

Use my example above but this time apply it to the attacker. Decide whether the attacker legally caused death in the following situations:

1. The attacker left her badly injured and lying in the road. She is run over by a car and killed.

2. The attacker left her badly injured but a passer-by stops and calls an ambulance. She is taken to hospital and starts to recover. However the treatment is wrong and she dies.

3. She was only slightly injured but (not a good day!) she is struck by lightning as she recovers from the attack.

We will come back to this, but first we'll look at some cases.

In **Smith1959**, a soldier stabbed in a fight was dropped twice on the way to the treatment centre and then left untreated for some time. Although the court recognised that this contributed to the death they found Smith, who had stabbed him, guilty of murder. As Lord Parker LCJ put it, his act was "still an operating cause and a substantial cause" of the death. A case where D's act was *not* found to have caused the death in similar circumstances is **Jordan 1956**. Here the stab wounds were healing well, but the doctor gave the victim treatment which caused an allergic reaction from which he died. The doctor's act was found to have broken the chain of causation. It is more likely that **Smith** will be followed nowadays, as in the next case.

## Key case

In **Cheshire 1991**, due to negligent treatment by the hospital, complications arose after an operation on the victim of a shooting. The victim subsequently died. The person accused of the murder argued that his act had not caused the death of the victim, the hospital had done so. The court rejected the argument, following **Smith**. They said that as long as D's action was a 'significant and operative' cause of the death it need not be the sole cause. The jury should not regard hospital treatment as excluding D's responsibility unless it "was so **independent of his acts,** and in itself so **potent in causing death,** that they regard the contribution made by his acts as insignificant."

This principle was followed by the CA in **Mellor 1996.** An elderly man was taken to hospital following an attack in which he suffered broken ribs and other injuries. He died from bronchial-pneumonia brought on by his injuries. The hospital had failed to give him oxygen which may have saved him. The words 'operating' (**Smith**) and 'operative' (**Cheshire**) are used in the sense of 'still having an effect on', and the injuries were still having an effect, so D's conviction for murder was upheld. It is clear from these cases that the courts are reluctant to allow medical treatment to break the chain of causation and thus prevent D being found guilty of the killing.

In **Pagett 1983** D armed himself with a shotgun and took a pregnant girl hostage in a flat. Armed police called on him to come out. He eventually did so, holding the girl in front of him as a human shield. He then fired the shotgun at the police officers who returned fire, killing the girl hostage. The actions of the police did not break the chain because shooting back at D was held to be a 'natural consequence' of his having shot first. D was convicted of manslaughter.

**Key Case**

In **Roberts 1971**, D – in a moving car – committed an assault on the victim by trying to take off her coat. She jumped out and was injured. He was charged with actual bodily harm. The court had to decide whether the assault caused the injury, or whether her actions broke the chain of causation. It was held that only if it was something that no reasonable person could foresee would the chain of causation be broken by the victim's actions. Here this was not the case so he was liable for her injuries. This means a magistrate or jury may take into account that the victim may do the wrong thing on the spur of the moment.

It was recognised in **Roberts** that V may do the wrong thing in the agony of the moment. In **Williams & Davis 1992** the CA said that only if V does something "so daft or unexpected" that no reasonable person could be expected to foresee it, would the chain of causation be broken. In **Corbett 1996,** the victim was trying to escape an attack by D, when he fell and was hit by a car. V died so it was a homicide case, but the same principle applies. His action came within a foreseeable range of consequences so did not break the chain.

Before looking at the final rule on causation what did you decide in the task? Remember legal causation turns on how significant a contribution the attack made and whether the 'intervening act' (the car, the hospital treatment or the lightning) was foreseeable. You can therefore ask:

> **Whether it is foreseeable that a car will come along and hit her – yes, she is lying in the road. The chain is not broken by the car.**

> **Whether it is foreseeable that hospital treatment may be inappropriate – yes, it happens enough for it to be foreseeable. The chain is not broken by the hospital treatment.**

> **Whether it is foreseeable that she is struck by lightning – not likely; it is very rare. Also, as she was only slightly injured the attack did not make a significant contribution to her death. The chain is broken by the lightning.**

Note that in the last one this does not mean the attacker gets off completely. He will still be liable for the attack, but not the death.

**The 'thin skull' rule**

This appears to be an exception to the 'foreseeability' rule. The term a 'thin skull' means something which makes V more vulnerable than other people. If a particular disability in the victim means that they are more likely to be harmed, or die, D is still liable. As Lawton LJ said in the case below, "those who use violence on other people must take their victims as they find them".

**Key case**

This comment was made by in **Blaue 1975.** He went on to say "This in our judgement means the whole man, not just the physical man". The victim was stabbed repeatedly and rushed to hospital where doctors said she needed a blood transfusion to save her life. She was a Jehovah's Witness and so refused to have one. She consequently died. D was convicted of manslaughter; her refusal of treatment did not break the chain of causation because he had to take his victim as he found her. The 'disability' is more often physical (like a pre-existing medical condition such as a 'thin skull') but here it was the fact that she was a Jehovah's Witness.

### Food for thought

If you were on the jury would you know what acts should be considered 'independent' or 'potent' enough to break the causation chain? How significant is significant? What amounts to a 'daft' act by the victim? There may be a thin line between doing 'something wrong in the agony of the moment' and doing something 'daft'. Also, consider whether the thin skull rule is fair to D, who is unaware of any vulnerability in the victim.

### Examination pointer: problem questions

In a problem question look out for anything that D can argue broke the chain. For example, D attacks someone and as they are running away they are hit by a car or bus. **Roberts** can be used to say that this is unlikely to break the chain. Look out for words like 'near the road' or 'in the bus station'. These suggest it is foreseeable. If V refuses treatment you may need the 'thin-skull' rule. Here look out for the reason. If it is a completely idiotic decision then **Blaue** may be distinguished, if it is due to religious beliefs it will be followed.

### Examination pointer: evaluation questions

All the matters 'food for thought' discussions are ones which can be discussed in an essay, using the cases to illustrate what you say. There are usually valid arguments on both sides so don't strive to write what you think examiners want to see; they will be much more impressed with a balanced argument. Have an opinion, but look at the issue from the other point of view too, this shows you have considered the arguments before reaching your own opinion.

### Summary

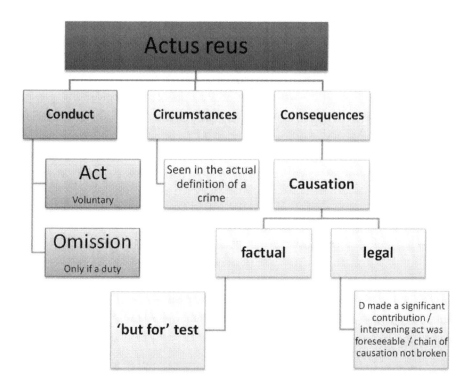

**Task**

Draw a diagram like the one above for your files. Add a case to each of the principles and keep it as a revision guide.

**Self-test questions**

*What '3 Cs' may be included in the actus reus of a crime?*

*On what basis did the court find liability in Fagan?*

*Give 2 examples of when an omission can result in criminal liability.*

*What is the thin skull rule?*

*From which case did the opening quote come?*

For answers to the tasks and self-test questions, please go to my website at www.drsr.org and click the button 'Answers to tasks'. For a range of free interactive exercises, click on 'Free Exercises' and then the OCR book.

"I attach great importance to the search for a direction which is both clear and simple ... I think that the **Nedrick** direction fulfils this requirement admirably"

*Lord Hope*

By the end of this Chapter, you should be able to:

> *Explain the term mens rea*
>
> *Explain how the law on mens rea has developed and how it applies in practice*
>
> *Identify possible criticisms*

*Mens rea* basically means a guilty mind and refers to the state of mind of the accused at the time the *actus reus* is committed. Thus *mens rea* and *actus reus* must exist at the same time.

There are 2 **main** types of *mens rea*. These are:

> **Intention**
>
> **Recklessness**

Other types of *mens rea* can be seen in particular offences. **Knowledge** comes into many of the property offences, as does **dishonesty**. **Gross negligence** is the *mens rea* for one type of manslaughter only, which we will also look at later with the specific offence.

It is important to be able to identify both the *actus reus* and the *mens rea* of each offence when answering a problem question. Each and every part of a crime has to be proved beyond reasonable doubt.

Crimes are sometimes divided into 'specific intent' and 'basic intent' offences. This can seem misleading, as basic intent offences don't require intent to be proved. Essentially, specific intent crimes are those requiring a *mens rea* of intention and nothing less. Basic intent crimes are those where the *mens rea* is intention *or* recklessness. Don't worry about this for now. It is mainly relevant to the defence of intoxication, and is discussed with this defence.

## Intention

This is the highest form of *mens rea*. It applies to, e.g., theft and murder. The *mens rea* of theft is intention to deprive someone of property permanently. If it can be shown that the property was taken absent-mindedly, D can argue that there was no *mens rea*.

## Example

You borrow your friend's mobile 'phone because you have run out of credit. You forget to give it back. You have no *mens rea* so are not guilty of theft. If you borrowed it, took it home and put your own SIM card into it, this would be evidence that you intended to deprive your friend of it permanently. In these circumstances you could be guilty of theft. Think of your own example and make a note now.

A case example is **Madeley 1990**. The host of the *Richard and Judy* television show was charged with shoplifting. He was able to show that he was suffering from stress and merely forgot to pay for the goods. The court accepted his argument and found him not guilty.

The *mens rea* for murder is an intention to kill or seriously injure someone. Many cases dealing with intention are homicide cases. This is because it is essentially the *mens rea* that differentiates murder from manslaughter. It is only murder where the killing is intentional. Intention can be direct or oblique (indirect).

### Direct Intent

Direct intent is where the result is D's aim or purpose. This is what most of us would understand by intention. If you pick up a loaded gun and fire it at someone with the aim of killing them it can be said without any difficulty that you intended to do so. Intention was defined in **Mohan 1975** as 'a decision to bring about [the prohibited consequence] no matter whether the accused desired that consequence or not'.

### Oblique intent

The courts have given intention a wider meaning, to include oblique, or indirect, intent. This is where the consequence isn't the aim but is 'virtually certain' to occur as a result of D's actions.

### Example

One night, two animal rights activists set fire to a shop which sells fur coats. The shop is closed but a security guard dies in the fire. Are they guilty of murder? They do not have the *mens rea* of *direct* intent, as their purpose is to make a political point, not to kill. They may have *oblique* intent. This will depend on the evidence. We will come back to this. For now, just make a note of what you think.

The issue of intent has been problematic. S8 **Criminal Justice Act 1967** provides that the jury *"shall not be bound in law to infer that D intended or foresaw a result of his actions by reason only of its being a natural and probable consequence of those actions"*. It also requires the jury to refer to *"all the evidence, drawing such inferences from the evidence as appear proper in the circumstances"*.

### Example

Don fires a gun. The bullet kills someone. So, according to **s 8** what do the jury have to do?

The first bit means that just because it's likely to happen, it does not mean that the jury should infer that D intended it to happen. If Don fired into a crowded room, the jury may think death is a likely result, but this is *not enough by itself* to *prove* that Don intended it.

The second bit means that the jury must look at everything else. Where did it happen? What time of day was it? Did Don know there were people about? This will help them to decide what Don 'intended'. There is a difference between firing a gun into the air in the middle of an empty field and doing the same thing in a schoolroom. Even in the latter case, it may be that the school is closed and Don is the caretaker shooting at a rat not realising anyone is about. There is no answer that's always going to be right. That's what juries are for.

There has been a long line of cases on intent. Words like 'foreseeable', 'probable', 'likely' and 'natural' have all been used along the way. In **Smith 1960**, the HL had said that whether a result was probable was an objective test (what the reasonable person would "contemplate as the natural and probable result"). S8 makes the test subjective, whether the *defendant* saw it as probable. In **Hyam v DPP 1975**, a woman poured petrol through the letterbox of a rival and set fire to it. Two children died. She argued that she had only intended to frighten the other woman. The HL rejected her appeal but made clear the test was subjective. It was whether *she* saw the result as 'highly probable'. However, they also suggested that this was proof of intent, not just evidence of it. This point was rejected in **Moloney 1985**. It is now only a matter of evidence, not proof in itself.

In **Moloney**, D and his stepfather were having a drunken competition to see who could load and draw a shotgun the quickest. D won, and his stepfather said 'I didn't think you've got the guts, but if you have, pull the trigger.' D said he didn't aim the gun but just pulled the trigger. His murder conviction was quashed. The judge had directed the jury that they could find intent if D foresaw the result as 'probable' and the HL said that this was not enough; it needed to be a certainty. Lord Bridge gave an explanation of intent in terms of 'moral certainty'. However, in his later summing up he said that a consequence was 'virtually certain' if it was a 'natural consequence', hardly the same thing at all. Many 'natural' consequences are far from certain. Death from a lightning strike is a natural consequence of a storm, but not very likely – let alone certain!

In **Hancock and Shankland 1986**, two striking miners had pushed concrete blocks off a bridge to prevent a miner going to work. They said they only intended to scare him, but the driver of the taxi in which he was travelling was killed. Their conviction for murder was quashed. Both the CA and HL held that 'natural consequence' was misleading and that even awareness of the consequence as 'virtually certain' was only evidence and not proof of intent.

The law on oblique intent was clarified somewhat by the HL in **Woollin 1998**, which confirmed the direction given by the CA in **Nedrick 1986**.

### The 2 key cases: Nedrick 1986 and Woollin 1998

In **Nedrick**, D poured paraffin through V's letterbox, circumstances not unlike those in **Hyam**, and set it alight. He said he only intended to scare her, but her child died in the resulting fire. He was convicted of murder and appealed on the basis of lack of *mens rea*. The CA quashed his conviction because the jury had not been properly directed on intent. A conviction for manslaughter was substituted. The court provided a standard direction for the jury as to intent in a murder trial in all cases of oblique intent. Lord Lane said,

*"The jury should be directed that they are not entitled to infer the necessary intention unless they feel sure that death or serious bodily harm was a **virtual certainty** (barring some unforeseen intervention) as a result of the defendant's actions and that **the defendant appreciated** that such was the case ... The decision is one for the jury to be reached on a consideration of all the evidence."*

The opening quote comes from the HL in **Woollin**. A father was convicted of murder after throwing his baby son across the room in a fit of temper. He argued that he had thrown the baby towards his pram but had not intended to kill him. His conviction was again substituted for one of manslaughter, this time by the HL. They confirmed the **Nedrick** direction. Thus, for murder, the two questions the jury must consider are:

**was death or serious bodily harm a virtual certainty?**

**did the defendant appreciate that such was the case?**

If the answer to both these questions is 'yes' then the jury may find intent. Although the HL used the word 'find' instead of 'infer', this seems of little import.

One other point. In some appeal cases you may feel that the jury would have found intent. You could well be right. Many appeals are allowed because the jury was misdirected, not necessarily because intent could not be proved. The jury may have found sufficient evidence of intent, but were not directed correctly on the law.

**Back to our example**

If the defence can show that the two activists thought the shop was empty then the jury are unlikely to be convinced they appreciated that anyone's death or serious injury was a virtual certainty. They could be convicted of manslaughter but not murder. If the prosecution can prove that they knew there was a guard on duty this will be evidence for the jury that they did appreciate that death or serious injury was a virtual certainty, so a conviction for murder is possible.

I have made both **Nedrick** and **Woollin** 'Key cases' because the law was *established* by the CA in **Nedrick**, but *confirmed* by the HL in **Woollin**, and a precedent carries greater weight once the HL has approved it. Also, the **Nedrick** test has not been followed consistently. In **Walker and Hayles 1990,** although the CA held the test to be correct, they said that the use of the phrase 'a very high degree of probability' sufficed. More confusion! In **Woollin** itself there was some confusion in the CA as to the application of the test (perhaps caused by the **Walker** decision). The Law Commission produced a report and **Draft Code,** in which it gave a definition of intent, between the cases of **Nedrick** and **Woollin**. There was therefore some doubt as to whether, if a case reached the HL, the LC's definition would be preferred to the **Nedrick** one. Apparently not.

### Food for thought: Intention

The **Draft Code** definition is that D acts intentionally with respect to a result *"when he acts either in order to bring it about or being aware that it will occur in the ordinary course of events"*. In **Woollin**, Lord Steyn referred to the **Draft Code** but thought the **Nedrick** test was "very similar". It is arguable that the HL should have adopted this if they thought it so similar. It seems quite clear and would become the law if the **Code** were ever adopted.

The test was followed again in **Matthews and Alleyne 2003**. The Ds had thrown V from a bridge into a river. He drowned. There was evidence that he had told them he couldn't swim. They appealed against their conviction for murder. The CA rejected their appeal but again said that foresight of death as a virtual certainty does not automatically prove intent, it is merely evidence (often very strong evidence) for the jury.

In **Stringer 2008**, D appealed against his convictions for both murder and arson with intent to endanger life. A fire had been started at the bottom of the stairs in his house, where several of his family were sleeping, his brother died. He had denied starting the fire. At the time he was 14 and had a low IQ. The CA accepted that when directing the jury on the question of intent based on **Woollin**, the judge did not make clear the distinction between the two parts of the test (the inevitability of death or injury, and D's appreciation of it). However, on the facts, there could be only one answer to the question whether it was a virtual certainty that somebody would suffer death or serious injury from a fire in these circumstances. As to the second part of the test, even taking account of his age and low IQ, *"the inference that he must have appreciated it on that morning was also overwhelming. The jury's conclusion that [he] had the necessary intent was bound to follow"*. So firstly, death or serious injury was a virtual certainty, and secondly, he must have appreciated that this was the case. He therefore had indirect intent.

### Examination pointer

When applying the law you need only use **Nedrick** and **Woollin,** and only then in cases of oblique intent, not where it is direct. This was made clear in **Woollin**. D's knowledge will be an important factor. Look carefully at the facts for information such as 'they knew that ..........' or 'unknown to them ............'. These comments will help you to apply the test as in my example.  The cases leading up to **Woollin** would be useful for an essay question on either *mens rea* or murder generally.  A summary of these follows.

**Summary of the development of the law on intent**

| Summary of the development of the law on intent | | | |
|---|---|---|---|
| Case | Development | Probable, possible or certain? | Objective / subjective Proof or evidence |
| DPP v Smith 1960 | HL held that the *mens rea* for murder is intention to kill or cause grievous bodily harm | Foresight of death or serious injury as a natural and probable result | Objective (what the 'reasonable man or woman' would contemplate) |
| Hyam 1974 (similar facts to Nedrick) | Changed to a subjective test by HL | Foresight of death or serious injury as highly probable | Noted that s8 had amended this to subjective It proved intent (this seems to contradict s8 which refers to evidence) |
| Moloney 1985 | HL disapproved **Hyam** Foreseeing death as 'probable' was not proof of intent | Foresight of death or serious injury as a moral certainty or natural consequence | Foresight was *evidence* of intent rather than *proof* of intent |
| Hancock and Shankland 1986 | **Moloney** guidelines were followed but HL held that 'natural consequence' was misleading | The greater the probability the more likely it was foreseen and thus intended | Evidence |
| Nedrick 1986 | CA provided a new test | Death or serious injury was a virtual certainty and D appreciated this | Evidence from which the jury can 'infer' intent |
| Walker and Hayles 1990 | CA followed **Nedrick** but added | very high degree of probability sufficed | Evidence from which the jury can 'infer' intent |
| Woollin 1998 | HL confirmed **Nedrick** test | Death or serious injury was a virtual certainty and D appreciated this | Evidence from which jury can 'find' intent |
| Matthews and Alleyne 2003 / Stringer 2008 | Applied **Nedrick** test | Death or serious injury was a virtual certainty and D appreciated this | Evidence of intent is not proof of intent |

*Recklessness*

There were 2 types of recklessness.  Subjective recklessness is used for most crimes as an alternative *mens rea* to intent.  Objective recklessness was used for criminal damage until 2003, but is now abolished.  Subjective means looking at what was in the *defendant's* mind. Objective means looking at what the *reasonable person* would think.  Although this no longer applies, you need to know a little about it for possible use in an essay on the developments.

**Key case**

**Cunningham 1957** provides the test for subjective recklessness. D ripped a gas meter from a basement wall in order to steal the money in the meter. Gas escaped and seeped through to an adjoining property where an occupant was overcome by the fumes. D was charged with maliciously administering a noxious substance, and argued that he did not realise the risk of gas escaping. The CA quashed his conviction having interpreted 'maliciously' to mean with subjective recklessness. The prosecution had failed to prove that D was aware that his actions might cause harm. The test for subjective recklessness is therefore that:

**D is aware of the existence of a risk (of the consequence occurring) and deliberately goes ahead and takes that risk.**

Objective recklessness was defined in **Caldwell 1982**. D, whilst drunk, set fire to a chair in the basement of the hotel where he worked. He was charged with arson (a type of criminal damage) endangering life. He argued that in his drunken state he had not thought about the fact that there could be people in the hotel. In the HL Lord Diplock extended the meaning of recklessness to include the situation where either

> **D saw a risk and ignored it (as in Cunningham, subjective recklessness)** *or*

> **D gave no thought to a risk which was obvious to a reasonable person, (a new meaning, objective recklessness).**

In **Gemmell and Richards 2003,** the HL confirmed that recklessness is subjective and that the **Caldwell** test was wrong. Overruling its previous decision in **Caldwell,** the HL said that the *defendant* had to have recognised that there was some kind of risk.

**Key case**

In **Gemmell and Richards 2003** two boys aged 11 and 13 set light to some papers outside the back of a shop. Several premises were badly damaged. They were convicted of arson on the basis of **Caldwell**, i.e., that the risk of damage was obvious to a reasonable person. In other words, objective recklessness. Their ages were therefore not taken into account. They appealed. The CA cannot overrule a decision of the HL and D's argument under the Human Rights Act also failed. They appealed further to the HL, which used the **1966 Practice Statement** to overrule its previous decision. The *mens rea* for criminal damage is now subjective (**Cunningham**) recklessness.

Thus, to prove recklessness it must be shown that *D is aware of a risk, but deliberately goes ahead and takes it.*

**Food for thought: recklessness**

Consider whether **Caldwell** or **Gemmell** is to be preferred. **Caldwell** itself can be supported on the basis that being drunk shouldn't mean you can get away with a crime. There were other cases that followed it which are harder to justify though.

In **Elliott 1983**, a 14-year old girl, who was in a special needs class at school, set fire to shed not realising the risk of lighting white spirit. The magistrates acquitted her. However, the prosecution successfully appealed on the basis of **Caldwell**. A reasonable person would have seen the risk that she took, so she had sufficient *mens rea*. This case shows the difficulties of applying the objective test to a child, or a person who lacks the capacity of a 'reasonable person'. However, **Gemmell** solves this problem.

**Examination pointer**

For a problem question involving recklessness you only need to discuss subjective (**Cunningham**) recklessness. This is now the law as stated by the HL in **Gemmell**.

**Task**

Using the summary of the developments above, draw up a diagram and add a column to it. Use this column for a brief comment of your own, either on the principle or the facts. Keep the diagram as a guide for essays. It might look nice on the bedroom wall.

### Transferred Malice

*Mens rea* can be transferred from the intended victim to the actual victim. This means that if you intend to hit Steve but miss and hit Joe you cannot say 'but I didn't intend to hit Joe so I had no *mens rea*'. In **Latimer 1886** D aimed a blow at X with his belt but missed and seriously wounded V. He had the intent (*mens rea*) to hit X, and this intent was transferred to the wounding (*actus reus*) of V. Thus he had both the *mens rea* and the *actus reus* of wounding. Although usually referred to as 'transferred intent' it applies to *mens rea* generally, both to intention and recklessness. The *actus reus* and *mens rea* must be for the *same* crime.

**Example**

I throw a brick at someone but it misses and breaks a window. I had *mens rea* for an assault and *actus reus* for criminal damage. This *mens rea* can't be transferred. I am not guilty of either crime. If I throw the brick at someone but it hits someone else then this *mens rea* can be transferred. I had *mens rea* and *actus reus* for the *same* offence.

**Coincidence of actus reus and mens rea**

We saw in **Fagan** that *actus reus* and *mens rea* must coincide, but that the court may view the *actus reus* as **continuing.** A similar reasoning can be seen in **Thabo Meli 1954.** Planning to kill him, the Ds attacked a man and then rolled what they thought was his dead body over a cliff, to make it look like an accident. He was only unconscious at this point, and the actual cause of death was exposure. The Ds were convicted of murder and argued that there were two separate acts. The first act (the attack) was accompanied by *mens rea* but was not the cause of death (so no *actus reus*). The second act (pushing him over the cliff) was the cause of death, but was not accompanied by *mens rea*. The *mens rea* of murder is intention to kill or seriously injure. They said there could be no such intention if they thought that the man was already dead. The court said that it was "impossible to divide up what was really one **series of acts** in this way", and refused their appeal.

**Summary**

| Level of *mens rea* | Explanation | Cases | Example crimes |
|---|---|---|---|
| • Direct Intention | • D's aim or purpose, a decision to bring about the result | • Mohan 1975 | • Murder, theft, grievous bodily harm and wounding with intent |
| • Indirect Intention | • Result is a virtual certainty and D appreciates this | • Nedrick 1986 CA<br>• Woollin 1998 HL | • Murder, theft, grievous bodily harm and wounding with intent |
| • Subjective Recklessness | • D recognises a risk and goes on to take it | • Cunningham 1957 | • All other assaults, criminal damage |

**Self-test questions**

*From which case did the quote at the beginning of this chapter come?*

*What are the two types of intent?*

*What is the **Nedrick** test for oblique intent?*

*Is recklessness now a subjective or objective test and in which case was this decided?*

*What is the principle in **Latimer**?*

For answers to the tasks and self-test questions, please go to my website at www.drsr.org and click the button 'Answers to tasks'. For a range of free interactive exercises, click on 'Free Exercises' and then the OCR book.

> *"... there has for centuries been a presumption that Parliament did not intend to make criminals of persons who were in no way blameworthy in what they did. That means that whenever a section is silent as to mens rea there is a presumption that, in order to give effect to the will of Parliament, we must read in words appropriate to require mens rea"*

Lord Reid

By the end of this Chapter, you should be able to:

*Explain the rules on strict liability*

*Show how the law has developed by reference to cases*

*Identify the arguments for and against strict liability, in order to attempt an evaluation*

## Strict and absolute liability

Most crimes require *mens rea* for one or more parts of the *actus reus*. Thus, even if D has carried out a criminal act, there will usually be no liability unless it happened with *mens rea*. However, some crimes do not require *mens rea* in any form. These are called **strict liability** crimes. In these crimes, only the *actus reus* must be proved.

As we saw, *actus reus* must be voluntary, so it is a defence if the offence was not committed voluntarily. In **Leicester V Pearson 1952**, the driver was acquitted of failing to give precedence to a pedestrian on a zebra crossing because his car had been pushed onto it by another car hitting him from behind. However, there are exceptions here too. Crimes of **absolute liability** arise where there is no defence to D's action. Some crimes do not require either *actus reus* or *mens rea*. Crimes which involve a 'state of affairs' can be committed without any apparent voluntary act by D. We saw in the first chapter that in **Larsonneur 1933**, the state of affairs was 'being found', so as soon as she landed in the UK without the required permission she committed the offence. It was no defence that she had not acted voluntarily. Also in **Winzar v Chief Constable of Kent 1983**, where he was arrested for being found drunk on the highway. The state of 'being found' was again enough. These crimes, where there is neither *mens rea* nor *actus reus* are called *absolute liability* crimes. They are fairly rare, but should they exist at all?

### Food for thought

State of affairs crimes can be criticised. They mean D can be liable without being at fault (no *mens rea*), or even acting voluntarily (no *actus reus*). One of the arguments for imposing liability without having to prove fault is that it saves lengthy investigations and court time, but is it fair to D? Should someone be convicted just for being in the wrong place at the wrong time as in **Winzar** and **Larsonneur**?

### *Statutory nature of strict liability*

Strict liability most often applies to regulatory offences, i.e., offences that are not truly criminal in nature such as traffic offences. In addition, offences covering areas of social concern or public health, such as the sale of food and alcohol, pollution and protection of the environment, are often strict liability offences. These offences are usually governed by statute. The statute will impose certain requirements on the relevant people and if these requirements are not satisfied, an offence will be committed. The **Health and Safety at Work**

**Act 1974** is a good example. It imposes requirements on an employer to ensure a safe environment, competent staff and safe equipment. Other statutes cover trading standards and the sale of goods. Although these statutes are often seen as dealing with civil issues, because the person affected can sue for damages, they also create criminal offences. An employer or shopkeeper can be prosecuted as well as sued.

### Example

In **Meah v Roberts 1977,** two children were served lemonade that had caustic soda in it. D was not responsible for it being there, but was found guilty under the **Food and Drug Act 1955**, even though not at fault herself.

Even though most such crimes are statutory, the courts must interpret the statutes, so case law is still important.

### *interpretation by the courts*

In **Harrow LBC v Shah 1999**, a newsagent was convicted for selling a lottery ticket to a person under 16 even though it had told its staff to ask for proof of age if there was any doubt, and the member of staff who actually sold the ticket believed the boy was over 16. It was held that the offence under the **National Lottery Regulations 1994** was one of strict liability, so there was no need to prove an intent, or even recklessness, as regards the age of the buyer of the ticket. The act of selling it to someone under 16 was enough.

Most strict liability crimes are fairly minor, and not usually seen as truly criminal. Someone convicted may have broken the law but there is little social stigma attached to the act, even though illegal. In 'real' crimes there is more controversy, and this can be seen in **Sweet v Parsley 1970**. The opening quote came from this case.

### Key case

In **Sweet v Parsley**, a woman let rooms to students. The police raided the premises and found cannabis. She was charged with being *'concerned in the management of premises used for the purpose of smoking cannabis'* under the **Dangerous Drugs Act 1965**. She was found guilty even though not at fault – she was completely unaware of the cannabis smoking. The HL eventually acquitted her and established the rule that strict liability could only be imposed where the Act specifically made the offence one of strict liability. In all other cases, a need for *mens rea* would be presumed. This means that if the Act is silent on the issue of *mens rea*, it will be interpreted so that D must either intend or be reckless regarding the criminal act.

In **B v DPP 2000**, D had been convicted of inciting a child of 14 to indecency. He argued that he believed the child was older so did not intend to commit the illegal act, nor was he reckless. The HL reversed the conviction based on the principle in **Sweet v Parsley**, saying the presumption of *mens rea* was particularly strong in serious offences. Thus, the prosecution should have proved *mens rea* in order to achieve a conviction. The matter appeared to be put beyond doubt the following year.

### Key case

In **K 2001,** D (who was aged 26) had sexual activity with a girl of 14 and was charged with indecent assault. He argued a mistaken belief that she was over 16. The HL accepted that he did not have *mens rea* and said the offence was not one of strict liability, so he was not guilty. This case indicated that the old case of **Prince 1875**, where D had been convicted of taking a girl under the age of 16 out of the possession of her parents, was wrong. She had told him she was 18 and, as she looked much older than she actually was, he believed her. D was convicted even though he had acted without *mens rea*. Lord Steyn described the decision in **Prince** as "a relic from an age dead and gone". The HL confirmed that there was an overriding presumption of statutory interpretation that *mens rea* was needed unless there were express indications to the contrary in the statute.

However, in not dissimilar circumstances a conviction was upheld. Here the charge was rape.

**Key case**

In **G 2008**, a boy of fifteen had sexual intercourse with a girl of 12 without her consent but believing her to be 15. He was charged with rape of a child under 13, for which there is no requirement of *mens rea* as to age (only as regards intention to penetrate). The CA upheld his conviction on the basis that Parliament clearly intended the offence to be one of strict liability as regards age. There was a defence available where the child was over 13 and this made it clear that the defence *only* applied in the case of older children.

**Food for thought**

It is clear that the law must protect children but it seems unfair when D is also a child. This does not seem to be as serious a crime as that in **K**, where the age difference was much greater. The problem is that the courts can only presume *mens rea* is needed if the Act is not clear (as stated in **Sweet v Parsley**). Here, because the Act made a difference between those over 13 and those under, the court could not presume *mens rea*.

*social utility*

One of the main arguments for imposing strict liability is that it is beneficial to society as a whole because it makes people more careful and protects people from harm. An example is **Meah v Roberts** above. Thus, offences covering areas of social concern such as the sale of food and drink, pollution and the protection of the environment are strict liability offences and this can be justified by the nature of the offence. The decision in **Shah** could be justified on the basis that underage gambling is a matter of social concern.

In **Alphacell v Woodward 1972**, the HL held that the offence of causing polluted matter to enter a river, contrary to **s 2** of the **Rivers (Prevention of Pollution) Act 1951**, was a strict liability offence because pollution was a matter of the "utmost public importance".

The rules on strict liability were set out in **Gammon (Hong Kong) Ltd v AG of HK 1985**.

**Key case**

In **Gammon**, builders were held liable for carrying out building works in a way likely to cause damage, where they had not followed the original plans exactly. Safety regulations had prohibited 'substantial changes' and they argued that they hadn't known the changes they made *were* substantial. The offence was said to be one of strict liability because it was aimed at protecting public safety. Lord Scarman laid down guidelines in this case:

**there is a presumption that *mens rea* is required**

**it is particularly strong if the offence is 'truly' criminal**

**it can only be displaced if the statute clearly states or implies this (e.g., with words such as 'knowingly' or 'maliciously')**

**it can only be displaced if the statute deals with an issue of social concern and public safety is an issue**

**Policy issues**

A related issue is that of public policy. The last point in **Gammon** is based on policy. It would be against public policy for people to be unsafe. Therefore, if the matter involves safety it is more likely the courts will accept it is a strict liability offence.

The approach in **Gammon** was followed in **Blake 1997**. D was a disc jockey who was convicted under the **Wireless Telegraphy Act 1949** for broadcasting without a licence. D was in his flat at the time of the broadcast and argued that he thought he was making tapes and not transmitting. The CA felt that as unlicensed transmissions could interfere with the emergency services and air traffic control, the issue was one of public safety. On this basis, the offence could be classed as one of strict liability.

In **Jackson 2006**, the CA held that flying an aircraft at a height lower that 100 feet was a strict liability offence under the **Air Force Act 1955**. The Judge referred to both **Sweet v Parsley** and **Gammon** and ruled that there was no wording in the **Air Force Act** which required proof that D knew that he was flying below the permitted height. This meant the statute created an offence of strict liability. D's argument that the prosecution needed to prove at least recklessness was rejected. The creation of the offence was to protect the public and the public interest overrode the need to prove *mens rea*.

**Examination pointer**

In a question on strict liability you should not only be able to discuss what it is and when it applies, but also provide an evaluation. The OCR specifications state that candidates "are expected to have a general appreciation of the role of criminal law in modern society and to be able to relate this to specific issues, e.g. whether it is justifiable to have crimes of strict liability". There are several arguments for and against imposing strict liability and the following section will give you a base on which to build. Try to develop your own arguments too.

*Arguments for and against imposing strict liability*

**Arguments against:**

>   it is unfair to convict D of a criminal offence without proving *mens rea*

>   it leads to the punishment of people who have taken all possible precautions

>   it also means such people have a criminal record

>   imposing a requirement of negligence would be fairer to D, but is a low level of fault so would still protect the public by making D careful

**Arguments for:**

>   it makes people more careful

>   it protects the public

>   most such offences are minor and carry no social stigma

>   proving *mens rea* is hard in many minor offences so time and money is saved

>   the judge can address the issue of fault when sentencing

**Example**

30

It has been snowing and there are piles of snow at the side of the road. I manage to park my car and go shopping. When I come back, I have a parking ticket. It turns out I have parked on a double yellow line, but I couldn't see it. It would be very hard to prove I *knew* I had parked on a yellow line in the snow, that I had *mens rea*. It would take up a lot of court time for what is only a minor matter.

## Task

Choose one argument for and one against strict liability and develop them. Use a case for each to support your views and keep this for essay practice.

### *no negligence and due diligence*

There may be a defence where D can prove that there was no negligence or that 'due diligence' or, more simply put, 'all due care' was taken. Some statutes specifically provide a defence to strict liability crimes, e.g., the **Licensing Act 1964** (as amended by the **Licensing Act 1988**) makes it a strict liability offence to sell alcohol to a person under 18. The **Act** then provides that it will be a defence if D can prove there was no reason to suspect the person was under 18. The **Licensing Act 2003 s 139** allows a defence if D can prove that an offence under the Act was committed

> '... due to a mistake, or to reliance on information given to him, or to an act or omission by another person, or to some other cause beyond his control' **and** 'he took all reasonable precautions and exercised all due diligence to avoid committing the offence'.

The courts have been reluctant to develop this approach. No such defence was available in **Shah**, and the courts found the newsagent guilty even though he had taken care. In **Barnfather v Islington Education Authority 2003**, it was said that the courts should not import a defence into strict liability crimes where none was provided in the relevant statute.

One new offence under the **2003 Act** is that of 'persistently selling alcohol to anyone under the age of 18 years'. The defence of due diligence is not available to this new offence which came into force in April 2007. This means licence holders will be strictly liable for selling alcohol to youngsters on three or more occasions within a period of three months.

## Food for thought

In Australia, for crimes of strict liability, the courts have ruled that it is a defence if D can show that all due care has been taken to avoid the offence being committed. This applies even if there is no defence in the statute itself. It can be argued that this would be an improvement in England. Continuing to have crimes of strict liability would retain the public safety aspect, but allowing a defence would be fairer to a D who has done all that is possible to ensure that safety. Although a few Acts do provide some defence there are still many areas where there is none, and the courts have shown that they are reluctant to imply a defence into a statute.

In some cases, the 'due diligence' defence is linked with mistake. The **Trade Descriptions Act 1968** allows a defence if D can prove the offence was committed due to a mistake or to reliance on information supplied by a third party, **and** that they exercised all due diligence to avoid committing the offence.

Note that where there is a defence the burden of proof moves from the prosecution to D. Once the prosecution has proved the offence occurred, it is for D to prove that all due care was taken to avoid it and there was no negligence.

**Task**

Do you think strict liability should apply in the following situations? Write a sentence saying why it should, or should not, be imposed.

**polluting the river**

**jumping a traffic light**

**murder**

**selling food which is not fit for human consumption**

**selling alcohol to a 15-year old**

**Summary**

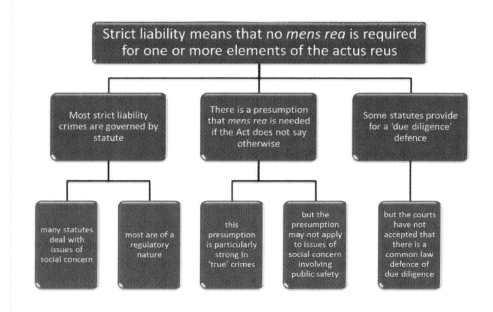

**Self-test questions**

*State three areas of social concern where strict liability applies*

*Which case established that there is a presumption of mens rea in most criminal offences where the Act is silent on the matter?*

*In which case were the guidelines set out for imposing strict liability where the Act is silent?*

*State three reasons for imposing strict liability*

*State three reasons for not imposing strict liability*

For answers to the tasks and self-test questions, please go to my website at www.drsr.org and click the button 'Answers to tasks'. For a range of free interactive exercises, click on 'Free Exercises' and then the OCR book.

**Actus reus can include:**

*conduct (which is voluntary)*

*circumstances*

*consequence (causation)*

**The prosecution must prove causation both factually and legally**

*Factually – the 'but for' test White 1910*

*Legally – D's action made a 'significant' contribution to the result (Cheshire) and any intervening act was foreseeable (Roberts)*

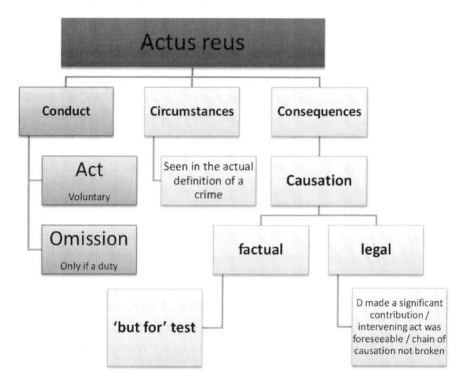

Finally don't forget the 'thin skull' rule – where V has a particular weakness D will be liable for the full consequences (**Blaue**)

*Mens rea*

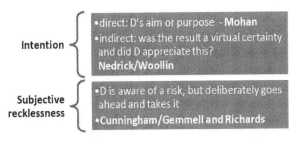

*Task*

Note the principle and brief facts of the following cases

    **Fagan**

    **Stone and Dobinson**

    **Roberts**

    **Cheshire**

    **Blaue**

    **DPP v Smith**

**Summary of strict liability**

*no mens rea is required*

*most strict liability crimes are statutory*

*many deal with issues of social concern and regulatory crimes*

*there is a presumption that mens rea is needed if the Act does not say otherwise*

*this presumption is particularly strong in 'true' crimes*

*but the presumption may not apply to issues of social concern involving public safety*

*some statutes provide for a 'due diligence' defence but the courts have not accepted that there is a common law defence of due diligence*

**Key criticisms of *actus reus*, *mens rea* and strict liability**

D is not usually liable for an omission but can be in certain circumstances. There is a degree of uncertainty in such cases e.g., Bland, Gibbins & Proctor

Sometimes questions arise about whether someone who is 'brain dead' or a foetus in the womb is a human being. In AGs Reference (No 3 of 1994) 1997, the HL held that a foetus was not a human being for the purpose of a murder conviction. However, if the foetus is injured, and dies from that injury after being born, that could amount to murder. Arguably, there should be greater clarity on this.

The rules on what will break the chain of causation may be difficult for a jury to understand

It may be unjust to convict the original actor when the victim (Blaue) or a medical operation (Cheshire) has actually caused the death

Words such as 'highly likely' and 'highly probable' blur the distinction between intent and recklessness

The law on intent has developed with Nedrick and Woollin but is arguably still unclear and should be clarified by Parliament

D can be convicted of a strict liability offence without proving mens rea

This can apply even to serious offences like rape, as in R v G 2008

People who have taken all possible precautions can still be convicted

People who have taken all possible precautions can still get a criminal record

Imposing a requirement of negligence would seem more just

### Sample examination question

'In general the criminal law prohibits the doing of harm but does not impose criminal liability for an omission. However, there are justifiable exceptions to this general principle'.

Assess the truth of this statement by reference to situations where a failure to act may result in criminal liability. 50 marks

### Special study unit – possible connections

Where you are asked to discuss developments in the law you can use the *Food for thought* sections to help you find ideas for an evaluation of any developments, and to discuss critically particular cases. Although there is little substantive law studied in this block there are still plenty of developments. I've included a few ideas here.

The use of the rules of **precedent** can be discussed in relation to *mens rea*. The **1966 Practice Statement** was used in **Gemmell & Richards** to overrule the earlier case of **Caldwell**.

Note also the development of the law in relation to the *mens rea* for murder. Several cases were distinguished in the lead up to **Woollin** on intent. There is a full summary of these developments in Chapter 2. In addition, the interpretation of the **Criminal Justice Act** can be discussed within these developments.

Earlier cases were *distinguished* and the law developed in regard to liability for omissions and *actus reus*. An example is **Fagan**: by allowing the *actus reus* to be seen as continuing, his act was not treated as an omission.

As regards strict liability, you can discuss the presumption that *mens rea* is needed. This was established in **Sweet v Parsley**. If the Act is silent on the issue of *mens rea*, it will be interpreted so that D must either intend or be reckless as regards the criminal act. This may reflect the intentions of Parliament, but it can be argued that if *mens rea* is needed the Act would say so. Of course, the alternative argument is that if it was a strict liability offence it would say so. The presumption was further developed in **Gammon (Hong Kong) Ltd** where guidelines were set out. **Sweet** was followed in **B v DPP** and in **K 2001**. In the latter case the HL confirmed that there was an overriding presumption of statutory interpretation that *mens rea* was needed. The old case of **Prince 1875**, was disapproved, but not specifically overruled.

**Chapter 4:** Attempts

This Study Block covers the preliminary crime of attempt. Such crimes are called *inchoate* offences. This means that they are incomplete, there is an **attempt** to commit a crime but the crime has not actually been completed. D can be convicted of the preliminary crime even if the main offence never occurs. Thus if D tries to kill someone but fails, there can be a charge of **attempted** murder. This would also apply where there is a problem with causation. Thus in **White**, D was not guilty of his mother's murder because she died of a heart attack before the poison he gave her took effect. He had not caused her death so his conviction was for attempted murder.

There is no separate summary for this Study Block as it only covers one offence. The summary is at the end of the Chapter.

"... a person may be guilty of attempting to commit an offence to which this section applies even though the facts are such that the commission of the offence is impossible"

Criminal Attempts Act 1981 s 1 (2)

By the end of this Chapter, you should be able to:

**Explain the actus reus of attempt**

**Explain the mens rea of attempt**

**Explain how the law applies in practice by reference to cases**

### What is an attempt?

It is defined in the **Criminal Attempts Act 1981 s 1(1)** which provides:

"If with intent to commit an offence to which this section applies, a person does an act which is more than merely preparatory to the commission of the offence, he is guilty of attempting to commit the offence"

The *actus reus* is that D 'does an act which is more than merely preparatory'. The *mens rea* is 'intent to commit an offence'.

### Example

In **Holt and Lee 1981**, two people in a restaurant made a plan to avoid paying for their meal by telling the waiter they had already paid another member of staff. They were overheard discussing this plan by an off duty policeman. They were charged with attempt (at inducing the restaurant to forgo payment). They had gone far enough with their plan to be seen as doing *an act which is more than merely preparatory* and they *intended* to induce the restaurant to forgo payment.

### *Actus reus: more than merely preparatory*

Although attempt is now a statutory offence, case law still has some relevance. Cases will not be binding as the definitions are set out in the Act, however they may be persuasive in deciding, for instance, what is *'more than merely preparatory'*.

Whether an act is 'more than merely preparatory' is a matter for the jury. Cases based on the common law before the Act was passed had produced various tests for attempt. Most of these required that D had reached the point of no return and many convictions failed because D was not sufficiently close to committing the crime. The Law Commission felt that there was no 'magic formula' and the test in **s 1** is based on their proposals. It is still not always easy to know where to draw the line. If D shoots someone and leaves them for dead, but they survive, then D can be charged with attempted murder without any problem. In **White 1910** (see Chapter 1), D gave his mother poison but she died before it took effect. He had not caused her death so the murder charge failed. He was found guilty of attempted murder. Difficulties arise where it is not so clear-cut. In **Gullefer 1987**, D had put a bet on a dog race and, seeing that his dog was clearly going to lose, jumped on to the track to try and stop the race. He would then have got his stake back. A charge of attempted theft failed because D had done no more than prepare to get his money back. He had not started on the act of stealing, which would have entailed going to the bookmaker and obtaining a refund.

In **Campbell 1991**, a conviction of attempted robbery was overturned on appeal on the basis that D's act was no more than preparatory. He was arrested within a yard of a post office carrying a fake gun. He said he had intended to rob it but had changed his mind and was walking away.

A controversial case on this issue is **Geddes 1996.** D was found in a boy's toilet in a school. He then ran off when challenged by a teacher. He left behind a bag containing a large knife, a roll of tape and rope. He was convicted of attempted false imprisonment but this was again overturned on appeal. He had *mens rea* but insufficient *actus reus* because he had not at the time approached any victim.

**Food for thought**

It can be said that this offence causes problems for the police. If they arrest D too early the charge will fail. However, if they wait until the act is clearly 'more than merely preparatory,' they could be putting people in danger, which was one of the problems with the old law. Take **Campbell**, for example. Should the police have waited until he entered the post-office? If the gun had been real, they would have been risking people's lives. This will often be a difficult operational decision to make. The same can be said with **Geddes**. There was held to be no attempt because he had not approached any victim but there was clear evidence of his intentions and if he had not been challenged by the teacher, someone might have been abducted.

### *Attempts to do the impossible*

The Act states in **s 1(2)** that a person may be guilty of attempting to commit an offence: *"even though the facts are such that the commission of the offence is impossible"*.

The Act seems clear, but in **Anderton v Ryan 1985**, the HL seemed to prefer to follow the earlier common law which was that there was no liability if a crime was physically or legally impossible. D had bought what she *believed* to be a stolen video recorder. It wasn't, in fact, stolen but she was charged with the attempted handling of stolen goods. The CA reversed the decision of the magistrates to acquit, and allowed the prosecution's appeal. The HL reversed that decision and the conviction was quashed. This meant that, despite the wording of the Act, impossibility could be a defence. This state of affairs did not last long. The HL accepted that it had made a wrong decision and in **Shivpuri 1987**, it used the *1966 Practice Statement* to overrule its own earlier decision. In **Shivpuri**, D had brought a substance into the UK believing it to be heroin. It turned out to be a harmless vegetable matter. He was convicted of attempting to deal in prohibited drugs and the HL upheld the conviction. Also in **Jones 2007**, D was convicted of attempting to incite an underage girl to have sex with him, even though the 'girl' was actually an adult policewoman who had responded to his advertisement for young girls to have sex with him in return for payment. Several texts were exchanged and eventually a meeting was arranged and he was arrested. He had argued that the offence was impossible as the girl did not exist; it was an adult he had incited. The CA followed **Shivpuri** and rejected his appeal against conviction.

Impossibility therefore no longer seemed to be a defence to an attempt to commit a crime. However, in **Pace and Rogers 2014**, the CA held that the *mens rea* for attempt was intent to commit the offence. This meant 'all the elements' of the offence. In this case, the police had mounted an operation with the idea of clamping down on the sale and disposal of stolen scrap metal. They offered some goods to scrap metal dealers indicating they were 'a bit naughty'. The appellants purchased the goods and were subsequently charged and convicted of attempting to convert criminal (stolen) property. In allowing their appeal the CA said that the principal offence was only committed where the property actually was criminal property. Here it was actually the property of the police and not stolen. This meant they could not be guilty of attempt because there was no intent to convert criminal property, so no *mens rea*.

## Food for thought

The CA recognised in **Pace and Rogers** that the decision could have significant effects on later cases and that the courts "do not always reveal a consistency in approach". This shows that the **Criminal Attempts Act** has not sufficiently clarified the law on this area.

## Examination pointer

Look for clues in a problem scenario, particularly as to whether the main crime takes place. If D tries to commit an offence but fails, there may be an attempt. D can be convicted of the preliminary crime even if the main offence never occurs. Note that attempt can come into a question with one of the other crimes. Thus, you should discuss attempted murder if D tries to kill someone but fails, or attempted theft if the *actus reus* of theft cannot be proved. In these cases, you should use the **Criminal Attempts Act** once you have established that the main crime has not been proved.

### Mens rea

The Act says "with intent to commit an offence" so the *mens rea* is intent and nothing less. Intent was defined in **Mohan 1975** as a decision to bring about the prohibited consequence no matter whether the accused desired that consequence or not.

Intention is required for attempt even if recklessness would be enough for the principal offence. This was confirmed in **Millard & Vernon 1987**, where some football fans had been convicted of attempted criminal damage. The CA allowed their appeal on the basis that even though recklessness was enough for criminal damage, it was not enough for an attempt to commit this offence. *Mens rea* is therefore more limited in an attempt than in the main offence. In **Whybrow 1951**, it was held that for attempted murder intent to kill is required, even though intent seriously to injure is sufficient *mens rea* for murder itself.

In **Pace and Rogers**, the CA again made clear that the *mens rea* was intent and that a suspicion (that the goods were stolen) was not enough. It also made clear that it must be intent to commit *all* the elements of the main offence.

One other point on *mens rea* and impossibility is that it will not be attempt if D intends to carry out an offence only in certain conditions, which then do not exist. An example of a 'conditional attempt' is where D intends to steal something but it is not there. D will not be guilty of attempted theft even though there was intent to steal.

## Summary

Actus reus is an act which is **more than merely preparatory**

**Impossibility** is no longer a defence to an attempt – **Shivpuri/Jones**

Although there must be intent to complete all the elements of the main offence – **Pace and Rogers**

Mens rea is **intent** to commit the main offence

This means intent to complete all the elements of the main offence – **Pace and Rogers**

The main offence need not occur

**Key criticisms**

*The line between what is and is not 'more than preparatory' is still unclear*

*The difficulty this poses for juries leads to inconsistency*

*Geddes shows the problem of waiting for a final act*

*Had the teacher not challenged the man people would have been put at risk, but the court held he had not passed the 'more than preparatory' test*

*Similarly, in Campbell, lives could have been put at risk by waiting for D to do more*

*D will not be guilty of attempt even though there was intent to commit the main offence. This seems illogical, as D can be guilty of the full offences of theft, robbery or burglary with only intent to steal even if nothing is actually taken*

*The Law Commission suggested adding a new offence of 'criminal preparation' in 2007 but the proposals were not accepted*

*Having an offence of criminal preparation would have meant a conviction in cases like Campbell and Geddes*

*The Law Commission in their 2009 report said that the 'more than merely preparatory' definition of attempt should stay but still maintained the offence needed amending as regards attempted murder and conditional attempts*

*The level of mens rea is high, making it more difficult to convict someone of attempt than of the main offence*

*This is especially illogical in murder cases where attempted murder is harder to prove than murder itself, as in Whybrow 1951, where it was held that for attempted murder intent to kill is required, even though intent seriously to injure is sufficient mens rea for murder itself*

*It remains to be seen how far the law on mens rea has been clarified by Pace and Rogers 2014*

*The sentence is the same as for the full offence even though that offence has not occurred*

**Self-test questions**

*What were the facts of **White**?*

*His mother died so why was he convicted of attempted murder rather than murder?*

*On what issue did **Shivpuri** overrule **Anderton v Ryan?***

*How is attempt defined? In which Act?*

*What was confirmed in **Millard & Vernon** on the issue of mens rea?*

For answers to the tasks and self-test questions, please go to my website at www.drsr.org and click the button 'Answers to tasks'. For a range of free interactive exercises, click on 'Free Exercises' and then the OCR book.

**Chapter 5** Murder

**Chapter 6** Special defence to murder – diminished responsibility

**Chapter 7** Special defence to murder – loss of control

**Chapter 8** Involuntary manslaughter – constructive manslaughter

**Chapter 9** Involuntary manslaughter – gross negligence manslaughter

Murder, the killing of a human being with intent to kill or seriously injure, is probably the most socially unacceptable crime. It carries a mandatory life sentence, which means the judge has no discretion when passing sentence. You should be familiar with many of the cases, as I have used several murder cases to illustrate Chapters 1 & 2.

The specific defences to murder are found in the **Homicide Act 1957,** and the **Coroners and Justice Act 2009**. If successful, they reduce murder to what is called 'voluntary manslaughter', and thus allow sentencing to be at the discretion of the judge. They ONLY apply to a murder charge. Chapter 6 covers situations where at the time of the killing D was suffering from *diminished responsibility*. Chapter 7 covers situations where at the time of the killing D has suffered a *loss of control* and killed in reaction to something done or said by the victim. Other defences to murder also apply to other crimes so are dealt with under general defences.

*Example*

Jane stabs Jenny, who dies. This is murder. If Jenny had taunted Jane in some way, Jane may be able to use the defence of loss of control. If she is suffering from severe depression at the time, Jane may argue diminished responsibility. If either of the defences is successful, Jane will be convicted of manslaughter, not murder. The judge can choose the sentence.

Neither the **Homicide Act** nor the **Coroners and Justice Act** *defines* murder. Murder, somewhat surprisingly, is not a statutory offence. It comes from the common law not an Act of Parliament. The Acts merely provide special defences to a murder charge. Murder and voluntary manslaughter both have the same *actus reus* and *mens rea*. The difference lies in these defences.

The other type of homicide, *involuntary* manslaughter, is often referred to as murder without *mens rea*, but this is a little misleading. It does require *mens rea*, just a different type. If specific intent cannot be proved then it is not murder, and manslaughter will be the appropriate charge. There are two main types, constructive manslaughter (also called unlawful act manslaughter) and gross negligence manslaughter. We will also look at a third possibility, reckless manslaughter.

*Example*

Jane throws a brick at a passing car. The driver swerves to avoid it and hits a lamppost, killing herself. This would be constructive manslaughter. Throwing a brick at the car is unlawful, and this act has caused the driver's death.

Jenny is driving her motor boat too fast and she hits another boat, killing the occupants. This would be gross negligence manslaughter, and at one time would have been reckless manslaughter. There is no unlawful act, but Jenny has been criminally negligent in not taking more care.

The problems of both types of manslaughter are considered at the end of this study block, along with reforms. Areas of law where there are problems and/or where there are current proposals for reform are popular examination topics so look carefully at these issues.

A final point:

'Voluntary' and 'involuntary' are terms used to distinguish between manslaughter following a murder charge, and manslaughter as a separate charge. There is no such charge as 'voluntary manslaughter' or 'involuntary manslaughter'. The first would be charged as murder, the second as manslaughter.

*"... if at the time of death the original wound is still an operating cause and a substantial cause, then the death can properly be said to be the result of the wound, albeit that some other cause of death is also operating"*

*Lord Parker CJ*

Can you remember in which case this statement was made? If not, look back at legal causation in Chapter 2.

By the end of this Chapter, you should be able to:

**Identify the actus reus and mens rea of murder**

**Explain how the law on causation (actus reus) applies in murder cases**

**Explain how intent (mens rea) is proved by reference to cases**

**Identify possible criticisms of the current law on murder**

There are definitions of murder going back to the 18th century and beyond. The most famous is that by Sir Edward Coke: 'the unlawful killing of a reasonable creature in being under the King's peace and with malice aforethought'. However, murder is a common law offence (not covered by an Act of Parliament), so the definition has changed through case law over time (for a start we now have a Queen not a King).

### Actus reus

The *actus reus* is essentially the same for both murder and manslaughter. The modern definition of murder is the "**unlawful killing of a human being under the Queen's peace**".

### Unlawful

Most killing will be unlawful. However, killing in self-defence (see defences) may make the act lawful and so not murder.

### Killing

People generally think of murder as involving an action (conduct) such as shooting or stabbing someone. However, murder can be committed by omission. In **Gibbins and Proctor 1918**, (a similar case to **Stone and Dobinson,** which was manslaughter), the D's lived together with the man's daughter. They failed to give her food and she died. The court held that where food was withheld with intent to cause grievous bodily harm then it would be murder if this caused death. The CA upheld their murder convictions.

The courts do draw a distinction between an act and an omission. In **Airedale NHS Trust v Bland 1993**, discontinuing medical treatment was treated as an omission rather than a positive action. This was a civil case so is not strictly binding on the criminal courts. It will be highly persuasive though. It can be compared to **Cox 1992**, where a doctor gave an injection to a patient begging for help to die. This is a positive act, and so amounts to murder. (On the facts, it was only attempted murder as the cause of death was not clear.) Intentionally accelerating death is still murder. Thus even if someone is going to die anyway you will be guilty of murder if you intentionally shorten their life. The only exception is what is known as the *de minimis* rule: if D's act is so small that it cannot be said to play a significant part in the death, there is no liability for murder.

### Example

V is in severe pain from an incurable illness. The doctor gives her a huge overdose of painkillers in order to end her suffering. Before these take effect, V's husband gives her two more painkillers.

The doctor's act would be murder. The husband's act *could* be murder as it probably hastened the death, but the court is likely to treat his act as '*de minimis*'.

### Food for thought

Any intentional act which causes death will be murder. Thus 'mercy killing', or euthanasia, is murder. You might argue that you were easing the suffering of someone incurably ill, but this argument will not succeed. Accelerating death is still murder. The motive for a crime is rarely relevant (it is as much theft to steal a loaf of bread for a starving child as it is to steal a £5,000 music system). The motive could affect the sentence, but with murder, the judge has no choice in this.

This is why the **Bland** case went to the House of Lords. Without a court order, it could have been murder.

A related issue for an essay is the sentence for murder. One argument against a mandatory life sentence is that if the jury see the killing as morally justified they may be reluctant to find someone guilty of murder. They would know that it would mean a life sentence and that the judge would be unable to consider the circumstances.

### Human being

This may seem obvious but questions arise about whether someone who is 'brain dead' or a foetus in the womb is a human being. In **AGs Reference (No 3 of 1994) 1997**, the HL held that a foetus was not a human being for the purpose of a murder conviction. However, if the foetus is injured and dies from that injury after being born, that could amount to murder.

### Under the Queen's peace

This part of the *actus reus* means that killing in war is not murder.

### Causation

Murder is a result crime so it must be proved that death resulted from D's actions. If D caused death then the charge can be murder or manslaughter depending on the *mens rea*. If D did not cause death then it can only be one of the non-fatal offences or an attempt. We have seen that the prosecution must show **factual causation**: 'but for' the defendant's conduct the victim would not have died. Also **legal causation**: that D's act was a 'significant' cause of death and there was no intervening act.

### Task

Before going any further, look up the following cases. Make a note of the facts.

**White**

**Roberts**

**Smith**

**Cheshire**

**Pagett**

Now make a note of the causation issue in each. Then read on to check these principles.

OK, let's have a quick recap of the causation principles involved.

## Factual causation

| R v White 1910 | 'but for' his actions would she be alive? No, she would have died anyway so he did not cause that death. |
|---|---|

## Legal causation

| R v Smith 1959 | If D's act was an **operating and substantial** cause of death, there is no break in the chain of causation. |
|---|---|
| R v Cheshire 1991 | Following **Smith**, if D has made a **significant contribution** to the death then hospital treatment will only break the chain of causation if it is **independent of the original act** and a potent cause in itself. |
| Roberts 1971<br><br>The prosecution relied on this case in **Corbett 1996**, to find that D caused the death of a victim who was hit and killed by a car when trying to escape from D's attack. | If the *victim's* act is **foreseeable**, it will not break the chain of causation, as long as it is not 'daft'. |
| R v Pagett 1983 | If a *third party's* act is **foreseeable** it will not break the chain of causation and the police returning fire was a **natural consequence** of D's actions. |

All these cases could be used to explain factual causation. In **Pagett** you would ask 'but for' his actions would she have died? No, so he factually caused death. (Note this test is sometimes reversed but the effect is the same: 'but for' his actions would she be alive? Yes, so he caused death.)

**Food for thought**

If V is easily scared and does something 'daft' then there is arguably a vulnerability that is no different from having a thin skull or being a Jehovah's Witness, as in **Blaue**. **Blaue** itself is somewhat controversial. If the victim does not have a life-threatening injury but refuses treatment, should D be liable for the resulting death?

In **Gnango 2011**, two people had been involved in a shoot-out in a car park on a housing estate. The first man fired at D who shot back, the man then fired again and his bullet killed a woman nearby. The prosecution argued that in returning fire D had caused the other man to shoot again, so had also caused the woman's death. The SC held that, although it may have made it more likely that the man would shoot again, this was not enough. The voluntary act of the other man had broken any possible chain of causation between D's return of fire and the death. The other man alone had caused the death. This can be compared to **Pagett**, where it was found to be foreseeable that the police would return fire so the chain of causation was not broken. The main difference seems to be that in **Gnango** the victim was not being held by D as a hostage, but was merely walking nearby. Also, in **Pagett**, D shot first which was not the case in **Gnango**.

## Mens rea

In Coke's 18th Century definition of murder, the unlawful killing must be done with *'malice aforethought'*. This expression is still used but has been interpreted as meaning with intention.

In **Vickers 1957**, the CA held that the *mens rea* for murder is satisfied by either an intention to kill, or an intention to cause grievous bodily harm. This was confirmed by the HL in **DPP v Smith 1960**, where they said that grievous bodily harm should be given its ordinary and natural meaning, that is to say, "really serious bodily harm". In **Saunders 1985**, it was said that the word 'really' did not add anything. Thus, the *mens rea* of murder is **intent to kill or seriously injure**. Intent can be direct or indirect as we saw in Chapter 2.

## Task

Look up the cases of **Nedrick** and **Woollin**. Make a note of the facts, and whether the murder charge succeeded, and why/why not.

Knowledge of the development of the law (set out in Chapter 2), is needed for a critique but, for a problem question, it is the current law that is important. We saw that this comes from the CA in **Nedrick 1986**. It was confirmed by the HL in **Woollin 1998** as being the correct direction for oblique intent. There is *evidence* of intent if:

**death or serious bodily harm was a virtual certainty as a result of the defendant's actions**

**the defendant appreciated that such was the case**

## Key case

In **Woollin**, the jury had to consider whether D appreciated that it was a virtual certainty the baby would be killed or seriously injured by being thrown in the direction of the pram. The HL confirmed the point that this is only evidence of intention, not proof. The jury should be directed on the **Nedrick** test and told to take into account ALL the circumstances.

The test was followed again in **Matthews and Alleyne 2003**. The CA confirmed the test and also that foresight of death as a virtual certainty does not automatically *prove* intent; it is merely *evidence* ("often very strong evidence") for the jury. The CA used the test again in **Stringer 2008** (see Chapter 2). It would now appear to be the established test as **Nedrick** was over twenty years earlier.

## Problems and reforms

In their 2006 report 'Murder, manslaughter and Infanticide' the Law Commission noted that

*"The law governing homicide in England and Wales is a rickety structure set upon shaky foundations. Some of its rules have remained unaltered since the seventeenth century, even though it has long been acknowledged that they are in dire need of reform".*

The LC recommended a three-tier structure for homicide, which would cover

*1st-degree murder (killing with intent to kill or with intent to cause serious harm knowing the conduct carried a serious risk of death)*

*2nd-degree murder (killing with intent to cause serious harm or where there is a defence of provocation (now loss of control) or diminished responsibility as now for voluntary manslaughter) and*

*Manslaughter (killing without intent, as now for involuntary manslaughter but with mens rea needed for some kind of harm)*

Only the first of these would have a mandatory life sentence. These recommendations have not been taken up.

See the Study Block summary for more on the problems and reforms of murder along with manslaughter, but here is a taster.

## Food for thought

The *mens rea* of murder is intent to kill or seriously injure (**Smith 1960**). This means you can be guilty of murder even if you did not intend to kill. This point was confirmed in **Cunningham 1981** (not to be confused with the 1957 case of the same name on recklessness). The HL criticised the rule but has refused to overrule it in several cases, preferring to leave that to Parliament.

The Law Commission has also criticised it but no government has yet suggested amending the law. In **Attorney-General's Reference (No 3 of 1994) 1997**, the HL, although not overruling the rule, refused to apply it so as to find someone guilty of murder where there was only intent to cause serious injury, however this was a case of transferred malice so may be of limited application.

Murder is the most serious offence, so it is vital that the law is clear. Look at the development of intent in Chapter 2. Has it produced a clear meaning of intent? Pretend you are on a jury. Could you decide what degree of probability is virtually certain? The **Cunningham** test for recklessness is that D knowingly takes a foreseeable risk. The **Nedrick** test for intent is foresight of something as a virtual certainty. At what stage does a foreseeable risk become a certainty?

The above can be discussed in an essay question on *mens rea* or a more general one on homicide. To practise for a problem question look at a case you are familiar with and apply the law you have learnt. Let's try this with **Pagett**.

## Summary of how to apply the rules

**Facts:**

1. D shot at the police whilst holding the girl in front of him.

2. The police returned fire.

3. The girl was killed.

**Application with cases in support:**

*Actus reus*

There is an unlawful killing, but did D cause it?

**'But for'** his action she would not have died (**White**). He factually caused death.

He also made a **'significant contribution'** (**Cheshire**) to the girl's death. The intervening act of the police shooting back was **foreseeable** and so did not break the **chain of causation** (**Roberts**). He legally caused death.

We have *actus reus* but is it murder or manslaughter?

*Mens rea*

Was D's **aim** to **kill or seriously injure** the girl? No, so there is no direct intent. Was death or serious injury a **'virtual certainty'** and did D **appreciate** this (**Nedrick**)? If the jury find this not to be the case there is no indirect intent. He will probably be found not guilty of murder due to lack of *mens rea*. However, if the jury believe that D intended to kill or seriously injure the police, whether directly or by appreciating it as a virtual certainty, then the principle of transferred malice means that this intent is transferred from them to the girl and he may be found guilty.

### Examination pointer

Decide what charge seems most appropriate, and then use the law to prove it. It may not be clear-cut so you could conclude with, "D could be charged with murder, but it may be hard to prove intent so a manslaughter charge may be more appropriate". Then go on to discuss involuntary manslaughter. However, read the question carefully. If you are *only* asked to discuss murder, don't go on to manslaughter.

### Intent and 'mercy killing'

In **Inglis 2010**, a mother was convicted of murder and sentenced to life imprisonment for killing her severely disabled son. There was clear intent to kill, so even though she acted in what she believed were her son's best interests the charge was murder. This can be compared with **Gilderdale** heard in the same week. Here a woman killed her daughter who had a chronic illness and who had tried to commit suicide herself on several occasions. She was cleared of attempted murder by a jury (attempted murder because it could not be shown if the drugs she gave caused the death or not). Again, she intended to kill her daughter so the charge had to be murder, but the jury were clearly sympathetic.

### Food for thought

These cases highlight the difficulties. Mrs Gilderdale was given a 12-month conditional discharge for aiding and abetting a suicide, whereas Mrs Inglis was given a life sentence for murder, even though there was little real difference in the facts and in both cases the mothers acted in what they believed was their child's best interests. The main difference seems to have been that in **Inglis** her son was too disabled to be able to communicate his own wishes, whereas in **Gilderdale** the daughter would probably have found a way to kill herself anyway. She had expressed a desire to end her life and this was taken into account by the jury, and by the judge when he said that the decision of the jury showed "*common sense, decency and humanity*".

However, the huge contrast in sentencing in these cases shows the problem of having a mandatory life sentence where the judge has no discretion.

In their 2004 report 'Partial Defences to Murder' the Law Commission said

*"the Government should undertake a public consultation on whether, and if so to what extent, the law should recognise either an offence of "mercy" killing or a partial defence of "mercy" killing".*

Making it a separate offence or a partial defence (as with diminished responsibility and loss of control) would allow for discretion in sentencing and perhaps make juries more willing to convict. No Government has yet felt able to tackle these issues and the law remains unchanged.

### Task

Practise your application of the law using my example with **Pagett** as a guide. Choose a case you know quite well and go through the stages step by step. This will produce the kind of logical structure you need for problem exam questions in other areas too. Keep it as a template for answering exam questions.

**Summary**

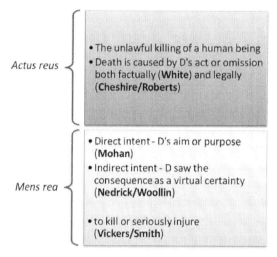

*Actus reus*
- The unlawful killing of a human being
- Death is caused by D's act or omission both factually (**White**) and legally (**Cheshire/Roberts**)

*Mens rea*
- Direct intent - D's aim or purpose (**Mohan**)
- Indirect intent - D saw the consequence as a virtual certainty (**Nedrick/Woollin**)
- to kill or seriously injure (**Vickers/Smith**)

*Self-test questions*

> What is the actus reus and mens rea of murder, and how have the courts interpreted the latter?

> What is a result crime and what is the significance in terms of actus reus?

> Can you explain the law on causation using two murder cases?

> In which CA case was the 'virtual certainty' test for mens rea established, and which HL case confirmed this?

> Have you achieved the aims not only of this Chapter, but of the Chapters on actus reus (especially causation) and mens rea (intent) too?

For answers to the tasks and self-test questions, please go to my website at www.drsr.org and click the button 'Answers to tasks'. For a range of free interactive exercises, click on 'Free Exercises' and then the OCR book.

*"... a state of mind so different from that of ordinary human beings that the reasonable man would term it abnormal"*

*Lord Parker*

By the end of this Chapter, you should be able to:

> *Explain the main legal requirements in proving diminished responsibility*
>
> *Explain how the law applies in practice by reference to cases*
>
> *Identify possible criticisms*

Diminished responsibility comes under the **Homicide Act 1957 s 2(1)** as amended by **s 52** of the **Coroners and Justice Act 2009**. This section came into force in October 2010 and states:

*"A person who kills or is a party to the killing of another is not to be convicted of murder if he was suffering from an abnormality of mental functioning which:*

> **(a) arose from a recognised medical condition,**
>
> **(b) substantially impaired D's ability to:**
>
>> **understand the nature of his conduct; or**
>>
>> **form a rational judgement; or**
>>
>> **exercise self-control.**

*and*

>> *(c) provides an explanation for D's acts and omissions in doing or being a party to the killing"*

### The legal requirements under the amended s 2

> **D suffers from 'an abnormality of mental functioning'**
>
> **The abnormality arises from a 'recognised medical condition'**
>
> **The abnormality substantially impaired D's ability to do one or more of three specified things**
>
> **The abnormality of mental functioning provides an explanation for D's acts and omissions**

Let's look at each of these.

### An abnormality of mental functioning

As this expression indicates, there is an overlap with the general defence of insanity. It covers more than 'defect of reason' though, which is the test for insanity. In **Byrne 1960**, Lord Parker CJ defined abnormality of mind (the old expression) as "a state of mind so different from that of ordinary human beings that the reasonable man would term it abnormal". D was described as a sexual psychopath. While suffering from powerful urges he strangled and then mutilated a young woman. These urges did not prevent him knowing what he was doing (he would have therefore failed on insanity) but he found it difficult, if not impossible, to control them. His defence of diminished responsibility succeeded and he was acquitted of murder.

Cases on the old law will still be relevant in deciding whether there was an abnormality of mental functioning, as the phrase is very similar. It is a matter for the jury based on medical evidence. It is likely that **Byrne** will be followed so that 'abnormality of mental functioning' will be interpreted as a condition which is so different from that of ordinary people that reasonable people (and the jury) would regard it as abnormal.

### Arising from a recognised medical condition

In all cases, medical evidence will be needed because the abnormality of mental functioning must arise from a 'recognised medical condition'.

This is perhaps wider than the old law (and a lot less complex) and covers both physical and psychiatric conditions. Disorders such as post-traumatic stress disorder, Gulf War syndrome, paranoid personality disorder, battered woman's syndrome and pre-menstrual stress are all likely to be recognised medical conditions.

### Case examples

In **Thornton 1992 and 1996**, Sara Thornton had gone to the kitchen to calm down after a violent argument. Whilst there she picked up a knife and sharpened it. She then went to where her husband was lying on the sofa and stabbed him. Her conviction for murder in 1990 was upheld by the CA in 1991. In a later appeal in 1995 fresh medical evidence was introduced which showed she had a personality disorder and 'battered woman syndrome'. The CA ordered a retrial. This took place in the Crown Court in May 1996 and she was convicted of manslaughter due to diminished responsibility.

(I have included the dates as this case and its various appeals and retrials may seem confusing. 1992 and 1996 are the dates the case was reported (All England Law Reports).)

In **Martin 2001**, a Norfolk farmer was convicted of murder after killing an intruder. On appeal he succeeded in arguing diminished responsibility due to a 'paranoid personality disorder'.

In **Freaney 2011**, a woman was cleared of the murder of her severely autistic 11-year-old son. Her son needed 24-hour care and help with dressing, washing, brushing his teeth and eating. He was not toilet trained and still wore nappies. She murdered him using her coat belt and when she was sure he was dead, she lay down on the bed beside him and tried to commit suicide. She denied murder but admitted his manslaughter on the grounds of diminished responsibility. The jury accepted that she was suffering under 'extreme mental stress' at the time she strangled her son and her plea of diminished responsibility succeeded. She was given a supervision order.

Reference to a recognised medical condition is clearer than the old law, which was complex and hard for juries to understand. However, one problem that remains is one that the Law Commission recognised. They had recommended that developmental immaturity in those under 18 should be included within the definition of diminished responsibility as a recognised medical condition. This was because there is evidence to show that parts of the brain which play an important role in the development of self-control do not mature until 14 years of age. The Government did not act on this suggestion. To an extent it is covered where the lack of maturity is caused by a medical disorder such as autism, but this clearly won't cover all young defendants so a child of 10 or over who kills can be convicted of murder even where there is evidence they had an abnormality of mental functioning due to their undeveloped maturity.

### Food for thought

In **Inglis 2010**, (see murder) a mother was convicted of murder and sentenced to life imprisonment for killing her disabled son. Once murder is established the judge has no discretion, so Mrs Inglis was given life even though it was accepted she acted in what she believed were her son's best interests (although this was reduced to a starting point of 9 years rather than the usual 15, on compassionate grounds). The vast difference in the sentences in **Freaney** and **Inglis** shows the difficulty in having a mandatory life sentence.

### Diminished responsibility and intoxication

In **Tandy 1989**, an alcoholic strangled her 11-year-old daughter after learning that she had been sexually abused. She had drunk almost a whole bottle of vodka and was suffering from an abnormality of mind at the time of the killing. The CA upheld the conviction for murder and held that the abnormality had to be caused by the disease of alcoholism rather than by the voluntary taking of alcohol. It could succeed if the first drink was involuntary but on the evidence, this was not the case. The CA established the principle that drink is only capable of giving rise to this defence if it either causes brain damage or produces an irresistible craving so that consumption is involuntary.

So an abnormality caused by taking drugs or drink would not suffice unless there is an associated medical condition such as alcoholism, now usually referred to as alcohol dependency syndrome. However, if D is intoxicated *as well as* suffering from one of the above causes the defence may succeed. This was stated in **Fenton 1975**, confirmed in **Gittens 1984** (where she was drunk but also suffered from chronic depression,) and approved by the HL in **Dietschmann 2003**. It is thus a well-established rule which will still apply under the new law.

### Key case

In **Dietschmann**, D had savagely attacked someone whilst suffering depression following the death of his girlfriend. He was also drunk. The HL made clear that D had to show that even without the drink he had sufficient 'abnormality of mind' (as in **Fenton** and **Gittens**). However, they added that he did not have to show that he would have killed even if not intoxicated, because the 'abnormality' did not have to be the *only* cause of the killing. This means D only needs to satisfy the jury that, as well as (but not *because of*) being drunk, he had an abnormality which substantially impaired his responsibility. He need not show he would still have killed even if he had been sober. The HL held that the jury must ask themselves whether D had satisfied them that, *despite the drink*, his mental abnormality substantially impaired his responsibility. If so the defence may succeed, if not the defence is not available.

### Food for thought

These are difficult issues. Not least if you happen to be on the jury! You will have to try to ignore the intoxication and determine whether the other causes were enough substantially to impair D's ability. Not an easy task. The **Dietschmann** case highlights the difficulties. Does it solve any? Would you be able ignore the intoxication in such cases if you were on the jury?

If alcoholism as a disease is argued, you will have to decide if the first drink taken was voluntary or involuntary.

The rules were clarified in the next case.

In **Wood 2008**, the CA confirmed that **Dietschmann** did not alter the principle that voluntary consumption of alcohol does not amount to an abnormality of the mind, but said that it did establish that a defence of diminished responsibility would not fail merely because D had consumed alcohol voluntarily before killing. The CA agreed that **Tandy** should be re-assessed in cases where there was 'alcohol dependency syndrome'. In **Wood**, D had been diagnosed with this syndrome and killed in a frenzied attack whilst drunk, having woken after a party to find a man attempting to have oral sex with him. The CA held that it was not a requirement that the syndrome caused brain damage (as required in **Tandy**). The only question for the jury was whether it constituted an abnormality of mind (now mental functioning). If it did not, diminished responsibility based on the consumption of alcohol would fail. If it did, the jury must consider whether D's responsibility was substantially impaired because of the syndrome. The jury should focus exclusively on the effect of alcohol consumed as a direct result of the illness or disease and ignore the effect of any alcohol consumed voluntarily.

In **Dowds 2012**, in an appeal to the CA after the **2009 Act** came into force, D argued that acute intoxication was a recognised medical condition. He and his partner had a long history of drunkenness and violence, and both had been drinking when he attacked her with a knife and killed her. His appeal failed and the CA held that the new law was not intended to change the rule that voluntary intoxication was not capable of establishing diminished responsibility.

So, if D has a medical condition and is also drunk the jury should ignore the drink and just consider the medical condition (**Dietschmann**).

If the intoxication *results from* a medical condition, such as alcohol dependency syndrome, the jury can consider the drink but must ask whether it amounts to an abnormality (**Wood**).

The **Coroners and Justice Act 2009** does not change the rules on this (**Dowds**).

### Example

After Tony came back from fighting in the war in Iraq he was diagnosed with post-traumatic stress disorder (PTSD), which causes him to have violent outbursts. One night, after several drinks, he gets into a fight and kills someone. He is charged with murder and pleads the defence of diminished responsibility. The PTSD will be a recognised medical condition, so the jury will then have to decide whether the PTSD itself substantially impaired his ability to exercise self-control, ignoring the effect of the drinks he had consumed.

### Substantially impaired D's ability

Substantially impaired will be interpreted in the way same as the old law. The judge will usually direct the jury as to the meaning of 'substantial' in relation to the facts of the case. In **Lloyd 1967**, the court said the impairment need not be total but must be more than trivial or minimal. In **Campbell 1987**, the medical evidence was that D had epilepsy which could make him "vulnerable to an impulsive tendency". The defence failed because 'vulnerable to' indicates that it was not substantial.

There is some difference with the previous law. Under **s 2** as amended by the **Coroners and Justice Act**, it is not D's mental responsibility that must be substantially impaired, it is D's ability to do one of three things:

> **to understand the nature of his conduct, or**

> **to form a rational judgement or,**

> **to exercise self-control**

Although not specified in the old law, these matters are much as before. Someone with learning difficulties may not understand the nature of the act, nor be able to form a rational judgement, nor exercise self-control. **Byrne** succeeded because he was unable to exercise self-control. Severe stress, as in many of the mercy killing cases, would perhaps prevent D being able to form a rational judgement.

Note that only one of the three things is needed, not all.

### Provides an explanation for D's acts and omissions in doing or being a party to the killing

That the abnormality of mental functioning must 'provide an explanation for D's acts and omissions' is clarified in **s 52(1)(C)** of the Act as meaning that it 'causes, or is a significant contributory factor in causing, D to carry out that conduct'.

This was introduced to the defence by the amendments made by the **Coroners and Justice Act 2009**. It means that there must now be some causal connection between D's abnormality of mental functioning and the conduct. The abnormality must cause the killing or make a significant contribution to it.

### Example: Applying the 2009 Act to Wood, above.

Alcohol dependency syndrome was confirmed to be a recognised medical condition in this case.

The jury would also need to be convinced that:

D was suffering an abnormality of mental functioning which arose from his alcohol dependency syndrome

This abnormality substantially (not trivially, but not necessarily totally, using **Lloyd**) impaired his ability to do **one of** the following:

understand the nature of his conduct: quite likely, the evidence showed he did not know what he was doing at the time

form a rational judgement: also likely as it was doubtful he could form any judgement at all

exercise self-control: not clear on the facts but we only need one of these not all three

Finally, the abnormality of mental functioning must provide an explanation for his acts. An issue of causation, and again quite likely as he would not have killed if not suffering from the syndrome, so this made a significant contribution to his actions

### Task

Go to the Law Commission website at http://lawcommission.justice.gov.uk/ and look at the 2004 report on 'Partial defences to murder' or the 2006 report on Murder, manslaughter and infanticide' (listed in the A-Z). Quotes and discussions from these will enhance an essay and help you see how far the **Coroners and Justice Act** took up the LC's suggestions.

### Burden of proof

D must prove that the defence applies. The standard of proof is the balance of probabilities, i.e., the civil standard. D will need to provide medical evidence to support a plea of diminished responsibility.

### Food for thought

There may be a sense of injustice where a jury decision is made based on what is justified rather than by using the legal tests. The defence may succeed or fail for moral reasons, rather than legal ones. A jury may accept a plea of diminished responsibility even where there is little evidence for it. Examples can be seen in cases of 'mercy killings', such as **Bailey 2002** where a

74-year-old man killed his wife, who had motor neurone disease and wanted to die. He had not lost control but the jury accepted his defence of diminished responsibility.

This may be due to sympathy for the accused, or because the mandatory life sentence means that if the defence fails, the sentence will be life for murder. Accepting the defence means that a discretionary sentence can be given, taking into account the circumstances. Whilst this may 'do justice' in a particular case, it is arguably stretching the law to fit the facts.

It also works both ways. In **Sutcliffe 1981**, the 'Yorkshire ripper' case where D had committed a series of brutal murders, the defence was rejected by the jury (on the direction of the judge) despite strong medical evidence to the contrary and the fact that both the defence and prosecution accepted it. Presumably, the brutality of the murders persuaded the jury that a life sentence was appropriate.

Abolishing the mandatory life sentence for murder could be discussed in an evaluation. It would perhaps avoid the uncertainty of relying on the jury's sympathy or revulsion.

**Summary**

| | |
|---|---|
| Abnormality of mental functioning: will be interpreted as for abnormality of mind ... | ... so different from that of ordinary human beings that the reasonable man would term it abnormal **Byrne 1960** |
| Substantially impaired | Impairment need not be total but must be more than trivial or minimal **Lloyd 1967** |
| It is D's ability to do one of three things which must be substantially impaired | These are:<br>   to understand the nature of his conduct;<br>   to form a rational judgement;<br>   to exercise self-control. |
| Alcoholism, or alcohol dependency syndrome, may lead to a successful defence but only if the first drink was involuntary | **Tandy 1989/Wood 2008** |
| If D is intoxicated *as well as* suffering from a abnormality of mental functioning the defence may succeed, but the jury must ignore the intoxication | **Dietschmann 2003** |
| The **Coroners and Justice Act 2009** does not change the rules on intoxication | **Dowds 2012** |
| The abnormality of mental functioning must provide an explanation for D's conduct | A causation issue; did the abnormality of mental functioning cause D to act that way? |

**Self-test questions**

*Have you achieved the aims set out at the beginning of the Chapter?*

*From which case did the opening quote come?*

*What type of evidence will be required for this defence?*

*Who has the burden of proving the defence?*

*Which Act amended the **Homicide Act s 2** on the defence of diminished responsibility?*

For answers to the tasks and self-test questions, please go to my website at www.drsr.org and click the button 'Answers to tasks'. For a range of free interactive exercises, click on 'Free Exercises' and then the OCR book.

*"Would a sober man, in relation to that drunken observation, batter his friend over the head with a nearly two pound-weight ashtray?"*

*Newell 1980*

By the end of this Chapter, you should be able to:

**Explain the main legal requirements in proving the s 54 defence**

**Explain how the law on loss of control applies in practice by reference to cases**

**Identify possible criticisms**

Loss of control replaces the previous defence of provocation. The law is now found in **s 54** and **s 55** of the **Coroners and Justice Act 2009** which came into force in October 2010.

**S 54** states:

*'(1) Where a person ("D") kills or is a party to the killing of another ("V"), D is not to be convicted of murder if —*

*(a) D's acts and omissions in doing or being a party to the killing resulted from D's loss of self-control,*

*(b) the loss of self-control had a qualifying trigger, and*

*(c) a person of D's sex and age, with a normal degree of tolerance and self-restraint and in the circumstances of D, might have reacted in the same or in a similar way to D.'*

The **Coroners and Justice Act 2009** repealed **s 3** of the **Homicide Act** and changed the name of the defence to loss of control. You will come across the previous defence of provocation in cases prior to 2010, and some of the old law still applies.

The burden of proof is on the prosecution. If D raises loss of control as a defence, then the prosecution have to prove beyond reasonable doubt – the criminal standard of proof – that the case is *not* one of loss of control. (With the alternative defence to murder of diminished responsibility, the burden is reversed and D must prove the defence.)

**Examination pointer**

Remember these defences ONLY apply to a murder charge. Don't try to apply them to other crimes. Where there is a death combined with intent to kill you can deal with any murder issues and then look at these defences. If intent and causation are clear, you don't need to discuss these in detail, move quickly to the defences having briefly explained why the charge is likely to be murder. Only if the facts indicate it is necessary, for example, if there is a possible break in the chain of causation, or if intent may be hard to prove, should you discuss these. Examiners know you cannot discuss everything in the time so questions are usually set which address specific issues. Be selective!

*The three questions to consider under s 54*

*did D lose self-control?*

*was the loss of self-control triggered by something specified in s 55?*

*would a normal person of D's sex and age have reacted in the same way in D's circumstances?*

### Did D lose self-control?

**S 54(1)** states:

*'D's acts and omissions in doing or being a party to the killing resulted from D's loss of self-control'.*

Note the words 'resulted from'. This means the killing must have been caused by the loss of self-control; this is a new requirement under the 2009 Act.

Whether D lost self-control is initially a matter for the judge. If there is evidence of loss of control the judge will put it to the jury to decide on the facts whether in the circumstances D lost self-control and whether the killing resulted from this, and may do so even if D does not raise it as a defence. This was seen in **Thornton 1992**, below.

Under the old law, the loss of control had to be 'sudden and temporary'. In several cases women who had suffered years of abuse killed their partners. Accused of murder, they argued the provocation defence. Many failed on the 'sudden and temporary' point because there was a 'cooling-off' period between the provocative conduct and the killing. Under **s 54(2)** there is no longer a need for the loss of control to be sudden so these cases could succeed now, however it may be difficult to prove any loss of control after a cooling off period.

### Key case

In **Thornton**, she didn't raise what was then the defence of provocation at her original trial but the judge put it to the jury and it was rejected. The evidence was that she had cooled down by the time she stabbed him. Her conviction for murder in 1990 was upheld by the CA in 1991. In a later appeal in 1995 fresh medical evidence was introduced which showed she had a personality disorder and 'battered woman syndrome'. The CA held that the jury should have been allowed to consider whether a reasonable woman with these characteristics would have acted as Mrs Thornton did. However, Lord Taylor said that D *"cannot succeed in relying on provocation unless the jury consider she suffered or may have suffered a sudden and temporary loss of self-control at the time of the killing"*.

It is possible that she would now succeed with the loss of control defence, but unlikely. Although there is no longer a 'sudden and temporary' requirement, there must be a loss of control, and she does not appear to have lost control at all, she went into the kitchen to calm down before getting the knife. The Law Commission had advised not keeping the loss of control requirement and this is understandable considering the need to extend the defence to 'battered women' cases such as **Thornton.**

In **Ahluwalia 1992**, D set fire to her husband's bed when he was asleep. The defence of provocation again failed on the 'sudden and temporary' point, and again could still fail as she waited until he was asleep, so arguably did not lose control.

NB: At both subsequent retrials, the defence of diminished responsibility succeeded so these cases are relevant to both partial defences to murder.

There must be loss of *control* not just *self-restraint*. In **Cocker 1989**, D had finally given way to his wife's entreaties to ease her pain and end her life. His defence failed as the evidence showed he had not lost control. This would still apply for the new law.

Two differences with the law under the **Coroners and Justice Act 2009** are that:

**S 54(2)** states that the loss of self-control does not need to be sudden

**S 54(4)** states that the defence is not allowed if D acted in a 'considered desire for revenge'

Revenge is usually carried out after a period of time, so the defence could have failed under the sudden and temporary rule in the old law, now it would fail because revenge is excluded by the Act.

In **Ibrams and Gregory 1981**, the Ds and a girl had been terrorised by V. They planned to entice V to the girl's bed and then the Ds would attack him. They carried out the planned attack several days later, and killed V. At their appeal against a conviction for murder, the CA held that the defence failed because there was no sudden loss of control, the attack was planned and carried out over several days. Under **s 54(2)**, although there is no need for the loss of self-control to be sudden, any such time delay may indicate that there was no loss of control at all. It could also indicate a 'considered desire for revenge' and so be excluded by **s 54(4)**. Finally, it may fail because even if there was a loss of control at the start, it is unlikely to have caused D to kill several days later, so the killing did not 'result from' the loss of control as required by **s 54(1)**.

Another case relevant to these issues is **Baillie 1995**. In **Baillie**, D's son was getting drugs from a dealer who had threatened him with violence. When D found out, he drove to the dealer's house armed with a razor and a sawn-off shotgun. They had an argument and D shot the dealer as he left, killing him. The trial judge refused to allow the defence (then provocation) to be put to the jury and D appealed. The CA allowed the appeal because there was sufficient evidence for the matter to be put to the jury. This case could go either way now. There is no need for the loss of control to be sudden, but there is an element of revenge in D's act of driving to the dealer's house in response to the threat to his son. Much would depend on whether the jury saw it as a 'considered' desire for revenge. In **Baillie**, unlike in **Ibrams**, D drove to V's house whilst still angry, so any desire for revenge may not be deemed 'considered', also the killing could have 'resulted from' the loss of control as there was not a long gap between the two.

In one of three appeals heard together under the new Act, **Evans 2012**, the loss of control defence was considered. D had killed his wife after she had goaded him. He said she had stabbed him, but it was not clear if this was the case, or whether he had done it himself. The prosecution case was that he killed her because she told him that she was going to leave him. The defence case was that she had stabbed him, and he had lost control and stabbed her. The main issue was whether he had 'acted in a considered desire for revenge'. The judge summed up in accordance with the Act and said:

*"If you conclude so that you are sure either that this was a considered act of revenge by the defendant or that he had not lost the ability to control himself, this defence does not apply and your verdict would be guilty of murder".*

He was found guilty of murder. The CA dismissed his appeal (heard together with **Clinton** and **Parker**, see below) and held that there was sufficient evidence that he had acted in revenge so the jury decision was correct. The judge had summed up both the prosecution and defence arguments as regards the possibility of it being an act of revenge, so the conviction was fair.

**Was the loss of self-control triggered by something specified in s 55?**

Under **s 54(1)(b)** there must be a 'qualifying trigger'; this refers to whether something triggered D's loss of control – and what that something was. Under the old law, there was no specific restriction on what caused D to lose control

**S 55(1)** of the Act sets out the qualifying triggers. The loss of control must be triggered by:

*D's fear of serious violence from V against D or another identified person; or*

*a thing or things done or said (or both) which—*

*(a) constituted circumstances of an extremely grave character, and*

*(b) caused D to have a justifiable sense of being seriously wronged.*

*Or a combination of both of these*

So what will amount to a qualifying trigger? Fear of serious violence suffices, e.g., reacting to someone threatening to attack you, as long as 'serious' violence is feared. The defence may succeed where it failed before, in the case of women who fear violent abuse, as long as it caused a loss of control.

The violence need not be directed at D. In **Pearson 1992**, a boy killed his father because of the father's ill treatment, not of himself but of his brother, and the defence succeeded. This is still the case, fear of violence against D or *'another identified person'* will be enough. The 'things done and said' means the loss of control can be caused by both actions and words. Again, this is the same as the previous law. In **Doughty 1986**, the crying of a baby was said to amount to what was then called provocation.

It is unlikely that **Doughty** would succeed now. This is because the 'things done or said' must be 'extremely grave' and 'justifiably' cause D to feel 'seriously' wronged. The crying of a baby is unlikely to be deemed *extremely grave* nor is a jury likely to be persuaded that it caused D to have a *justifiable* sense of being *seriously* wronged.

In **Parker 2012**, D had killed his wife during an argument. The evidence was that he had placed knives close to hand in preparation for the attack. However he argued that he had 'lost it' when she told him she didn't love him. The judge summed up the new law to the jury as follows:

*'When D stabbed his wife had he lost self-control?*

*If not then go no further. Otherwise, consider whether his loss of self-control was caused by a qualifying trigger. The qualifying triggers are things said or done by his wife which*

*a. constitute circumstances of an extremely grave character and*

*b. caused the defendant to have a justified sense of being seriously wronged.*

*If neither was the case then he is guilty of murder, otherwise consider whether a man of D's age with a normal degree of tolerance and self-restraint would have reacted in the same or in a similar way to the way that the defendant reacted'.*

The jury reached a verdict of murder. In dismissing D's appeal (heard with **Clinton** below) the CA held that the matters relied on by D could not reasonably be treated by any jury as circumstances of an extremely grave character which caused him to have a justifiable sense that he had been seriously wronged.

The Act specifically excludes sexual infidelity as a qualifying trigger. Under the old law, it would have been allowed as a cause of the loss of control, in fact the original law was introduced to cover such cases. Under **s 55(6)**, if the thing 'done or said' constituted sexual infidelity it is to be disregarded.

In **Holley 2005**, (discussed below) D killed his girlfriend with an axe after she had slept with another man and had also taunted him about his lack of courage. The fact that she had slept with someone else would be irrelevant as sexual infidelity is excluded by **s 55(6)** but the taunt about his lack of courage would be 'a thing said' so would be relevant.

### Key case

In the third of the three cases appeals together, **Clinton 2012**, D had killed his wife during a heated exchange and claimed both diminished responsibility and loss of control. She had told him she was having an affair and he had seen graphic pictures of her and her lover on Facebook. They also had financial difficulties and were undergoing a trial separation. The evidence was that he had planned the death having done some research on the internet. The jury rejected the diminished responsibility plea and the judge held that there was no loss of control due to one of the 'qualifying triggers' as required by the **Coroners' and Justice Act**, and also that the wife's infidelity should be ignored as this was specifically excluded by the Act. He was convicted of murder and appealed. The CA held that the judge had misdirected herself about the possible relevance of the wife's infidelity. Under **s 54(1)(c)** regard should be had to 'the circumstances of D'. The CA said this meant all the circumstances should be taken together. In this case, the sexual infidelity was an essential part of the whole, and had had sufficient impact on D to suggest the defence should have been put to the jury. A retrial was ordered. Strangely, at this retrial he changed his plea to guilty and did not rely on the defence. He was given a life sentence for murder.

Also excluded under **s 55(6)** are situations where D has incited either the fear of violence or the thing done or said, in order to have the excuse to use violence.

### Example

Alan gets into an argument with Imran and says, "Come on then, come and do your worst." Imran then attacks Alan and Alan is now scared, he loses control and picks up a poker and hits Imran with it, killing him. Can Alan rely on loss of control if charged with murder? No, because he incited Imran to cause the fear.

### Food for thought

In **Thornton** the trial judge directed the jury on provocation and then added "… *it may be difficult to come to the conclusion that that was, and I use the shorthand, a reasonable reaction*". He then went on to suggest it wasn't reasonable to stab someone when "*there are other alternatives available, like walking out or going upstairs*".

Do you think his comments influenced the jury too much? Many people say abused women should simply walk away but life is rarely simple. Arguably, issues of fact like this should be left to the jury alone.

The question the jury had to ask themselves in **Thornton** was whether a reasonable woman would have done the same in her position, which brings us to the last point.

### Would a normal person of D's sex and age have reacted in the same way in D's circumstances?

**S 54(1)(c)** asks whether '*a person of D's sex and age, with a normal degree of tolerance and self-restraint and in the circumstances of D, might have reacted in the same or similar way*'. This is further clarified by **s 54(3)** which allows for '*reference to all of D's circumstances other than those whose only relevance to D's conduct is that they bear on D's general capacity for tolerance or self-restraint*'. This means age and sex are relevant in deciding the level of control expected and what the 'reasonable person' would do, but the addition of 'in the circumstances' means others matters can be looked at for the latter as long as they don't relate to D's capacity for tolerance or self-restraint. A medical problem like an addiction, or a history of abuse would be a 'circumstance' but a short temper would not because this relates to D's capacity for restraint.

Many of the old cases will still be relevant and will anyway be needed for evaluation and discussion of reforms.

The question is objective, what 'a person' would do, not what D did. The Act refers to these persons having the same age and sex as D. What other personal characteristics can be attributed to this hypothetical person has caused many problems. In **Camplin 1978**, a 15 year-old boy hit V with a chapatti pan after being homosexually assaulted and then taunted about it. V died and D was charged with murder. The HL said the question was whether a reasonable person of his *age* and *sex* would have done as he did. The **2009 Act** confirms this.

It was not fully clear from **Camplin** whether characteristics other than age and sex could be taken into account. Earlier cases centred on physical characteristics; this was later extended to mental ones. One of the reasons for ordering a retrial in **Thornton** was that this development had occurred since her original trial. In addition, the characteristics had to be both *relevant* and *permanent*. In **Newell 1980**, an alcoholic was in an emotional state and was provoked by his friend making homosexual advances. He hit him over the head with a heavy ashtray and killed him. The court held that although alcoholism was a possible characteristic it was not to be taken into account, as it wasn't related to the provocation. The fact that he was drunk and emotional wasn't attributable because this was a temporary state. The court asked the jury the question in the opening quote.

In **Morhall 1995**, glue sniffing was said by the CA not to be a characteristic to be attributed to the reasonable man but this was reversed by the HL. It was held that as D was addicted this would be attributable, in the same way that alcoholism is, but being drunk isn't. D had been taunted by V about his addiction and they got into a fight, during which he stabbed V. Here the addiction was both relevant and permanent.

In **Luc Thiet Thuan 1996**, the Privy Council took a more restrictive view. D killed his girlfriend after she teased him about his sexual prowess. There was evidence he was mentally unstable and had difficulty controlling his impulses. The Privy Council held that such mental factors could not be attributed to the reasonable man.

However, in **Smith 2000**, the HL widened the law again. D and a friend, both alcoholics, spent the evening drinking. D accused the friend of stealing his work tools and selling them to buy drink. They argued and D picked up a kitchen knife and stabbed his friend to death. At his murder trial, he argued provocation and said the jury should take into account the fact that he had been suffering from severe depression which reduced his powers of self-control. The judge rejected this argument but the HL accepted D's appeal. Lord Hoffman said that if the jury thought that there was some characteristic which affected the degree of control which society could reasonably have expected of him, it would be unjust not to take that into account. However, he did carry on to say that characteristics such as jealousy and obsession should be ignored, and Lord Clyde added 'exceptional pugnacity or excitability'.

So, this hypothetical person seemed to be getting quite a number of possible characteristics. In **Smith** Lord Hoffman referred to "monsters" being produced by attributing characteristics like glue sniffing to the reasonable person. The decision was only by a 3/2 majority. In particular, Lord Hobhouse produced a lengthy and reasoned argument against the decision. **Smith** is no longer likely to be good law; see **Holley** below where it was disapproved. The old law will be useful for evaluation questions though. The need for reforms and how far the Act has addressed the problems can be discussed.

## Food for thought

That this has been a problematic defence is clear. In 2003, the Law Commission said, "its defects are beyond cure by judicial development of the law". Some improvements are made in the **Coroners and Justice Act** but it is still complicated. Groups such as Justice for Women have long argued that the defence of provocation favours men as it can be used only by those strong enough to fight back. The women who suffer years of abuse and finally kill in desperation – but not in the heat of the moment – failed on the 'sudden and temporary' requirement. The removal of the need for a 'sudden and temporary' loss of control is an improvement but there must be a loss of control and the killing must result from this, so many of these cases would still not succeed. . The fact that loss of control must be shown goes against the Law Commission's proposals and prevents the defence clearly extending to cases of abuse against women, who may be physically weaker and liable to even greater abuse if they lose control and fight back

The Privy Council looked at the issue again in **AG for Jersey v Holley 2005**. Although this was an appeal from a trial in Jersey, decisions of the Privy Council are highly persuasive on English law because the judges are Law Lords.

## Key case

In **Holley 2005**, D, who was an alcoholic, killed his girlfriend with an axe whilst drunk. She had slept with another man and had also taunted him about his lack of courage. The CA substituted his conviction for murder for one of manslaughter, on the basis that the jury was misdirected on provocation. The prosecution appealed to the Privy Council, who held that **s 3** of the **Homicide Act** provided that provocation should be judged by one standard, not a standard that varied from D to D. **Smith** was held to be wrong on this point. D was to be judged against the standard of a person having 'ordinary powers of self-control', not against the standard expected of a particular D in the same position. Alcoholism is therefore no longer a 'relevant matter' for the jury when deciding whether a reasonable person would have done what D did. Note that Lord Hoffman dissented, but as his was the leading judgement in **Smith**, this is not surprising. It would seem that the law is back to **Luc Thiet**.

In **James; Karini 2008**, the CA followed **Holley** and disapproved **Smith**. It was noted that although decisions of the Privy Council are only persuasive, in **Holley**, the Council had consisted of nine law Lords so it was clear that in any appeal to the HL the decision would be the same.

### The subjective and objective elements

**Holley** also highlights the subjective and objective elements of the characteristics issue

The subjective element means D's characteristics and particular circumstances can be taken into account when assessing the gravity of whatever triggered the loss of control

The objective element is that only age and sex are taken into account in deciding what a reasonable person would do

This is confirmed by the **Coroners and Justice Act** which clarifies the circumstances to be taken into account in deciding whether 'a person' would have acted in a similar way to D. **S 54(1)**

states that D is to be judged against a person of the same age and sex, having ordinary levels of tolerance and self-restraint in the circumstances of D. **S 54(3)** further adds that "the circumstances of D" is a reference to all of D's circumstances other than those whose only relevance to D's conduct is that they bear on D's general capacity for tolerance or self-restraint.

We saw that in **Newell 1980**, alcoholism was a possible characteristic, but was not allowed as it wasn't related to the taunt, and being drunk wasn't allowed because it was a temporary state. The Act will apply in a similar way. If he had been taunted about his alcoholism that could be one of the 'circumstances of D'; his drunkenness in itself would be ignored as this merely relates to his capacity for self-restraint.

In **Asmelash 2013**, D had been drinking with another man and got into a fight, during which D stabbed and killed him. He said the deceased had made him so angry that he lost control. The judge applied **s 54** of the **Coroners and Justice Act 2009** and said the jury should consider whether a person of D's sex and age with a normal degree of tolerance and self-restraint and in the same circumstances, but unaffected by alcohol, would have reacted in the same or similar way. D was convicted and appealed. The CA agreed with the judge that the consumption of alcohol should be ignored. The judges noted that in **Dowds 2012** (see previous chapter), the new law was held not to change the rule that voluntary intoxication was not capable of establishing diminished responsibility. It was "inconceivable" that different criteria should apply to voluntary drunkenness depending on whether the partial defence under consideration was diminished responsibility or loss of control. This did not mean D could not use the loss of control defence; it simply means that the defence had to be approached without reference to the voluntary intoxication.

### Examination pointer

The old law will be useful in evaluating the defence for an essay question. For problem questions, it is the later cases and the Act that are important. Also, as you will have seen, there is an overlap between diminished responsibility and loss of control, so you may well have to apply both. Look carefully at the given facts and watch for words like 'abuse' or 'depression'. Long-term abuse may be relevant to loss of control or result in a recognised medical condition such as 'battered woman's syndrome' or trauma. Look at the following example.

### Example

A man's wife is dying and in terrible pain. Over a period of several months, she begs him to end her suffering. He is getting very upset and severely depressed. One night she screams at him "for once in your life act like a man and help me die". He finally snaps and smothers her. This could be 'loss of control' so you would apply the law under **s 54** and **s 55**. There is evidence of loss of self-control, by things 'done or said', a person with normal levels of tolerance and restraint will be someone who had gone through several months of being tormented by such requests and so arguably would act in the same way. What if he had spent a couple of days thinking about it, trying to find the courage? Under the old law, he may fail due to the 'sudden and temporary' rule. This no longer applies – but a loss of control defence may still fail if there was a cooling-off period so you can refer to his 'severe depression' and bring in **s 2** as an alternative.

### Case examples

In **Bailey 2002**, (see last chapter) D had not lost control but his defence of diminished responsibility succeeded

In **Zebedee 2011** (unreported), D had killed his father who was suffering from Alzheimer's disease. He admitted killing him but denied murder. He said that he snapped after remembering alleged abuse by his father that he had suffered as a child, but there was no evidence to support this. He argued both diminished responsibility and loss of control, saying that his ability to exercise control had been impaired by an adjustment order resulting from the earlier abuse. As for loss of control he said this was caused by his father whistling a tune over and over, soiling himself and making a gesture which recalled the abuse. Both defences were put to the jury but rejected.

### A quick recap

### Would a person of D's age and sex have reacted in the same way?

The level of control expected is that of a person of the same age and sex with normal levels of self-restraint. This is an objective test.

### In the circumstances of D

This is partly subjective, D's particular circumstances, such as a history of abuse or alcoholism, can be taken into account, because these will relate not to the ability to retain control but to the reason for losing it. According to **Clinton**, sexual infidelity can be taken into account at this point as it will affect the gravity of the circumstances as a whole, and their impact on D.

### Other than those whose only relevance to D's conduct is that they bear on D's general capacity for tolerance or self-restraint

Things that made D lose control more easily, such as being drunk or aggressive by nature, will be irrelevant.

In **Mohammed 2005**, D found a young man in his daughter's bedroom. The man escaped but D killed his daughter with a knife. He was very strict and had a reputation for being violent and short-tempered. D was convicted of murder and appealed. The CA had to decide whether his violence and short-temper were relevant to the question of how a normal person would have reacted. Lord Justice Scott Baker said that D's temperament was not relevant and that

*"... the reasonable man is a fixed rather than a variable creature. The yardstick is a person of the age and sex of the appellant having and exercising ordinary powers of self-control."*

This is similar to the new law. Violence and short-temper would relate to D's capacity for self-restraint or control, so cannot be taken into account when deciding whether a person would have reacted in a similar way.

Similarly, in **Luc Thiet Thuan 1996**, the evidence that he was mentally unstable and had difficulty controlling his impulses would not be taken into account. It is not clear whether the taunts about his sexual prowess would constitute circumstances of an 'extremely grave character' (and so be a qualifying trigger) but if so then they may be considered as a 'circumstance'. Following **Clinton**, it is unlikely these should be excluded even if they amounted to sexual infidelity.

It seems clear that things like a violent nature, short-temperedness, glue-sniffing, taking drugs or being drunk will be irrelevant as these affect D's capacity for tolerance and self-restraint. It is likely that (as in **Newell**) the 'particular circumstances that D was in' would have to be relevant to the loss of control, i.e., constitute a reason for the reaction. This was previously referred to as affecting the *gravity* of the provocation, rather than the *capacity for self-control*, and it would be similar under the new law.

### Example

I am very embarrassed about a big growth on my back. Recently the doctor told me I needed an operation and I am very depressed and upset. Whilst drinking in the kitchen at a party someone calls me a hunchback. I pick up a large knife and stab them. I am charged with murder and plead loss of control.

There is evidence of 'things said', and I clearly lost control, but would a reasonable person have acted like I did? The jury will have to decide whether a person of my age and sex, with a normal degree of tolerance and self-restraint, would have done the same in my circumstances. My growth is a circumstance which can be taken into account as it affects the gravity of the comment, i.e., its effect on me. A person with no growth wouldn't be upset by the comment, so it is fair that this circumstance is taken into account. My drunkenness would not be allowed as it bears on my capacity for tolerance or self-restraint.

Following **Holley** and the **Coroners and Justice Act** my depression may not be allowed as a circumstance. I am not taunted about this so it is not likely to be seen as a relevant circumstance (it does not affect the gravity of the taunt or its effect on me), it is more likely to be seen as only it affecting my capacity for tolerance or self-restraint.

In the guidelines to the Act put out by the Ministry of Justice an example is given of a 23- year old woman who has killed her partner, who has beaten her frequently. It says the jury must consider whether a woman of that age with that history and with an ordinary level of tolerance and self-restraint might have done the same or a similar thing to their partner.

### Problems and reforms

In their 2004 report 'Partial Defences to Murder' the Law Commission said

*"Over the centuries the law of homicide, including the law of murder, has developed in a higgledy-piggledy fashion. The present law is a product of judge made law supplemented by Parliament's sporadic intervention. The outcome is a body of law characterised by a lack of clarity and coherence."*

The **Coroners and Justice Act** only addresses a few of the problems seen in their report. See the Study Block summary for more on these.

### Task

Go to the Law Commission's website and see what they say concerning murder in 'completed projects' or 'publications'. You will find lots of information which you can refer to in an essay. You can see how far the Coroners and Justice Act took up the LC's suggestions. Quotes and discussions from this will help and will enhance an essay.

### Examination pointer

Look for clues like 'goaded by what X said' or 'in reaction to what X did'. Remember to explain that there must be a qualifying trigger State and apply the law and then say "D may be charged with murder, but if the jury are satisfied that a reasonable person would have done the same the conviction will be for manslaughter"

### Summary of the developments

The characteristics which can be attributed to D to decide if a reasonable person would do as D did have caused some inconsistencies, which have now been clarified to some extent. Age and sex are attributable in all cases, other characteristics will be part of 'the circumstances of D', so can be taken into account as long as they do not only relate to D's capacity for tolerance or self-restraint

| | |
|---|---|
| DPP v Camplin 1978 | only age and sex attributable |
| Morhall 1993 | CA said glue-sniffing was not a characteristic to be attributed to the reasonable person, but this was reversed by HL |
| Luc Thiet Thuan 1996 | mental factors could not be attributed |
| Smith 2000 | everything but excitability, jealousy, obsession and exceptional pugnacity could be attributed |
| AG v Holley 2005 | the jury should not take into account D's mental state, just age and sex, but can then consider how a person would have acted in D's circumstances |
| S 54 & 55 Coroners and Justice Act 2009 | as for Holley, as long as D's circumstances don't relate to the ability to show tolerance or self-restraint |
| Clinton 2012 | sexual infidelity can be a 'circumstance' as long as it is part of the whole |

Remember, there are two things the new law excludes that the old law did not, one under **s 54** and one under **s 55**.

**Excluded matters**

**S 54(4) Revenge**: The defence is not allowed if D acted in a 'considered desire for revenge'. It is not clear yet how far this reflects the old law. Revenge is usually carried out after a period of time so would have failed under the sudden and temporary rule in the old law, now it could fail because revenge is excluded by the Act.

**S 55 (6) Sexual infidelity**: this cannot be a qualifying trigger. Under the old law, it would have been allowed as a cause of the loss of control. However, note that the law was interpreted liberally in **Clinton 2012**, where sexual infidelity was accepted as a 'circumstance' as long as it was integral to the whole situation and not a trigger on its own.

## Summary of the provisions under the Coroners' and Justice Act 2009

| | |
|---|---|
| Did D lose control s 54(1)? However the defence cannot be used where acted in a 'considered desire for revenge' s 54(4) | D must have lost self-control but this need not be sudden s 54(2), however any sign of calming down and/or planning an attack is likely to mean the defence fails |
| D's act must have resulted from the loss of control s 54(1)(a) | A causation issue, did the loss of control cause D to kill? |
| There must be a qualifying trigger 55 | Did D lose control because of a fear of violence s 55(3)? Did D lose control because of things done or said s 55(4)? Or a combination of these s 55(5) |
| If the trigger was 'things done or said':- (this is narrower than the old law) | These 'things' must be of an 'extremely grave character' and have caused D to have a justifiable sense of being seriously wronged 55(4)(a) and (b). |
| Was the trigger excluded by the Act? | If D acted in a considered desire for revenge s 54(4) or the thing 'done or said' constituted sexual infidelity s 55 (6) the defence fails |
| A person of the same sex and age would have reacted in the same way as D in the same circumstances. The jury should ignore matters that affect the ability to retain control. | The old case law is clarified here, i.e., the jury should not take into account mental characteristics which might have made losing control more likely, like a short temper |
| Did D lose control s 54(1)? However the defence cannot be used where acted in a 'considered desire for revenge' s 54(4) | D must have lost self-control but this need not be sudden s 54(2), however any sign of calming down and/or planning an attack is likely to mean the defence fails |

## Self-test questions

*To what charge does the **Coroners and Justice Act 2009** apply?*

*What three things need to be proved for **s 54**?*

*What amounts to a qualifying trigger?*

*State two 'characteristics' which are not attributable to the reasonable man*

*What 'trigger' is excluded by the Act?*

> *"the unlawful act must be such as all sober and reasonable people would inevitably recognise must subject the other person to, at least, the risk of some harm resulting therefrom, albeit not serious harm".*

By the end of this Chapter, you should be able to:

*Explain the three legal requirements in proving the actus reus of constructive manslaughter*

*Identify the required mens rea element*

*Explain how the law applies in practice by reference to cases*

*Identify possible criticisms*

The definition of 'dangerous' from the case of **Church 1967**

This type of manslaughter is 'constructed' from an act which is both unlawful and dangerous and which causes death.  It is called both constructive manslaughter and unlawful act manslaughter.

*Actus reus*

There are three separate issues to address in the *actus reus*

> **an unlawful act**
>
> **which is dangerous**
>
> **which causes death**

## Unlawful act

An act is only unlawful for the purposes of constructive manslaughter if it is a crime.  Criminal damage is a common example, as in **Hancock and Shankland**.  Assault is another.

In **Lamb 1967**, D pointed a loaded gun at V, his friend, as a joke.  They did not understand how a revolver works, and thought that there was no danger in pulling the trigger.  D did so and V died.  The court said the unlawful act must be a crime and so he was not guilty.

It must be an act not an omission.  In **Khan and Khan 1998**, the charge of unlawful act manslaughter failed because there was no act, just an omission to get medical help.

## Task

Look up these cases and identify the unlawful act.  Then make a note of how causation in fact and in law is proved and how these apply.

**Hancock and Shankland 1986**

**Pagett 1983**

**Nedrick 1986**

## Which is dangerous

This is an objective test.  It was stated in **Church 1967** that the unlawful act is dangerous if '*all sober and reasonable people*' would see it as resulting in some harm.  The opening quote came from this case.

**Key case**

In **Church**, D had knocked a woman unconscious and then, wrongly believing her to be dead threw her in the river to dispose of the 'body'. The CA held that it did not matter that D did not see any risk of harm. In this case, D did not see any such risk as he thought she was dead! The principle is that if reasonable people would see the risk of harm, this will be enough. D was guilty of manslaughter because reasonable people would see that throwing someone into a river risks harm.

In **R v M (J); R v M (S) 2012**, two Ds were involved in a violent incident at a nightclub after being asked to leave. One of the doormen collapsed from shock shortly afterwards and died. The CA rejected their appeal against a manslaughter conviction and confirmed that it was not necessary for D to have foreseen any specific harm to the victim. What mattered was whether 'reasonable and sober people' would have recognised that the unlawful activities subjected the victim to the risk of some harm. On the facts, it was clear that sober and reasonable people observing the events would have recognised that the doormen involved in the effort to control the Ds were at the risk of some harm.

Physical assaults will usually be deemed dangerous, unlawful acts like robbery and burglary will depend on the circumstances.

In **Dawson 1985**, during an attempted robbery of a garage, the Ds had frightened V with an imitation pistol. He suffered from a heart condition and subsequently died. They were found not guilty of manslaughter because a reasonable person would not have been aware of the heart condition, and so would not see the act as dangerous. The court recognised that fear could be foreseen, but as physical harm could not be, the act was not dangerous in the true sense.

**Food for thought**

Both **Church** and **Dawson** show that for an act to be deemed dangerous, there must be a risk of physical harm. It appears that this does not include psychiatric harm. In many other areas of law, physical harm has been extended to include psychiatric. It can be argued that 'dangerous' should include an act which could cause psychiatric harm. **Dawson** can be criticised on the basis that a robbery with imitation firearms could be construed as dangerous. The reaction of a victim to such a robbery could be unpredictable. Someone might decide to 'have a go' and this would certainly be dangerous, whether the guns were real or not. **Dawson** was *distinguished* in the next case.

In **Watson 1989,** burglars entered a house and saw an elderly man, but continued with their act of burglary. They were charged with manslaughter when he died of a heart attack. The man's frailty was obvious and the Ds saw this. Their knowledge could be attributed to the reasonable person who could therefore see the danger of the act, thus **Dawson** could be distinguished. (Note that on the facts their conviction was quashed on the causation issue, because there was not enough evidence that the shock of seeing burglars caused death).

In **Bristow 2013**, a man died after intervening in a burglary at an off-road vehicle repair shop. The Ds argued that the burglary was not dangerous until after V arrived and the escape car was driven dangerously, i.e., the risk of harm became apparent. At this point there was no evidence as to who was driving so no-one was guilty. The CA held that this was not like **Dawson** or **Watson,** and although burglary was not dangerous in itself, the particular circumstances could make it so. Here the risk was obvious from the outset of the burglary because of the nature of the premises and their geography. There was a limited escape route with nearby residential accommodation. The reasonable person would see a risk of harm being caused to anyone trying to intervene or prevent escape.

In **Dawson** the robbery was not dangerous because V's heart condition was not obvious – reasonable people but would not see any risk of harm.

In **Watson** the burglary became dangerous once the man's frailty was obvious – reasonable people would see the risk of harm.

In **Bristow** the burglary was dangerous from the start because the risk was obvious to reasonable people at that stage

### Food for thought

Whether the unlawful act is dangerous is an objective test, based on what a reasonable person would see as dangerous. It is not relevant that D didn't see it as dangerous. For such a serious offence it can be argued that a subjective test should be used.

### Examination pointer

Take care when applying the rules in a problem scenario. Students often misunderstand the point of **Dawson** and confuse it with the thin skull rule. This rule may well be relevant but it will only apply once the act is found to be unlawful and dangerous. It is a causation issue. In **Dawson**, the question was whether the act was dangerous. The answer was 'no' because a reasonable person would not know of the heart condition. If the act *had* been dangerous then D would 'take the victim as he finds him'. Thus, D would be liable for the death even though a person without a heart condition would not have died.

### Example

Consider the following imaginary cases:

*1. You are angry and wave your fist at Cathy. She is of a very nervous disposition and dies of fright.*

*2. You are angry and throw a brick at Kate, which misses. She is of a very nervous disposition and dies of fright.*

In the first case, your action may be unlawful (causing fear is an assault), but is unlikely to be seen as dangerous. Much may depend on whether you know she is of a nervous disposition, if not, you are not guilty of Cathy's manslaughter. It ends there.

In the second, your act is both unlawful and dangerous. The next question is whether you caused Kate's death. You cannot argue that most people would not have died, and that Kate's nervous disposition caused her death. Under the thin skull rule you must 'take your victim as you find her'. You are guilty of manslaughter.

### Causes death

The usual rules of causation apply, i.e., D must make a significant contribution to the death and the chain of causation must not be broken. Let's look at the cases in your task.

### Examples

**Hancock and Shankland** – throwing concrete blocks onto a taxi would be criminal damage, thus unlawful. Throwing concrete blocks off a bridge is dangerous. The damage caused the driver's death.

**Nedrick** – setting fire to something belonging to someone else is a type of criminal damage (arson) and so again unlawful. It is also clearly dangerous and the fire caused death.

**Pagett** – shooting at the police is both unlawful and dangerous. D made a significant contribution to the girl's death and the police didn't break the chain of causation by firing back because it was a natural reaction (foreseeable). The shooting caused death.

Causation is not always easy to prove and problems have arisen in several cases. Compare the following two decisions.

In **Cato 1976**, D supplied, and assisted V to take, heroin which resulted in death. It was held that he had unlawfully administered a drug which caused death and so was guilty of manslaughter.

In **Dalby 1982**, the CA quashed the conviction because although D had supplied drugs (an unlawful act) this had not caused death. V had injected himself and this broke the chain of causation.

In **Kennedy 1999**, D mixed the drug and handed the syringe to V and this sufficed even though, as in **Dalby**, V injected himself. In **Dias 2002**, V injected himself, as in **Dalby**. The CA quashed D's conviction on the issue of causation and criticised the decision in **Kennedy**. The conflicting case law led to the CCRC referring **Kennedy** back to the CA on the issue of causation. In **Kennedy 2005**, the CA said causing your own death was not unlawful, so nor was encouraging another to. However, participating in the administration of a 'poison' or 'noxious thing' is a crime, and so forms the basis for a manslaughter charge. The case then went to the HL.

**Key case**

In **Kennedy 2007**, the HL quashed the conviction and held that in the case of a fully informed adult self-administering the drug it would never be appropriate to find the supplier guilty of manslaughter. D had not administered the drug so this was not an unlawful act. He had committed an unlawful act in supplying the heroin, but this did not cause the victim's death.

In **Cato**, D actually injected V so there was no break in the chain of causation. In **Dalby**, V's own act broke the chain and this was approved in **Kennedy 2007** by the HL.

Application of the three essentials can be seen in **Carey and Others 2006**. A teenage girl died from a heart attack following an attack on her and three other girls. The group who carried out the attack were charged with manslaughter. The CA confirmed the three elements, (i) that there was an unlawful act, (ii) which was dangerous in the sense that the unlawful act subjected V to the risk of physical harm, and (iii) that the unlawful act caused her death. As regards the unlawful act, the prosecution relied on the public order offence of 'affray'. This is using or threatening unlawful violence towards another, which would cause a person of reasonable firmness present at the scene to fear for his/her personal safety. The CA confirmed, following **Church**, that 'dangerous' was an objective test. Affray was not dangerous in the required sense because it would not have been recognised by a 'sober and reasonable bystander' that an apparently healthy 15-year-old was at risk of suffering harm as a result. On causation, both **Dawson** and **Watson** were discussed. It was agreed that it was not foreseeable that an apparently healthy 60-year old man would suffer shock and a heart attack as a result of an attempted robbery (**Dawson**). However, it was foreseeable that an obviously frail and very old man was at risk of suffering shock leading to a heart attack because of a burglary committed at his home late at night (**Watson**). The current case involved a healthy young girl, so was nearer to **Dawson** than **Watson**. It had been argued that V was running from the attack so, as in **Roberts**, this did not break the chain of causation. However, the CA felt that she was not running away, merely running home, because there was no longer any threat by then. Although V had suffered a punch to her face, an unlawful act, this minor injury did not cause her death. The act of affray was unlawful but not dangerous, so the manslaughter charge failed.

This can be compared to **R v M (J); R v M (S) 2012**, above. A similar violent incident was held to be a substantial cause of the doorman's shock and had significantly contributed to his death. The shock and the increase in blood pressure led to his collapse and an internal rupture, from which he died. Shock was foreseeable, and there was found to be no break in the chain of causation between the violence and the death.

Before going on to *mens rea,* let's recap with an imaginary scenario.

### Example

Vic decides to kill himself and jumps off a tall building, checking before he does so that no one is underneath. Dave is a resident of the building who is having a violent row with his wife. He fires a gun at her and misses, hitting Vic as he passes the window. Vic is thrown off course by the blow and lands on a pedestrian, Sue, killing her. Vic survives. Can anyone be charged with manslaughter?

Look at the three requirements. Vic's act is *dangerous* and *caused her death*, but is not *unlawful*. Vic is unlikely to be found guilty of manslaughter. Dave's act is both *dangerous* and *unlawful*. However, did it *cause death*? Unlikely, Vic's jumping would be the cause. Dave is also unlikely to be found guilty of manslaughter.

### Mens rea

There is no special *mens rea* for this type of manslaughter. It is the *mens rea* for the unlawful act. There is therefore no need to prove *mens rea* as regards the death, only the unlawful act. Let's take one of the earlier examples a step further.

### Example

Going back to **Nedrick**, the unlawful act was arson, a form of criminal damage. The *mens rea* for this is intent or recklessness. There is no need for D to intend, or to recognise a risk of, death, only to intend or see a risk of the damage. Arson was clearly intended, so *mens rea* is easy to prove for a manslaughter charge to succeed.

The only other point on *mens rea* is to remember that it must coincide with the *actus reus*. As we saw this is widely interpreted. Thus in both **Thabo Meli** and in **Church**, the Ds were guilty of unlawful and dangerous act manslaughter based on a 'series of acts'.

### Food for thought

The Law Commission has criticised the fact that the *mens rea* for this type of manslaughter may be for some quite different offence. Manslaughter is a very serious offence but the *mens rea* may be for a minor crime, such as criminal damage. Arguably, manslaughter should have a *mens rea* of its own and D should at least be subjectively reckless about causing death or serious injury.

### Summary

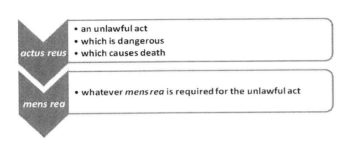

**actus reus**
- an unlawful act
- which is dangerous
- which causes death

**mens rea**
- whatever *mens rea* is required for the unlawful act

## Task

Refer to the last task you did in the Chapter on murder, where you followed my examination pointer as a guide to applying the law. Now go on to apply the rules you have just learnt on manslaughter. Use the recap, but be sure to add cases.

## Self-test questions

*What were the facts and principle in **Church**?*

*What is the difference between **Cato** and **Dalby**?*

*What did the HL decide in **Kennedy 2007**?*

*What is the mens rea for unlawful act manslaughter?*

For answers to the tasks and self-test questions, please go to my website at www.drsr.org and click the button 'Answers to tasks'. For a range of free interactive exercises, click on 'Free Exercises' and then the OCR book.

*"A verdict of manslaughter may, depending on the circumstances, be appropriate both by reason of an unlawful and dangerous act, and by reason of gross negligence".*

*Rose LJ*

By the end of this Chapter, you should be able to:

**Explain the four legal requirements in proving gross negligence manslaughter**

**Explain how the law applies in practice by reference to cases**

**Identify possible criticisms**

This type of manslaughter occurs when someone owes a duty to another person, but is 'grossly negligent', with the result that the person dies.

## Example

Kylie is looking after a 2-month-old baby for the evening. She gets very drunk and falls over whilst carrying the baby. Kylie passes out and the baby is smothered. If the baby dies then Kylie may be guilty of gross negligence manslaughter. She will owe a duty to the baby in her care, and getting so drunk whilst looking after a young child is likely to be sufficiently negligent.

The rules on gross negligence manslaughter were clarified by the HL in **Adomako 1994**.

## Key case

In **Adomako**, an anaesthetist had failed to monitor a patient during an operation. The patient later died as a result. The doctor was accused of manslaughter.

The CA held that in order to prove gross negligence manslaughter there must be:

**A risk of death**

**A duty of care**

**Breach of that duty**

**Gross negligence as regards that breach, which must be sufficient to justify criminal liability**

The CA also gave examples of the type of conduct which might amount to such negligence. When the case went to the HL, the test was confirmed but the HL rejected the idea of setting out particular examples. Lord Mackay said that the jury would have to decide whether *"involving as it must have done a risk of death"* D's conduct fell below the standard expected to the extent *"that it should be judged criminal"*. On the facts, this was the case here, and the conviction was upheld.

*The Adomako requirements as confirmed in Misra 2004.*

*Key case*

In **Misra**, also a medical negligence case, it was argued that the uncertainty in the law of gross negligence manslaughter meant that it infringed the **European Convention on Human Rights**. The CA rejected this argument and held that the offence had been sufficiently clearly set out in **Adomako**. Grossly negligent treatment, which exposed a patient to the risk of death, and caused death, would make the doctor liable for manslaughter.

The CA also said that it had been 'clearly established' that a risk of death was needed; a risk of bodily injury or injury to health was not enough.

As well as a **risk of death**, the death must have occurred as a result of a **breach** of a **duty** owed by D to V. This means apply the usual rules on causation, both in fact and in law. Then the jury must decide whether D's breach of duty was **grossly** negligent and therefore criminal.

Let's look at these four requirements.

### Risk of death

In **Misra 2004**, the CA confirmed that a risk of death was needed, not just a risk of harm. This will still be quite wide. Activities which are dangerous in themselves, such as taking people mountaineering or white-water rafting would be included. Ordinary activities which have the potential to be dangerous could also involve a risk of death. This would cover driving a train or piloting a ferry. Such activities are not dangerous in themselves, but if a train or ferry is handled negligently or poorly maintained, there is a risk of death, so the driver or company may be liable.

### Duty

It was not made fully clear in **Adomako** whether the ordinary civil test for duty is enough. Later cases suggest that it is. In **Wacker 2003**, the Ds were transporting about 60 illegal immigrants in a lorry. For some time during the journey there was no ventilation. Most of the immigrants died and the Ds were charged with gross negligence manslaughter. The judge referred to **Adomako** and the 'ordinary principles of the law of negligence'. The CA held that they had assumed a duty of care for the victims and rejected their appeal against conviction.

### Task

Look back at Chapter 1 and reread the following manslaughter cases. What was the duty and how was it breached?

**Stone and Dobinson 1977**

**Pittwood 1902**

### Key case

**Khan and Khan** is a case worth knowing because gross negligence manslaughter, constructive manslaughter and omissions were all discussed. It also seems to confirm that there are only two types of manslaughter, so reckless manslaughter no longer exists. The Ds had supplied drugs to a young prostitute. She went into a coma but they left her and when they returned the next day, she had died. This would be a failure to act, an *omission* (not getting medical help). The trial judge referred to 'manslaughter by omission' and found them guilty. The CA allowed the appeal and stated that there were only two types of involuntary manslaughter. These were unlawful act manslaughter (which requires an act, not an omission) and gross negligence manslaughter (which requires a pre-existing duty, as in **Stone and Dobinson**). The CA held that there was no such duty between a drug dealer and a client. D could not be guilty of either type of manslaughter.

In **Khan**, the CA refused to find that a duty was owed by a drug dealer to a client. However, they did suggest that such a duty *could* arise. If the facts were capable of giving rise to a duty, then the judge should give the jury "*an appropriate direction which would enable them to answer the question whether on the facts as found by them there was such a duty*".

The CA restated this in **Evans 2009**. The judge will direct the jury as to whether the facts were *capable* of giving rise to a duty; the jury must then decide whether in fact they did.

In **Evans**, the CA held that if a person created, or contributed to, a situation which was life threatening then a duty to take reasonable steps to save that life would arise. D had supplied heroin to her 16-year-old half-sister, who had injected it herself. When she showed symptoms of having overdosed her sister took no action, fearing she would get into trouble. She and her mother put the girl to bed but she was dead the next morning. The CA held that the duty in cases of gross negligence manslaughter was not confined to family and professional relationships. The CA noted that cases had not been clear on whether the judge or the jury should decide on whether a duty was owed. The CA held that whether a duty of care could exist was a question of law for the judge. However, it was for the jury to look at the facts to decide whether such a duty had been established.

### Breach of duty / the conduct amounted to gross negligence

In civil law, breach means D has not reached the standard expected of a reasonable person. However only if D is *grossly* negligent will there be criminal liability. This is for the jury to decide. According to **Adomako**, the jury must look at the circumstances and decide whether D's conduct was sufficiently grossly negligent to be deemed criminal. This was confirmed in **Misra 2004**. First there must be a breach (has D acted like a reasonable person?), then this breach must be seen by the jury as sufficiently negligent to be deemed criminal.

In **Warner 2014**, a caretaker was convicted of gross negligence manslaughter when he failed to replace a gap in the barrier of a walkway and a child fell to her death. He had breached his duty of care to users of the walkway and the court said his failure to replace the barrier had been "thoroughly irresponsible".

In **Wood and Hodgson 2003**, a 10-year-old girl was visiting the Ds. She found some ecstasy tablets hidden in a cigarette packet and took some. She later died in hospital. They were charged with gross negligence manslaughter. Applying the rules:

**Risk of death**: It is known that ecstasy can kill so there is a risk of death

**Duty:** they owed her a duty as a visitor and/or as a child in their care.

**Breach**: There was evidence that they had hidden the tablets, and that they had attempted to treat her, but they did not call an ambulance for some time. They had **breached** their duty to her by not taking reasonable care.

**Gross negligence**: However, the jury found that they had not shown a sufficiently high level of negligence to be deemed criminal.

**Result**: They were not guilty of gross negligence manslaughter.

### Food for thought

In **Adomako**, the CA had set out a list of what type of conduct might be deemed sufficiently negligent. The HL rejected this on the basis that it could confuse juries who might think that only those situations would suffice. They thought it better to leave it to the jury to decide on the facts whether the conduct was sufficiently bad to be deemed criminal. It is therefore not at all clear what exactly does amount to criminal negligence. It is hard for a jury to decide what was sufficiently negligent if the law is not clear.

In **Willoughby 2004**, D was the owner of a disused public house in Canterbury. He had recruited a local taxi driver to help him set fire to the building for financial purposes. The taxi driver was killed when the building collapsed and D was convicted of gross negligence manslaughter. On appeal, the CA said that the judge should have directed the jury on unlawful act manslaughter rather than gross negligence manslaughter. They made it clear that either may be appropriate, depending on the circumstances. The opening quote came from this case. (On the facts, the jury had accepted that D had committed arson which is an unlawful act, and this caused death, so the manslaughter conviction was upheld).

## Examination pointer

For a problem question look for clues in the scenario; you may need to discuss both types. The CA in **Adomako** indicated that it could also be gross negligence manslaughter where, e.g., an electrician caused a death by faulty wiring. This was *obiter dicta* because it was not relevant on the facts of the case. It could be referred to if the given scenario involved such circumstances, or something similar. Although not binding, *obiter dicta* can be used as *persuasive precedent*.

As we saw in **Willoughby**, the two types of manslaughter overlap. If you think it is constructive manslaughter, discuss this first, but if, e.g., there is doubt as to whether there is an act or omission, or whether the act is unlawful, go on to gross negligence manslaughter as an alternative. If, as in **Willoughby**, there is some doubt as to whether a duty is owed, you could start with gross negligence manslaughter and go on to constructive manslaughter as an alternative.

## Food for thought

Although on the facts, the conviction in **Willoughby** was upheld, it does highlight the difficulties. The overlap is not always clear. If the judge has trouble identifying whether it is gross negligence or unlawful act manslaughter, then arguably the law is still too uncertain, as argued in **Misra**. It is also unclear whether the civil test for duty is enough. It would seem so, but if it is, then another criticism is that it should not be. The functions of the criminal and civil law are very different.

You could also consider how far the law should impose a duty on a drug dealer to his client. Although the CA declined to find there was a duty in **Khan**, there could arguably have been a common law duty, as in **Stone and Dobinson**. The decision may be one of policy rather than law. Taking on responsibility for an invalid is sufficient, responsibility for a prostitute to whom D had supplied drugs is not. This is another area that needs clarification.

## Task

Refer to the tasks you did in the Chapter on murder and followed up on in manslaughter, where you used my examination pointers as a guide to applying the law. Make up a new scenario and apply the pointers as before, then add these new rules. Keep the whole thing as a guide for problem questions on homicide.

It seemed that gross negligence replaced reckless manslaughter, which Lord Mackay said in **Adomako** no longer existed. However, he also said, "*I consider it perfectly appropriate that the word reckless be used in cases of involuntary manslaughter*". This left the matter somewhat uncertain.

### Reckless manslaughter

In **Seymour 1983**, D was driving recklessly, and crushed his girlfriend between his lorry and a car, killing her. The HL said that if there was an 'obvious and serious' risk of injuring someone (objective recklessness), D was guilty of manslaughter. However, in **Adomako**, the HL seemed to reject reckless manslaughter and as this was a unanimous decision, it could be taken as a statement of the current law. The judgement was, however, somewhat complex and matters were further complicated by use of the word 'reckless' by Lord Mackay.

Many objective reckless manslaughter cases involved driving incidents and there is now a statutory offence of causing death by dangerous driving, so arguably reckless manslaughter is not needed. However, some cases came outside the 'motor manslaughter' category and so are not covered by statute. In **Khan**, the CA said that there were only **two** types of involuntary manslaughter: unlawful act manslaughter and gross negligence manslaughter. This apparently confirmed **Adomako**, that reckless manslaughter no longer existed. However, doubt was again cast on this in **Lidar 2000**.

In **Lidar**, a group of men had a fight in the car park of a pub. When two of them got in a car and started to drive off, a 3$^{rd}$ leant in the window of the car and the fight continued. They drove off with him half in the window and at some point he fell off and suffered injuries from which he died. The jury were directed in terms of recklessness and the driver was convicted of manslaughter. The CA upheld the conviction, possibly relying on Lord Mackay's reference in **Adomako** to it being "perfectly appropriate" to use the word reckless. As a driver owes a clear duty to other road users there is no doubt a finding of gross negligence manslaughter would have been possible

### Food for thought

In such a serious crime it is less than satisfactory that there is still confusion about whether reckless manslaughter exists, and if it does, whether the test is subjective or objective. Since **Gemmell & Richards** overruled **Caldwell** on recklessness as the *mens rea* for criminal damage it would appear that the HL prefers the subjective test. Arguably it is time the matter was addressed, either by the HL or by Parliament.

### *Reforms*

Manslaughter is an area which has long been in need of clarification and reform. There have been many high profile cases illustrating one of the main problems with gross negligence manslaughter. The enquiries following the Herald of Free Enterprise ferry disaster and the King's Cross fire, both in 1987, showed a high level of negligence within the companies involved. Attempts at prosecution, however, were unsuccessful because it was impossible to find an individual on whom to place the required duty. Similarly, the Hatfield rail crash in 2000 caused four deaths and over 100 injuries, but at the trial of Balfour Beatty in October 2005 charges of manslaughter were dismissed, although the company was fined for its poor safety procedures. Cases such as this have produced a demand for changes in the law.

The Law Commission published a consultation paper on manslaughter in 1994, followed by a report in 1996: *Legislating the Criminal Code: Involuntary Manslaughter* (Report 237). They suggested that involuntary manslaughter should be abolished and replaced with three new offences:

**reckless (subjective) killing (D sees a risk of death or serious injury)**

**killing by gross carelessness (the risk of death or serious injury was obvious and the conduct fell far below what was expected)**

**corporate killing (similar to killing by gross carelessness but death is due to management failure)**

In 2006 the Law Commission produced a new report dealing with murder and manslaughter (see Task below). In this they suggested that manslaughter should consist of:

**unlawful killings caused by acts of gross negligence**

**unlawful killings caused by a criminal act that was intended to cause injury or by a criminal act foreseen as involving a serious risk of causing some injury**

### Task

Go to the Law Commission website at http://lawcommission.justice.gov.uk/ and look at the 2006 report on Murder, manslaughter and infanticide' (listed in the A-Z). Quotes and discussions from this will enhance an essay.

The first proposal would have simplified and clarified the law. The offence of killing by gross carelessness would solve the **Khan**-type problem, as there would be no need to prove a duty. The second proposal would not abolish manslaughter and replace it with new offences, but would at least require a *mens rea* of intent to cause injury. However the problems with gross negligence manslaughter would remain.

The government has concentrated on voluntary manslaughter reform and most of the suggested reforms of involuntary manslaughter have not been taken up. Much still needs to be done to meet the criticisms.

### Food for thought

Having such a serious crime relying on the common law for its development is questionable. The courts themselves have indicated it is the role of Parliament to create the law on such a major issue. The public have long called for change. The Law Commission proposals are no longer new. All these problems and calls for reform make this area a popular essay question. Another problem in relation to both types of involuntary manslaughter is that they cover such a wide range. The level of fault involved can vary enormously from something just short of intent to the virtually accidental. Justice requires greater clarity in the law. Even where changes have been proposed and accepted, the reforms have been not only been slow but arguably far too limited.

### Summary

The **Adomako** requirements as confirmed in **Misra** are:

| | |
|---|---|
| **a risk of death** | •A risk of death, not just harm – Misra |
| **a duty owed by D** | •A duty owed by D on the ordinary principles of negligence – Wacker |
| **breach of that duty** | •D has not reached the standard expected of a reasonable person Wood & Hodgson/Evans |
| **gross negligence** | •sufficiently negligent to be deemed criminal – Adomako/Wood & Hodgson/Misra/Evans |

### Self-test questions

*What are the elements for proving gross negligence manslaughter?*

*Can you commit either type of manslaughter by omission?*

*From which case did the opening quote come?*

*Why do you think a duty was found in **Evans** but not in **Khan**?*

*Bearing in mind the case of **Evans** and **Miller**, can you find an argument for establishing a duty in **Khan**?*

For answers to the tasks and self-test questions, please go to my website at www.drsr.org and click the button 'Answers to tasks'. For a range of free interactive exercises, click on 'Free Exercises' and then the OCR book.

**Murder**

*Actus reus:* The unlawful killing of a human being under the Queen's peace

*Mens rea:* Malice aforethought i.e., intention to kill or seriously injure

**Key criticisms of murder**

Sometimes questions arise about whether someone who is 'brain dead' or a foetus in the womb is a human being. In AGs Reference (No 3 of 1994) 1997, the HL held that a foetus was not a human being for the purpose of a murder conviction. However, if the foetus is injured, and dies from that injury after being born, that could amount to murder. Arguably, there should be greater clarity on this.

The rules on what will break the chain of causation may be difficult for a jury to

The law on intent for murder has developed but is arguably still unclear

The mandatory life sentence for murder means the judge has no discretion and cannot take into account the very different circumstances between some killings, in euthanasia cases. A discretionary sentence could remove the need for the special defences (voluntary manslaughter) as the circumstances could be taken into account by the judge

Murder is a common law offence. Should there be a statutory definition? If so should it contain more than one degree of murder as in the USA (and as recommended by the Law Commission – see below)? This could again remove the need for the special defences.

The mens rea for murder is intent to kill or seriously injure, for such a serious crime should it only be intent to kill?

Reforms

In their 2006 report 'Murder, manslaughter and Infanticide' the Law Commission noted four particular problems with the law on homicide and said:

If excessive force is used in self-defence this should come within the partial defences.

It is not right that duress cannot be a defence to murder in any circumstances

The serious harm rule is wrong and there should be intent to kill, or at least intent to cause serious harm knowing there is a risk of death

The two-category structure of murder or manslaughter is out-dated. The LC felt someone who killed e.g., under provocation should still be called a murderer but should not have a life sentence. They recommended a three-tier structure for homicide, which would cover

*1st-degree murder*

*2nd-degree murder (*

*Manslaughter*

Only the first of these would have a mandatory life sentence.

The LC also wanted a new Homicide Act not only to deal with the partial defences but also to clarify the law. They said that the new Act should provide clear and comprehensive definitions of the homicide offences and the partial defences.

These recommendations have not been taken up, although the self-defence issue is now covered by the 'fear of serious violence' trigger for loss of control in the **Coroners and Justice Act**.

## Voluntary manslaughter

## Loss of control

Under **s 54**, of the **Coroners and Justice Act 2009** there are three questions to consider:

**did D lose self-control?**

**was the loss of self-control triggered by something specified in s 55?**

**would a normal person of D's sex and age have reacted in the same way in D's circumstances?**

Under **S 55(1)** the loss of control must be triggered by:

**D's fear of serious violence from V against D or another identified person; or**

**a thing or things done or said (or both) which:**

**(a) constituted circumstances of an extremely grave character, and**

**(b) caused D to have a justifiable sense of being seriously wronged**

**Excluded matters**

**S 54(4)** revenge and **S 55 (6)** sexual infidelity (see **Clinton**)

## Diminished responsibility

**Under** s 2 **of the Homicide Act as amended by the Coroners and Justice Act 2009 there must be**

**an abnormality of mental functioning**

**which arises from a 'recognised medical condition'**

**and substantially impaired D's ability to do one or more of three specified things**

**and provides an explanation for D's acts and omissions**

The specified things are:

**to understand the nature of his conduct, or**

**to form a rational judgement or,**

**to exercise self-control**

*Task*

From which cases did the following principles come?

That sexual infidelity may be relevant to the circumstances of D, even though excluded by s 55

That an 'abnormality of mind' (now mental functioning) for diminished responsibility is one that reasonable people would term abnormal

An abnormality caused by alcoholism may be accepted as diminished responsibility

Impairment of responsibility need not be total but must be more than trivial

Where there is evidence of intoxication as well as another cause of 'abnormality' the jury should ignore the intoxication

In their 2004 report 'Partial Defences to Murder' the Law Commission said

> "Over the centuries the law of homicide, including the law of murder, has developed in a higgledy-piggledy fashion. The present law is a product of judge made law supplemented by Parliament's sporadic intervention. The outcome is a body of law characterised by a lack of clarity and coherence."

The **Coroners and Justice Act** only addresses some of the problems seen in their report

**Key criticisms of the special defences (voluntary manslaughter)**

The defence of provocation, now loss of control, has been improved by the Coroners and Justice Act, although some argue that it is still unclear. One improvement is that reacting in fear of serious violence is a stated to be qualifying trigger, thus clarifying this somewhat

The removal of the need for a 'sudden and temporary' loss of control is an improvement. However, the fact that any loss of control must be shown goes against the Law Commission's proposals and prevents the defence clearly extending to cases of abuse against women, who may be physically weaker and liable to even greater abuse if they lose control and fight back

The 'fear of serious violence' trigger addresses the 'all-or-nothing' nature of self-defence. If excessive force is used, there may now be a defence of loss of control

Diminished responsibility is not a satisfactory alternative for abused women as it indicates they are mentally unbalanced

Where there is evidence of intoxication as well as another cause of 'abnormality' the jury has to perform an almost impossible task of separating the one from the other – Dietschmann

'Abnormality of mental functioning' is difficult for the jury to understand and medical evidence is often complex and contradictory

Diminished responsibility is sometimes dependent on whether the killing was morally wrong – Bailey/Sutcliffe

Success may depend on which defence is raised in the first place. What was then provocation failed in the case of Cocker 1989, but diminished responsibility succeeded in Bailey 2002 in similar circumstances

For diminished responsibility the burden of proof is on D

There is an overlap between diminished responsibility and loss of control where the killing has been due to a mental state such as depression or long-term abuse (Aluwahlia and Thornton)

The difficulties of these defences for the jury could lead to inconsistency. Juries may differ in their decisions

Should the mandatory life sentence for murder be abolished? If it was, then it could be argued that these defences would not be necessary. On the other hand, abolishing them and leaving the issue as one of sentencing would remove the role of the jury. It is arguably better for a jury to decide, for example, how a 'reasonable man' would act

Should the LC's recommendations of a three-tiered system have been taken up? If it was, then again it could be argued that these defences would not be necessary.

*Task*

Pick out a few of the criticisms which make sense to you. Add a few sentences to expand on each of the points you choose. Where possible, refer to cases to support your comments. You'll soon find you have a good base for an examination question.

**Summary of involuntary manslaughter**

*Gross negligence manslaughter*

The **Adomako** requirements as confirmed in **Misra** are:

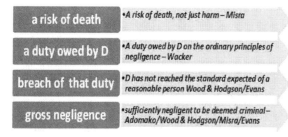

*Constructive or unlawful act manslaughter*

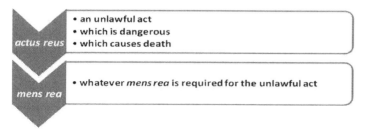

*Task*

Refer to the last task you did in the Chapter on murder, where you followed my examination pointer as a guide to applying the law. Now go on to apply the rules you have just learnt on manslaughter. Use the recap, but be sure to add cases.

**Key criticisms of unlawful act and gross negligence manslaughter**

> unlawful act manslaughter covers a wide range of behaviour
>
> it is hard to find an unlawful act and/or causation in some of the decisions on unlawful act manslaughter
>
> the mens rea for unlawful act manslaughter may be for a quite different offence
>
> whether the unlawful act is dangerous is an objective test, it can be argued that a subjective test should be used for such a serious offence
>
> identifying whether it is gross negligence or unlawful act manslaughter can be difficult, even for a judge – Willoughby 2004
>
> it is not fully clear what gross negligence amounts to

*Task*

Pick out a few of the criticisms which make sense to you. Add a few sentences to expand on each of the points you choose. Where possible refer to cases to support your comments. Look also at what proposals for reform are currently being pursued by the Law Commission (see their website). You'll soon find you have a good base for an exam question.

**Sample examination question**

'The *mens rea* of murder is too complicated both in theory and in practice. It needs to be simplified by Parliament'. Discuss the extent to which this statement is accurate. 50 marks

*Special study unit – possible connections*

Where you are asked to discuss developments in the law there is a lot of material within this study block to provide a base. The Food for thought sections and the key criticisms above can be used to provide some ideas for an evaluation of developments and particular cases which can be discussed critically.

The Law Commission's role in law-making can be discussed in relation to involuntary manslaughter. They suggest in 'Legislating the Criminal Code: Involuntary Manslaughter (Report 237)', that involuntary manslaughter should be abolished and replaced with 3 new offences:

> *corporate killing*
>
> *reckless (subjective) killing*
>
> *killing by gross carelessness*

The Law Commission's role in law-making can also be discussed in relation to murder and voluntary manslaughter. In 2004, the Law Commission published a report, 'Partial defences to Murder' (No 290). In May 2005, the DPP recommended the introduction of different degrees of homicide and the Law Commission published a consultation paper 'A new Homicide Act for England and Wales?' (No177) in December 2005. The consultation paper incorporates suggestions for the reform of murder, as well as the partial defences (voluntary manslaughter). Some of the latter have been incorporated in the **Coroners and Justice Act 2009**.

Prior to the judges became quite creative in their interpretation of **s3** of the **Homicide Act** and accepted most characteristics could be attributed to the reasonable man in **Smith**. The issue was clearer following **Holley**, which was a 'persuasive' precedent as it was a Privy Council case. Although not strictly binding, the fact that it was heard by nine Law Lords means it is likely to be followed instead of **Smith**.

In **James; Karini 2006** you can how a persuasive precedent can assist in the development of the law. The Privy Council had rejected the **Smith** decision on the law of provocation in **Holley** but it was arguable that the decision would not be followed as **Smith** was a HL decision. In the joint appeals of **James and Karini** the CA confirmed that the Privy Council decision should be followed. Both cases were referred by the Criminal Cases Review Commission on the basis that provocation had not been raised at the original trials. Both killers had psychiatric disorders and this was now relevant to the issue of provocation as the law had changed with **Smith**. Then in **Holley** the law seemed to change again. The CA heard the two appeals together as they were both based on the same point of law, and because it was such an important point there were five judges sitting. The CA accepted that the principle in **Holley** was the correct law. The **Coroners and Justice Act** has now put **Holley** into statutory form, and the only relevant characteristics in relation to the question of whether the reasonable person would have lost control and done as D did, are age and sex.

This area of law has seen many developments over the years and many cases can be discussed from **Camplin** through to **Holley**, as well as the 'battered women' cases. As discussed above with the key criticisms, the **Coroners and Justice Act** only addresses some of the problems seen in the Law Commission report

**Chapter 10**: Insanity and automatism

**Chapter 11**: Duress, necessity and duress of circumstances

**Chapter 12**: Intoxication

This study block covers general defences. Unlike the specific defences (which only apply to murder) these apply to most offences. The summary at the end of this Study Block will compare the defences and the different effect of each for the person using them.

Insanity, automatism and intoxication overlap, you will often have to discuss more than one defence.

**Example**

If Jane hears voices in her head which tell her to kill someone, she will argue insanity if she obeys the voices. If she is taking medication for her psychological problems, and this causes her to lose control of her movements, and she kills someone, it may be automatism. She is acting 'automatically'. The defence of intoxication includes drugs as well as drink, so if she is under the influence of drugs but not out of control, this defence could apply instead, although it very rarely succeeds.

Duress, necessity and duress of circumstances are used where D feels compelled to commit an offence because of a threat of some sort. There is an overlap between these too.

**Example**

Harry tells Andy that if Andy doesn't rob a bank he will beat him up. This is duress. If Andy drives into another car because he is being chased by a gang threatening to beat him up, this would be duress of circumstances. Here the threat isn't directly from another person but from the circumstances Andy finds himself in. It could also be seen as necessity but you will see that this defence is rare.

So, when discussing any possible defences, remember that you may have to discuss more than one when applying the law to a problem scenario.

*"... and it would be an unfortunate thing if it were left to juries to consider whether some particular act was morally right or wrong. The test must be whether it is contrary to law ..."*

Lord Goddard

By the end of this Chapter, you should be able to:

**Explain the different parts of these defences**

**Explain how the rules on both insanity and automatism apply in practice**

**Compare the 2 defences and explain their differences by reference to cases**

There is an overlap between these two defences so we will look at them in the same Chapter.

### Insanity

Insanity can be relevant at three points in time. Whilst awaiting trial, at the time of trial or at the time of the offence. The first two are not strictly defences as they mean D does not stand trial at all. It is the last one that concerns us here.

The burden of proving insanity to the jury is on D, on the balance of probabilities. The prosecution may however, raise insanity, in which case it must be proved beyond reasonable doubt.

Under the **Criminal Procedure (Insanity) Act 1964**, the result of a successful plea of insanity was committal to a secure hospital for an indefinite period. For this reason, it was not often raised in defence. The **Criminal Procedure (Insanity and Unfitness to Plead) Act 1991** amended the 1964 Act and increased the judge's powers to make four orders. The orders were then reduced to three by the **Domestic Violence, Crime and Victims Act** 2004, the judge may now give:

**a hospital order (which can also be accompanied by a restriction order)**

**a supervision order**

**an absolute discharge**

Until 2004 if the charge was murder a hospital order was the only option but this is no longer automatic.

### Examination pointer

If the defence is successful then there is a special verdict. This is "not guilty by reason of insanity". When discussing the effect of a plea of insanity you should refer to the judge's powers under the **1991** and **2004 Acts** as 'orders'. Avoid calling them sentences. Technically, D has been found not guilty.

The defence is based on **M'Naghten's case 1843**.

### Key case

M'Naghten fired his gun at the Tory Prime Minister Robert Peel but killed his secretary. Medical opinion showed that M'Naghten was suffering from 'morbid delusions'. He was found not guilty. Due to the public reaction to both the crime and the outcome, the House of Lords formulated a set of rules. The **M'Naghten Rules** are still used today. There are two main propositions of law.

Firstly, everyone is to be presumed to be sane until proved otherwise.

Secondly, insanity may be proved if, at the time of committing the act, D was *"labouring under such a defect of reason, from disease of the mind, as not to know the nature and quality of the act he was doing, or if he did know it, that he did not know he was doing what was wrong."*

Let's break this defence down into the different parts.

### Defect of reason

There has to be a complete deprivation of the powers of reason rather than simply a failure to exercise them. In **Clarke 1972**, D claimed that, due to depression, she had absent-mindedly put some items in her bag and so was not guilty of theft. The judge ruled that this argument amounted to insanity. She promptly changed her plea to guilty, (because this was before the **1991 Act** and it would have meant being sent to a mental hospital). On appeal, the CA held that temporary absentmindedness was not a defect of reason, but it did negate *mens rea*. As she had no *mens rea,* her conviction was quashed.

### Task

Look back at Chapter 2 on *mens rea* and the case of **Madeley** where the host of a TV show had a similar argument. The court decided he was not guilty. What was the reason in that case?

### Disease of the mind

The defect of reason must be caused by a disease of the mind. The meaning of 'disease of the mind' is a legal question for the judge. However, D will need medical evidence from two experts. This is a requirement of **s1 Criminal Procedure (Insanity and Unfitness to Plead) Act 1991.**

So what constitutes a disease of the mind? In **Bratty v A-G for Northern Ireland 1963**, D killed a D had killed a girl with a stocking during an epileptic fit. Lord Denning said a disease of the mind was *"any mental disorder which has manifested itself in violence and is prone to recur".*

In **Kemp 1957**, Devlin J said

> *"the condition of the brain is irrelevant and so is the question of whether the condition of the mind is curable or incurable, transitory or permanent".*

This means it is the mental faculties of reason and understanding that is important. It also indicates a temporary state can be insanity. In **Smith (Mark) 2012**, D was violent and abusive while travelling on an aircraft and had to be restrained by cabin staff. Evidence from psychiatrists was that he had a brief reactive psychosis characterised by delusions and hallucinations. He was charged with criminal damage and interfering with the performance of the aircraft crew in flight, and was found not guilty by reason of insanity, even though it was a temporary state.

It would appear, though, that it is more often accepted as insanity where the disease is of a permanent nature, or in Lord Denning's words "prone to recur".

A lot of case law turns on this issue of 'disease'. This has led to a distinction between *internal* factors and *external* factors. If the 'defect of reason' is caused by an internal factor (a disease), the defence is likely to be insanity. If it is caused by an external factor (like a blow to the head and concussion), then it is likely to be automatism (discussed below). The distinction is most easily explained by looking at some cases.

**Kemp 1957:** D had arteriosclerosis (narrowing of the arteries which reduces the flow of blood to the brain). This caused occasional lapses of consciousness. During one such period, he killed his wife by striking her with a hammer. His defence was treated as insanity.

**Quick 1973:** A diabetic nurse at a psychiatric hospital attacked one of the patients. He argued that this was because at the time he was suffering from hypoglycaemia as result of failing to eat after taking his insulin. The CA held the 'defect' was caused by an external factor, i.e., the insulin itself. This would be automatism not insanity.

**Sullivan 1984:** D hit out at someone trying to help him during an epileptic fit, and was convicted of actual bodily harm. The HL confirmed that the appropriate defence would be insanity and that epilepsy was a 'disease of the mind' which had caused a 'defect of reason'.

**Hennessey 1989:** D was a diabetic. He had taken a car and driven whilst disqualified. He argued automatism caused by failure to take his insulin. The CA upheld the judge's finding of insanity on the basis that the cause was the disease itself, an internal factor.

**Burgess 1991:** D claimed he was sleepwalking when he hit V over the head with a bottle. He was charged with wounding with intent and raised the defence of automatism. The judge held that the cause of his 'defect of reason' was an internal factor, a disease of the mind. He was found not guilty by reason of insanity and detained in a mental hospital. However, in **Bilton 2005 (unreported)**, the defence of automatism was successfully used when D raped a girl whilst sleepwalking.

**Task**

Look at the sequence of events in the diagram. If you take out any 'non-events' it is easier to see what caused the defect of reason. On the left, it is the insulin (external) on the right, the diabetes (internal). Do the same for **Quick** and **Hennessey** and then write a summary of each highlighting the differences.

*Diabetes example*

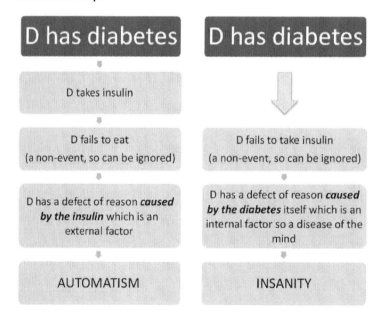

A 'defect of reason' caused by external factors (automatism) would usually be temporary whereas if caused by internal factors (insanity) it may be more permanent. This would need treating in order to protect the public, so a hospital order may be appropriate. In **Bratty**, Lord Denning said a disorder which led to violence and was prone to recur was "the sort of disease for which a person should be retained in hospital rather than be given an unqualified acquittal". **Burgess** shows that a temporary state can amount to insanity so there is a fine line between the two defences.

## Food for thought

In its 'scoping paper' (a paper setting out what is within the scope of the project) on insanity in 2012, the Law Commission said

> "... the law has not adopted a distinction between mental disorders and physical disorders, so that the latter are outside of the scope of the notion of "disease of the mind" in M'Naghten. Instead, it has adopted a distinction between internal and external factors which as we have seen leads to highly illogical results"

In cases like **Bratty** and **Kemp**, the defence of insanity may be appropriate. D's acts were to some extent purposeful and there is a danger to the public. The case of an epileptic thrashing out and hitting someone during a fit would be less easy to justify. There is a problem with finding insanity in respect of people whose conditions are not normally associated with mental disorder. Use the 'diabetes' cases to support a discussion of these problems. **Burgess** is also arguably too wide a definition. Should a sleepwalker be classed as insane? It leads to a second issue. Once insanity is raised – and remember this can be by the prosecution or the judge as well as D – D will often change the plea to guilty to avoid the insanity verdict. This is what happened in **Sullivan**. He pleaded guilty after the judge ruled the defence was insanity and was convicted of actual bodily harm. In **Quick**, on the other hand, the defect was held to be caused by the insulin itself. D's appeal succeeded because the defence of automatism should have been left to the jury.

A final point is that the stigma of an insanity verdict may also mean people who genuinely do have a mental problem do not plead the defence.

## Not knowing the nature and quality of the act

In **Codere 1916**, this was held to mean the physical nature of the act, not its moral nature.

In **Bratty**, a man who killed a girl with her stocking was found not guilty by reason of insanity because it was held that his epilepsy may have prevented him knowing the 'nature and quality' of the act.

In **Burgess**, the fact that he was sleepwalking meant he did not know the nature of his actions. Similarly in **Sullivan** and **Hennessy**, where they were not aware of what they were doing at the time.

If D is suffering from insane delusions the defence of insanity may succeed, however it will not succeed where D knows the nature of the act.

## Example

Derek is deluded and throws a baby onto the fire believing it to be a log. The defence may succeed, as Derek did not realise what he was doing.

Ahmed hears imaginary voices telling him to kill someone. He does this. The defence will fail, as he knew that he was killing someone.

## Not knowing the act was wrong

Even if D understands the nature of the act, the defence may succeed if this second part is satisfied. It is a question of whether D realises the act was *legally* wrong, not whether D believes it was morally right or wrong. In **Windle 1952**, D killed his wife with an overdose of aspirin. There was evidence of mental illness but on giving himself up he said 'I suppose they will hang me for this' thereby indicating he knew that what he had done was legally wrong. The conviction was upheld by the CA, where Lord Goddard gave the quote opening this Chapter. This made it clear that the question was a legal one; the jury were not to consider whether he believed the act was morally right or wrong. If D knows that the act is wrong, the defence fails.

## Example

Jack goes on a killing spree and murders several young prostitutes. He believes clearing the streets of prostitutes is morally justified. He could not plead insanity, as he knows killing is legally wrong.

The point was reiterated in the following case, where it was also made clear that there was no need for the judge to put the defence to the jury if it was clear D knew the act was legally wrong.

## *Key case*

In **Johnson 2007**, D forced his way into a neighbour's flat, while he was watching television. He shouted at him and became very aggressive. For no apparent reason he stabbed him with a large kitchen knife and was charged with wounding with intent. At his trial, he said that he did not know what he was doing. The medical experts agreed that, at the material time, he had been suffering from a disease of the mind, paranoid schizophrenia. However, the judge held that there was no question of insanity for the jury to consider because he knew what he did was legally wrong. The jury found him guilty and he appealed. He argued that the judge had been wrong to prevent the jury considering the **M'Naghten Rules**. The appeal was dismissed. Following **Windle**, the CA held that even if there was evidence of a disease of the mind, if he knew that what he did was legally wrong there was no issue of insanity to be left to the jury. The judge had therefore been entitled to prevent the jury considering the **M'Naghten Rules**.

## Exam pointer

There is an overlap with diminished responsibility so in a murder case you may need to discuss both. Until the 1991 Act, the only possible order following a successful insanity defence was detention in a mental hospital. It was therefore mainly used in murder cases. Since 2004 there are three possible orders, so the defence may be used for other crimes more often. The defence of diminished responsibility under the **Homicide Act 1957** is wider though (but only applies to murder cases).

## Food for thought and proposed reforms

The defence originates from an 1843 case and it is argued that because of medical advances it should be updated. Judges themselves have called for Parliament to look at the insanity defence.

There are arguments that the law could breach Article 5 of the European Convention on Human Rights which states that a person of unsound mind can only be detained where proper objective medical expertise has been sought.

The **1953 Royal Commission on Capital Punishment** recommended the abolishment of the **M'Naghten Rules**. The **Homicide Act 1957** introduced diminished responsibility shortly after this which addressed some of the criticisms made. In 1975, the **Butler Committee** favoured replacing the rules with a new verdict of 'mental disorder'. This would arise where D was suffering from 'severe mental illness' or 'severe mental handicap'. The burden of proof would also move to the prosecution.

The **Law Commission's Draft Code** adopted many of Butler's recommendations and specifically accepted that sleepwalking and spasms should come within automatism rather than insanity. The Commission made some further recommendations in 1995 but these were not acted upon, and they identified insanity as an area in need of reform again in 2008. In their 2012 scoping paper, it was noted that the law lagged behind psychiatric understanding. The LC also said *"English law has adopted an unusually, and arguably unjustifiably, narrow interpretation of the 'wrongfulness' limb"* as interpreted in **Windle**. Another point made in the 2012 paper was that the defence was very rarely used, but it was accepted that this did not necessarily mean it did not need attention; on the contrary, it was noted that the complexity of the law and the out-of-date tests were part of the reason for the lack of use. A project has been set up to consider the responses to the scoping paper in 2013 in order to identify *"better and more up-to-date legal tests"*.

Despite calls for reform for over half a century there is still no clear definition of insanity, though as the LC noted the one from Lord Denning in **Bratty** was the most often cited.

Lack of clarity leads to inconsistency as the defence may fail or succeed on moral rather than legal grounds, or simply through lack of understanding of the medical terminology.

### Insanity and intoxication

Intoxication is dealt with in Chapter 12 but it is often seen in conjunction with another defence. If the defect of reason comes about through intoxication, the insanity defence fails. If it comes from alcoholism, it could succeed as this can be classed as a 'disease'. In **Lipman**, D had taken LSD and hallucinated, he thought he was fighting snakes. He killed his girlfriend by stuffing a sheet down her throat. He did not know the quality of his act but, as the LSD was voluntarily taken, the defence failed. He was convicted of manslaughter.

### Automatism

We saw in Chapter 1 that the *actus reus* must be voluntary. The defence of automatism arises where D's act was 'automatic' and so was not voluntary. Thus, it is negating *actus reus* rather than *mens rea*.

### Insane and non-insane automatism

Automatism is also referred to as 'non-insane automatism' to distinguish it from insanity which can be called 'insane automatism'. Automatism is a very limited defence but if successful, it leads to a complete acquittal so it would be preferred to pleading insanity.

D has to show:

the act was involuntary

this was due to an external factor

### The act was involuntary

Automatism was defined by Lord Denning in **Bratty v Attorney General for N I (1963)**

*"... automatism means an act which is done by the muscles without any control by the mind such as a spasm, a reflex action or a convulsion or an act done by a person who is not conscious of what he is doing ..."*

This covers both insanity and automatism. The difference lies in what caused the lack of control. If it was a disease of the mind, the defence is insanity. If an external factor, like a blow to the head, the defence is automatism. The LC said in its 2012 paper

*"English case law has drawn a distinction between "insane automatism" (which it classifies as "insanity") and "sane automatism". It has done this by distinguishing between whether the cause of the accused's lack of control was due to an "internal factor" (i.e. some malfunctioning of the person's body) or an "external factor" (such as a blow to the head)".*

The LC recognised that this led to 'illogical results'. It also noted the defence had no clearly accepted definition, although the one in **Bratty** was the most often used.

There is a reluctance of the courts to accept the defence of automatism as it is a complete defence, so could mean releasing potentially dangerous people back into society. If there is a 'continuing danger' then it is more likely that the courts will refuse the defence and decide it is insanity instead.

**Food for thought**

As Lord Denning said in **Bratty**, a disease of the mind was *"any mental disorder which has manifested itself in violence and is prone to recur"*. If it is 'prone to recur' then D is a continuing danger to society. It is therefore right that insanity rather than automatism should be the defence, because automatism results in an acquittal. However, this does lead to inconsistency and arguably it would be better if automatism was a partial defence. The huge difference in the effect of the pleas of insanity and automatism is hard to justify.

The lack of control must be total.

**Key case**

In **Attorney-General's Reference (No2 of 1992) 1994**, D killed two people when his lorry crashed into a car on the hard shoulder of the motorway. He pleaded automatism on the grounds that driving for so long on a motorway had resulted in a 'trance like' state and he was suffering from what is called 'driving without awareness'. On referral to the CA, it was held that this did not amount to automatism because his lack of awareness was not total. Thus if D's behaviour is only partly automatic, there is no defence. This confirmed **Broome v Perkins 1987**, where a diabetic, suffering from hypoglycaemia, hit another car. It was held that, as D was able to exercise *some* control, automatism was not available.

**This was due to an external factor**

The essence of automatism is that the crime was the result of an external factor causing an involuntary act on the part of the defendant. If it was an internal factor then the defence is insanity. As we saw with insanity, this distinction has produced some fairly bizarre cases. The LC said in its 2012 paper that the *"line drawn between sane and insane automatism can never make medical sense"*.

External factors would include prescribed drugs, such as the insulin in **Quick**. In **Hill v Baxter 1958**, a hypothetical example was given of D being attacked by a swarm of bees whilst driving a car. If this caused a total loss of control, the automatism defence would succeed.

**Examination pointer**

The defences of insanity and automatism are closely linked so you may need to discuss both. However, note that the automatism defence would be better as it results in an acquittal.

### Self-induced automatism

As D must be acting involuntarily the defence cannot be relied upon if the automatism was self-induced, *e.g.*, by intoxication through drinking or taking drugs, as in **Lipman**.

In **Quick**, Lawton LJ said

> "A self-induced incapacity will not excuse ... nor will one which could have been reasonably foreseen as a result of either doing, or omitting to do something, as, for example, taking alcohol against medical advice after using certain prescribed drugs, or failing to have regular meals while taking insulin."

It would appear from this that if you knew you had a heart condition and then drove you could not argue automatism if you had a heart attack and crashed into someone. However, the rule has not been applied very consistently.

In **Hardie 1984**, D set fire to a bedroom after taking Valium. The court held that he could successfully plead automatism even though the pills were not prescribed by a doctor. A distinction was made between drugs which are meant to calm you and ones which are likely to lead to aggressive or unpredictable behaviour. In the latter case, the defence would fail.

In **Bailey 1983**, D was suffering from hypoglycaemia due to a failure to eat properly after taking insulin. He hit his ex-girlfriend's new boyfriend over the head with an iron bar and was convicted of GBH. The CA rejected his automatism defence, as there was clearly not a complete loss of control over his bodily movements (he went to the man's house armed with an iron bar). They restated that self-induced automatism by voluntarily consuming drink or drugs would not be acceptable. However, even though his state was arguably self-induced, because he could have eaten something, the CA made clear that the defence *could* succeed in such a case because it is not commonly known that failing to eat can cause such results.

**Food for thought**

The CA in **Quick** implied that failing to eat makes automatism self-induced. It was not fully clear as they merely held that the defence of automatism should have been left to the jury. In **Bailey**, the same court suggested that whilst drink or drugs would mean the defect is self-induced, failing to eat would not. This leaves the law insufficiently clear.

The rules on insanity and automatism have led to sleepwalkers and diabetics being labelled insane – sometimes. The difference between not taking insulin, and taking it but not eating properly, is small but has a major consequence. The result is either that D is found insane or goes free.

In **Quick** Lawton LJ said that the defence was a *"quagmire of law seldom entered nowadays save by those in desperate need of some kind of defence"*. Not very reassuring!

**Summary**

97

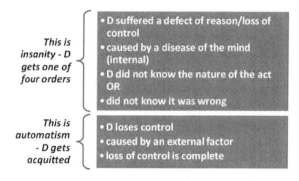

*This is insanity - D gets one of four orders*
- D suffered a defect of reason/loss of control
- caused by a disease of the mind (internal)
- D did not know the nature of the act OR
- did not know it was wrong

*This is automatism - D gets acquitted*
- D loses control
- caused by an external factor
- loss of control is complete

**Self-test questions**

*From which case do the insanity rules come?*

*From which case does the opening quote come?*

*Which defence applies when the cause is external?*

*Which defence applies when the cause is internal?*

*Give a case example for each of these defences to show this difference*

For answers to the tasks and self-test questions, please go to my website at www.drsr.org and click the button 'Answers to tasks'. For a range of free interactive exercises, click on 'Free Exercises' and then the OCR book.

*"Necessity would open a door which no man could shut"* – Lord Denning

By the end of this Chapter you should be able to:

**Explain these 3 defences and the limitations on them**

**Distinguish between these 3 defences, whilst noting the overlap between them**

**Explain how the law applies in practice by reference to cases**

**Identify possible criticisms**

In each of these 3 defences D is arguing that there was no alternative to committing the crime. It was 'necessary' due to a threat, or to the circumstances. In **Shayler 2001,** the CA suggested that duress and necessity were the same. Both were available to a charge under the **Official Secrets Act 1989**, although the argument that information had been revealed in the public interest was not enough, there had to be an imminent threat to life or limb. There is some difference between the defences. Necessity was used to justify a death in **Re A (Conjoined Twins)** but it is clear that duress cannot apply to murder. However, the dividing line between duress of circumstances and necessity, if any, is very faint and the terms have been used interchangeably by the courts. In fact in **Quayle 2005**, discussed below, a new term, 'necessity by circumstances' was used.

**Duress of threats** is where there is a specific threat of harm to D if a particular crime is not committed. **Duress of circumstances** is where there is also a threat of harm. However, here the threat comes, not from another person, but from the surrounding circumstances. **Necessity** is similar to the latter. The circumstances leave D no alternative but to commit a crime. There is no need for a threat of harm to D, though. It is rarely seen; most cases of necessity now come under duress of circumstances. For this reason we will look at necessity first and then look at duress in more detail.

### Example

Don tells Dave that if he does not rob a bank he will kill his family. Dave can use duress as a defence to a burglary charge.

Don finds that Dave's family are away so instead he says he will set fire to his house if he doesn't rob the bank. Dave can't use the duress defences here as there is no threat of harm. He can't use necessity because there are alternatives; he could go to the police.

Dave is attacked by a violent gang whilst waiting at the traffic lights. He jumps the red light to get away. Dave can use duress of circumstances to the driving offence. This could also be called necessity.

### Necessity

Necessity is rarely a defence in itself, though it may be used to reduce a sentence. Thus, stealing because you are starving is still theft, but your sentence may be less because you had some justification. In **Southwark London Borough v Williams 1971**, homelessness was not accepted as a reason for squatting (trespass). Lord Denning said that if it was, "no-one's house could be safe", and continued with the opening quote. He also said that if hunger could be used as a defence to theft, it would open another door through which "all kinds of lawlessness and disorder would pass".

In **Dudley and Stephens 1884,** the Ds had been shipwrecked and after several days in a lifeboat with no food they believed they would die. They killed and ate the cabin boy in order to save their own lives. The defence of necessity was rejected.

Duress of circumstances is really necessity in a modern form, but there are few 'real' cases of necessity. It may be allowed in particular circumstances laid down by statute. An example is **s 5(2)(b) of the Criminal Damage Act 1971**, which allows for it to be a defence where damage is 'necessary' in order to protect property. One of the very few cases where necessity was successfully raised is **Re A 2000.** A hospital sought a declaration that it would be lawful to operate on Siamese twins in the knowledge that one twin would die. The operation was the only way to save the life of the other twin. Although they may not have been prosecuted, they *could* have been charged with murder. They operated in the knowledge that one twin would die and so intended that consequence, even though they didn't desire it. The CA granted the declaration and confirmed they would have a defence of necessity. They made a distinction between cases of duress by threats or circumstances, and cases of real choice. In the latter, the question is one of justifying a choice between two evils. This is the defence of necessity. It would only succeed where the act *was necessary to avoid an inevitable evil, and the evil inflicted was not disproportionate* to the evil avoided.

### Food for thought

It is clear from case law that duress is not a defence to murder. This was stated in **Howe 1987,** and extended to attempted murder in **Gotts 1992. Dudley & Stephens** indicated this rule would also apply to necessity, although there was a special verdict in this case so it does not set a precedent. **Re A** suggests that it is possible that it could apply to murder. This case is seen as unique though, so again is unlikely to set a precedent. There is good reason for the limits on the defence. Nobody should be able to say that one person's life is any more important than another's is. The difference between **Dudley** and **Re A** is that in the latter the doctors were not choosing another life over their own.

It could be argued that necessity should apply to more minor crimes, but Lord Denning's comments show the dangers of this. If you can argue that you have some kind of right to commit a crime in certain circumstances, there is a danger that people will not feel safe.

It was confirmed in **Quayle 2005** that 'necessity' and 'necessity by circumstances' should be decided on a case-by-case basis. There are, however, certain requirements which will apply generally. We will look at duress first, as this is where the rules were established. Then we can look at some cases to illustrate duress of circumstances. Where these have developed, or reconfirmed, the law on duress generally I have included them in the discussion of duress. You should note in particular that the HL reconsidered the whole issue of duress in **Hasan 2005** (duress of threats), and this was applied by the CA in **Quayle 2005** (duress of circumstances) with approval.

It is for D to provide evidence of duress, but then the burden of proof is on the prosecution to disprove it. If the defence succeeds then D will be acquitted.

### Duress

The original defence of duress occurs where D is forced to commit a crime because of a threat. An example would be "if you don't steal the money, I will shoot you". It is sometimes called duress of threats. This is mainly to distinguish it from the more recently developed, duress of circumstances.

**Key case**

The test for establishing the defence was laid down in **Graham 1982**. D was a homosexual who lived with his wife and another man. He was charged with the murder of his wife. He alleged that the other man had threatened and intimidated him, and argued duress as a defence. The HL upheld his conviction and established the test for duress. It is a two-part question for the jury:

Was the defendant impelled to act as he did because he believed that he had good cause to fear that if he did not so act he would be killed or caused serious injury? If so have the prosecution made the jury sure that a sober person of reasonable firmness, sharing the characteristics of the defendant, would not have responded that way.

Put more simply:

**Did D believe that there was good cause to fear death or serious injury if the crime was not committed – subjective**

**would a sober person of reasonable firmness sharing the same characteristics have responded that way – objective**

The test is therefore in part subjective and in part objective. However, the first part is not fully subjective because D must have 'good cause to fear'. Unlike self-defence and mistake, where as long as a belief is genuinely held it need not be reasonable, for duress it must be a reasonable belief.

**The threat**

The threat has to be a serious one. Firstly, it must be a threat of *harm*. In **Valderrama-Vega 1985**, it was said that financial pressure and a threat of disclosing that D was a homosexual was not enough. In **Shayler 2001,** the CA said that duress was only available where the threat was to 'life or serious injury'. In **Wadsworth 2009** a woman pleaded duress to a charge of theft. She had stolen from the bank where she worked over a period of time, due to demands made by her boyfriend. She argued that she was in fear of violence and believed he would kill her or her family if she did not bring him the money. She had good cause to fear serious violence and the defence succeeded.

Secondly, the threat must be *imminent*. The rule was that if D could seek police protection or take evasive action then the defence was unavailable. Thus in **Gill 1963,** the defence failed because although there was a threat of harm if D did not steal a lorry, he had time to escape and seek help. This rule was relaxed in **Hudson and Taylor 1971.** Two young girls had lied in court because they were told they would be harmed if they testified against the accused. They successfully appealed against their conviction for perjury. The CA rejected the prosecution's argument that the threat wasn't imminent. They said that it was irrelevant that it could not be carried out immediately; it could be carried out on the streets late that night. The CA clearly recognised that the girls may not have received effective police protection from the threats. In **Abdul-Hussain 1999,** the Ds successfully appealed against a hi-jacking conviction. They believed they would be executed if returned to their own country, which they thought was imminent, and hi-jacked a plane to escape. The CA accepted duress of circumstances did not need an *immediate* threat, as long as it was *influencing* D at the time the crime was committed.

However, in **Hasan 2005**, Lord Bingham referred to both these cases and disapproved them on this point. He thought the limitation that D must have no chance of evasive action had been "unduly weakened". This HL case reaffirms that the threat must be immediate, or at least there should be no possibility of taking evasive action.

### Key case

In **Hasan 2005**, D had fallen in with a drug dealer who was known to be violent. He told the dealer about a house where there was a lot of money kept in a safe. The dealer then told him that if he didn't burgle the house his family would be harmed. When charged with burglary he argued duress. Lord Bingham said that the defence was excluded where, due to a 'voluntary association' with criminals "he foresaw, or ought reasonably to have foreseen, the risk of being subjected to any compulsion by threats of violence". He also said that if the harm threatened was not "such as he reasonably expects to follow immediately, or almost immediately", then there was little doubt that D should take evasive action "whether by going to the police, or in some other way, to avoid committing the crime"

In **Hasan 2005**, Lord Bingham restated the essential requirements for duress. These are:

> **The threat relied on must be to cause death or serious injury**
>
> **The criminal conduct which it is sought to excuse has been directly caused by the threats**
>
> **The threat must be directed to d or a member of d's family, or to "a person for whose safety the defendant would reasonably regard himself as responsible"**
>
> **D may rely on duress only if there was no evasive action that could reasonably have been taken (such as going to the police, disapproving Hudson & Taylor)**
>
> **The questions for the jury were both objective (did D 'reasonably believe' there was a threat, approving Graham)**
>
> **The defence is not available where, as a result of a voluntary association with criminals, D "ought reasonably to have foreseen" the risk of violence**

### Examination pointer

Look for any evidence of a threat in the given scenario. If there is a threat from a person then duress will be appropriate. You will need to apply each of the rules from **Hassan** to decide whether you think the defence will succeed.

### Sober person of reasonable firmness

In **Graham**, D had been drunk as well as threatened but the court said that voluntary intoxication could not be taken into account. The test refers to a 'sober person'. 'Of reasonable firmness', means factors such as timidity and susceptibility to threats will not be taken into account. In **Bowen 1996**, D had been charged with obtaining services by deception. He said he only did it after he and his family were threatened. The court refused to take his low IQ into account. However, as well as age and sex the CA did say that pregnancy, a recognised mental illness or serious physical disability could be relevant characteristics because these could affect D's ability to resist.

### Food for thought

In **Bowen**, the fact that his very low IQ made D particularly vulnerable to threats was not taken into account.  However, his low IQ clearly affected his ability to be 'firm'.  This can seem unjust.

### Self – induced duress

In **Sharp 1987** D had been involved in a plan with a gang to commit a robbery, he then tried to withdraw but was threatened.  Someone was killed during the robbery and his conviction for manslaughter was upheld.  The CA made clear that the defence would fail where D knew that the gang he had joined might put pressure on him to commit an offence.  This is self-induced duress as D had a choice in the first place.  The key issue is what is known about the gang.  In **Shepherd 1987**, the defence succeeded as there was no evidence of any violence prior to the threats.  It is now clear that this is an objective test.  Even if D didn't know of any violent tendencies, the defence will fail if these would have been obvious to anyone else.  This was made clear in **Hasan**, which is an example of self-induced duress.  The question is whether D *should* have known, rather than whether D *did* know, that there was a risk of being threatened.  The words "or ought reasonably to have foreseen" in **Graham** had indicated this.

In **Ali 2008**, D had been charged with robbery.  He did not deny the robbery but said that another man had forced him into it.  His parents had warned him the man was a criminal and to stay away from him.  He pleaded the defence of duress.  The CA held the defence was not available where, because of a voluntary association with others engaged in criminal activity, D foresaw, or 'ought to have foreseen', the risk of being subjected to any compulsion by threats of violence to commit criminal acts.  If so the duress will be deemed voluntary and the defence will fail.  The main question was whether he had voluntarily put himself in a position where such a risk was reasonably foreseeable, and it was made clear that this was an objective test.

### Duress of circumstances

Duress of circumstances is relatively new.  It arose during the 80's in driving offence cases.  Recognising that necessity was rarely allowed as a defence, lawyers had started to argue that duress could extend beyond the traditional 'threat by a person' to situations where D has no alternative but to commit a crime.  In **Conway 1988,** D was in his car when he was approached by two men.  He believed they were going to attack him and he drove recklessly to escape from the perceived threat.  The CA accepted the defence and said it was 'convenient' to refer to such a defence as 'duress of circumstances'.  In **Martin 1988**, D had driven his son to work whilst disqualified.  He argued that his son might lose his job if he was late and his wife had threatened to commit suicide if he did not take him.  The judge said that English law recognised a 'defence of necessity' in extreme circumstances.  In such cases, where the threat came from dangers other than a threat from another person, "*it is conveniently called duress of circumstances*".  In the early days, it was most commonly used for driving offences.  In **DPP v Bell 1992** D drove whilst drunk, again to escape from a threatening gang.  The defence succeeded because as soon as he was out of danger he stopped in a lay-by.  In December 1999, the footballer, David Beckham, was not so lucky.  He was being chased by the paparazzi and was charged with speeding.  His defence of duress was rejected on the basis that driving at over 75 mph in a 50 limit was not the only option available to him (e.g., he could have slowed down or changed lanes).  He appealed, and although the judge overturned his driving ban due to 'special circumstances', his conviction was upheld.

It is not confined to driving offences, though.  In **Pommell 1995**, D was charged with possession of a firearm and successfully argued duress.  He said that he had taken the gun from someone who was threatening to use it in a revenge attack.  As this was in the early hours of the morning, he kept it overnight, intending to take it to the police in the morning. The police had, he said, arrived before he could do so.

Although coming from circumstances rather than a person, in all these cases there was a threat of physical harm, either to D or to another. It will still not apply to the cases that concerned Lord Denning, theft and trespass.

### Examination pointer

If there is no evidence in the given scenario of a threat from a person, look for any circumstances that may be threatening, and consider necessity or duress of circumstances. There still needs to be a threat of physical harm, whichever defence is used. Duress of circumstances is more common, so apply the rules from **Hassan**. If there is any evidence that D belongs to a gang, look at how **Hasan** confirmed the rules on self-induced duress seen in **Sharp** and **Shepherd**.

### Task

Look at the following situations and decide if I can successfully use a defence of duress:

**I am threatened with being exposed as a cheat and a drunk if I do not steal a packet of smoked salmon from the supermarket. I do so and am charged with theft.**

**I am chased by a man who is threatening to hit me. I steal a car to escape. I drive to a nearby house where I have friends. I am charged with theft.**

**I am at a party and a bit drunk. As I live 30 miles away I intend to stay overnight. An old enemy turns up and threatens to beat me up. I run outside and see my car in the drive. I get in and drive all the way home. I am charged with driving with excess alcohol.**

### The overlap

It had seemed that necessity had been replaced by duress of circumstances. However, cases such as **Re A** show that there may still be occasions where only necessity can be used. In most cases, however, there is no difference between the defences except in the words used to describe them.

In **Quayle 2005**, D had argued necessity in defence to a charge of growing cannabis. He argued that it was necessary for medical reasons. He was in pain and it was the only drug that allowed him to sleep without knocking him out. He did not want to take anything that knocked him out as he had children to look after. The CA rejected his appeal. They referred to the "defence of necessity where the force or compulsion is exerted not by human threats but by extraneous circumstances". They relied on **Rodger and Rose 1998,** where the Ds had been suicidal because they were in prison and when caught escaping had argued duress of circumstances. The defence had failed and the earlier cases were distinguished on the basis that the threat was not from an extraneous source, it was the suicidal tendencies of the Ds themselves. The CA in **Quayle** confirmed that the threat could come from circumstances rather than a person but restated that it must come from an external source.

The CA in **Quayle** recognised the overlap between the defences and said that both "duress of threats and necessity by circumstances" should be confined to cases of threats of physical injury. They did point out, however, that there was no 'over-arching principle' which applied to all cases. They referred to the comments of the CA in **Abdul-Hussain,** that in the absence of parliamentary intervention, the law should develop on a case-by-case basis.

## Food for thought

Developing the law on a case-by-case basis may be achieving justice but is it at the expense of consistency? The courts have clearly stated that Parliament should address the issue. In **Safi 2003** (another hi-jacking case), the CA noted that the courts had 'repeatedly' emphasised the urgent need for legislation on duress. It appears from the detailed discussion in **Hasan** that the HL has decided to try to clarify the law itself.

## Task

The courts have called for Parliament to intervene. Read back over this chapter and ask yourself how you would draft a bill on the defence of duress. What features of duress would you keep? Would you add any new conditions? Write these out adding a few comments on your reasons. Keep this for a discussion for and against the defence. It can be used for an essay on defences or for the special study unit.

## Duress and mistake

**Conway** shows that D can use the defence even if there is no actual threat. It turned out that the people D thought were going to attack him were plain-clothes policemen. However, he was able to rely on duress even though he was mistaken as to the threat. He was judged on the facts as he honestly believed them to be.

In **Safi 2003,** the judge had suggested there had to *be* a threat but the CA said that this was wrong. They confirmed that the **Graham** test was still the law. Thus both types of duress could (as with self-defence) be used with mistake. However, there is a difference. With duress the mistake must be reasonable. This was implied by the test in **Graham** (did D have '*good cause to fear*'?) and has now been confirmed by the HL in **Hasan**. Lord Bingham said, "there is no warrant for relaxing the requirement that the belief must be reasonable as well as genuine".

## Food for thought

Lord Bingham suggested that the stricter requirements for duress were fair because, unlike self-defence and provocation, the victim was totally innocent. This is a fair point. However, it can be argued that the same is true in many cases of self-defence. If D mistakenly believes someone is being attacked and assaults the attacker, as in **Williams (Gladstone),** then that 'attacker' is as innocent as the victims in cases of duress.

### Limits to the availability of the defence of duress

We have seen some of the limitations in the cases discussed. They were restated by the HL in **Hasan 2000**:

> **Duress does not apply to murder – Howe 1987**
>
> **Nor attempted murder – Gotts 1992**
>
> **D may not rely on duress as a result of a voluntary association with others engaged in criminal activity where there was a foreseeable risk of being subjected to threats of violence – Sharp 1987**

In **Wilson 2007**, a teenager was accused along with his father, of murdering his mother, He argued that he only helped in the murder because he was scared of his father. The CA confirmed that however much duress a person was under the defence was not available for murder.

## Criticisms and reform

The defence has not been without its critics and in its **1978 Report** the Law Commission acknowledged several criticisms of the defence of duress. These included:

**It should not be justifiable to do wrong or cause harm**

**The defence could be used as an excuse to commit a crime**

**It should not fall upon an individual to balance wrong-doing against the avoidance of harm to themselves or to others**

**It could encourages terrorists and kidnappers**

There are some fair points here. However, the Commission proposed that legislation should provide a defence and recommended that:

**Duress should be a general defence applicable to all offences including murder and attempted murder**

**Threats of harm to individuals should be allowed but not threats to property. Self – induced duress should not be allowed**

**The burden of proof should be on the defendant to establish duress**

## Food for thought

Many of the Commission's recommendations have been incorporated by case law. The proposal in regard to murder is one that hasn't. It is somewhat contentious. It is arguable that it is not up to D to decide whose life is worth more. In **Hasan 2005** the HL noted the logic of the Commission's recommendation, but also noted that the recommendation had not been adopted *"no doubt because it is felt that in the case of the gravest crimes no threat to the defendant, however extreme, should excuse commission of the crime"*. One problem is that the defence results in an acquittal. It could be argued that allowing it to be used as a partial defence to murder, reducing murder to manslaughter, would be more satisfactory.

Essentially, the defence needs to be clarified by Parliament, as requested by the courts.

## Summary

| Defence | Requirements | Limits |
|---|---|---|
| Necessity | The evil avoided is greater than the evil done | Case by case basis. Could justify a killing (**Re A**) |
| Duress | Imminent threat of death or serious injury (from a person) D had 'good cause' to believe such a threat (**Graham/Hasan**) a reasonable person would have acted as D did | Not murder or attempted murder (**Howe/Gotts**) Not where D voluntarily associates with those foreseeably posing a risk of threats No evasive action possible (Hasan) |
| Duress of circumstances | Imminent threat of death or serious injury (from circumstances) D had 'good cause' to believe such a threat (**Graham/Hasan**) a reasonable person would have acted as D did | Not murder or attempted murder No evasive action possible (Hasan) The threat need not come from a person but must be external to D (**Quayle**) |

**Self-test questions**

*In which case was the test for duress established?*

*What did **Hasan** confirm in regard to the first part of this test?*

*What defence was used in re A and how does this differ from duress?*

*What point was confirmed in **Quayle** about the source of the threat?*

*Did David Beckham fail when using the defence duress?*

For answers to the tasks and self-test questions, please go to my website at www.drsr.org and click the button 'Answers to tasks'. For a range of free interactive exercises, click on 'Free Exercises' and then the OCR book.

*"If a man, whilst sane and sober, forms an intention to kill ... he cannot rely on this self-induced drunkenness as a defence to murder"* -Lord Denning

By the end of this Chapter, you should be able to:

*Distinguish between voluntary and involuntary intoxication*

*Explain how the courts treat different types of drug*

*Explain the difference between specific intent and basic intent*

*Show how the defence applies by reference to cases*

Although traditionally this defence only applied to drink, it is now clear that the rules on intoxication apply to both drink and drugs. In cases involving drugs a distinction has been made between those which are commonly known to cause aggressive or dangerous behaviour and those which are not.

**Key case**

In **Hardie 1985**, D was trying to get his ex-girlfriend to get back together with him. She gave him a sedative (Valium) to calm him down and then left him in her flat. Whilst she was out, he set fire to it. He claimed that he could not remember anything after he had taken the drug. The CA allowed his appeal against conviction and held Valium was *"wholly different from drugs which are liable to cause unpredictability and aggressiveness"*.

Thus, 'unpredictable' drugs are treated in the same way as alcohol. With sedatives, the courts will apply a test of subjective recklessness.

**Example**

D is given anti-depressant drugs by his doctor. They make him feel sick and he doesn't eat for several days. Together with the pills, lack of food has the effect of making him prone to outbursts of violence. During one such period, he lashes out at someone and is charged with assault. He argues intoxication as a defence.

The question will be whether he was reckless, i.e., appreciated the risk that taking the drug would lead to such aggressive and unpredictable behaviour. If he was not told about any possible side effects then it is unlikely he will be seen as reckless. However, if the doctor had warned him to eat regularly to avoid any side effects then his defence will probably fail.

Intoxication is only a defence if it can be shown that due to the intoxication D was incapable of forming the necessary intent. This was established many years ago in **Beard 1920**. The rules for the defence differ depending on whether D was drunk voluntarily or not.

*Involuntary intoxication*

This would occur where D did not knowingly take alcohol or drugs. An example would be drinking orange juice which someone had 'spiked', e.g., added vodka to. The intoxication must do more than make D lose their inhibitions, though, it must remove *mens rea*.

**Key case**

In **Kingston 1994**, D was given drinks which had been laced with drugs. He was then photographed indecently assaulting a 15-year old boy. He admitted that at the time of committing the offence that he had the necessary intent, but said that he would not have acted in that way had he been sober.  The HL overturned the decision of the CA and held that intoxicated intent was still intent.  Intoxication is therefore no defence if the defendant had the necessary *mens rea*, even if it is formed whilst involuntarily intoxicated.

In **Allen 1988**, the CA made it clear that the intoxication had to be totally involuntary; not knowing the strength of what you are drinking would not be enough.  D had drunk homemade wine not realising it was very strong.  He then pleaded involuntary intoxication when charged with indecent assault.  The CA held that he had freely been drinking wine, knowing it to be wine.  It was therefore voluntary intoxication.

### Task

Refer back to the Chapter on insanity and automatism.  Read the facts of **Lipman** again.  Make a note of which defence was argued and which succeeded.  Why was this?  We will come back to this case later to see the overlap between the defences.

### *Voluntary intoxication:  Basic and specific intent*

The basic rule on intoxication is that it can provide a defence to crimes of specific intent but not those of basic intent.  In simple terms, the distinction is this: if a crime can only be committed intentionally then it is crime of specific intent; if it can be committed with some other form of *mens rea*, e.g., recklessness, it is a crime of basic intent

### Key case

This distinction was made in **Majewski 1977** where the HL held that intoxication could not negate the *mens rea* where the required *mens rea* was recklessness.  Essentially getting drunk was seen as reckless in itself.  D had been charged with an assault after a pub fight.  He argued that he was too drunk to know what he was doing.  The HL upheld his conviction and stated that evidence of self-induced intoxication which negated *mens rea* was a defence to a crime requiring specific intent but not to any other crime.

### Example

Whilst drunk, Sue takes someone's bag and is charged with theft.  This is a specific intent crime.  Sue's intoxication defence can succeed if she can show that she lacked *mens rea*.  The *mens rea* for theft is 'intent to permanently deprive' another.  She might show that because she was drunk she thought it was hers and so she had no intent to deprive anyone else of it.

If she destroyed the bag, she could not use the defence to a charge of criminal damage.  This offence can be committed by 'intending ... or being reckless as to whether property is destroyed'.  The fact that this can be done by 'being reckless' makes it a basic intent crime.

The distinction seemed straightforward but some doubt was cast on it in **Heard 2007**.  D had sexually assaulted a police officer whilst drunk and argued intoxication as a defence.  He was convicted and appealed on the basis that the crime was 'intentionally' touching another person sexually and thus a specific intent crime.  The CA held that basic intent could include intention where the *mens rea* was only for the act itself and nothing further, as here.  Specific intent could include recklessness where the offence required *mens rea* for more than the illegal act itself, e.g., a consequence.  The CA also noted that not all offences could be categorised as basic or specific offences as some had elements of both.

### Food for thought and examination pointer

The Law Commission (in its 2012 paper on insanity) said

*"We define specific intent offences as those for which the predominant mens rea is one of knowledge, intention or dishonesty, and basic intent offences as all those for which the predominant mens rea is not intention, knowledge or dishonesty (this includes offences of recklessness, belief, negligence and strict liability)"*.

This is what many judges and academics had interpreted **Majewski** as meaning, but **Heard** has introduced some doubt. This provides useful material for a critical evaluation of the defence, but for a problem question I would use the earlier interpretation and just mention briefly that **Heard** has cast some doubt on this.

In **Dowds 2012**, (see diminished responsibility) the CA held that voluntary, or self-induced, intoxication was not capable of establishing a defence. Although the case involved the special defence of diminished responsibility, the CA made clear that the rules on intoxication apply to all defences, and to intoxication caused by drugs or other substances as well as alcohol.

Note that if you plead intoxication to a specific intent crime then you will still be guilty of any related basic intent crime. If charged with murder, this would be manslaughter. If charged with **s18 Offences against the Person Act 1861**, the result would be a conviction under **s20**. This is because you are using intoxication to negate the *mens rea* of intention. **Majewski** shows, however, that you will still be deemed 'reckless'. If there is no related basic intent crime then D may be acquitted. An example would be theft.

**Examination pointer**

Look carefully at the facts and at *how* D became intoxicated. First decide if it is voluntary or not. If it is then use **Majewski**, if not then use **Kingston**. You may need both if the matter isn't clear. Look at the type of intoxicant; if it is a drug, you will need to look at the distinction made in **Hardie**, between drugs likely to cause aggression and sedatives. Taking unpredictable drugs is likely to be seen as voluntary intoxication.

Did you do the task on **Lipman?** It can help identify the overlap between defences. Let's look at how:

A possible defence is insanity. He clearly had a 'defect of reason' and he did not know 'the nature and quality' of his act. He thought he was fighting snakes not strangling his girlfriend. However, the defect was not caused by a 'disease of the mind' but by the LSD. This is an external factor so consider automatism. The defence of automatism fails because the loss of control was self-induced (taking LSD). It was voluntary. The defence of intoxication can be argued. The effect of the drug meant he did not have the required *mens rea*. He had no intent to kill or seriously injure so was not guilty of the specific intent crime (murder), but as the intoxication was voluntary, he was guilty of the related basic intent crime (manslaughter).

**Food for thought**

As we saw when looking at *mens rea* in Chapter 2, the **Criminal Justice Act 1967** requires the jury to decide whether D did 'intend or foresee' the result by reference to 'all the evidence'. **Majewski** seems to dispense with this requirement. If D is drunk that is enough to prove recklessness. No other evidence is required. This favours the prosecution who will not have the usual job of proving *mens rea*. It is also wider than the usual test for recklessness. Usually the prosecution must prove that 'D recognised a risk and went ahead anyway'. Not quite the same as D was drunk.

## The 'Dutch courage' rule

What if D forms the required *mens rea* and *then* gets drunk and commits an offence? This may occur where D becomes intoxicated in order to summon up the courage to commit the offence. This is called the 'Dutch Courage' rule.

In **Attorney General for Northern Ireland v Gallagher 1963**, D decided to kill his wife. He bought a knife and a bottle of whisky. He drank the whisky and then stabbed her. The HL held that once a person formed an intention to kill then the defence would fail. Lord Denning made the main speech including the quote at the beginning of this Chapter. He also gave two examples of when intoxication might succeed. Firstly, where a nurse at a christening got so drunk that she put the baby on the fire in mistake for a log. Secondly, where a drunken man thought his friend, lying in bed, was a theatrical dummy and stabbed him to death. Lord Denning said that in both cases D would have a defence to a murder charge. This latter is not dissimilar to **Lipman**, where D thought he was fighting snakes and ended up strangling his girlfriend.

### Food for thought

In **Gallagher**, the HL held that once a person formed an intention to kill, then the defence would fail. At first glance, this seems fine. After all, D did have *mens rea* because he planned to kill her and went and bought a knife. That he was too intoxicated to possess intent when the act was carried out is arguably irrelevant. It can be seen as inconsistent with the normal rules of law though. The usual requirement is that *mens rea* and *actus reus* occur together.

Lord Denning's examples show that intoxication and mistake are closely linked. We will deal with mistake separately but for the moment let's just look at the overlap.

### Intoxication and public policy

Public policy is one reason why the courts will not allow intoxication as a defence. It is not in the public interest to allow people who get drunk and then commit an offence to be able to rely on intoxication as a defence. In **O'Grady 1987**, D hit his friend over the head in the mistaken belief that the friend was trying to kill him. Both of them were drunk at the time. He was convicted of manslaughter and appealed. The CA refused to allow the defence and said:

> "There are two competing interests. On the one hand the interest of the defendant who has only acted according to what he believed to be necessary to protect himself, and on the other hand that of the public in general, and the victim in particular who, probably through no fault of his own, has been injured or perhaps killed because of the defendant's drunken mistake. Reason recoils from the conclusion that in such circumstances a defendant is entitled to leave the court without a stain on his character".

In **Dowds 2012**, Hughes LJ said

> "... public policy proceeds on the basis that a defendant who voluntarily takes alcohol and behaves in a way in which he might not have behaved when sober is not normally entitled to be excused from the consequences of his actions".

### Food for thought

The law is complex and juries are confused by the different rules. The **Majewski** 'rules' are less than exact. It is not fully clear which crimes are specific intent, and which are basic. The jury will have to decide whether D was knowingly taking an 'unpredictable' drug or a sedative. This distinction is also unclear.

**Task**

Draw up a flow chart or diagram using the following cases. Note for each whether insanity, automatism or intoxication applied and why.

**Lipman 1970**     **Bailey 1983**     **Hardie 1984**     **Hennessy 1989**

### Intoxication and other defences

Intoxication is often seen with other defences so when revising this area look also at the chapters on diminished responsibility, insanity, automatism and mistaken self-defence to see how the intoxication defence applies alongside these other defences

**Summary**

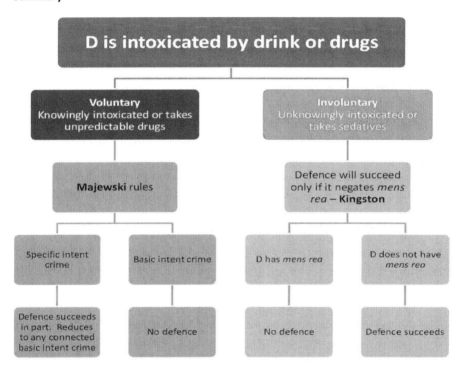

**Self-test questions**

*What is the difference between specific and basic intent?*

*Name a crime for each type*

*What is 'Dutch courage' and will it provide a defence?*

*If D successfully pleads intoxication to a specific intent crime such as murder what is the result?*

*From which case did the opening quote come?*

This summary looks at the application of the defences. An important thing to note is the *effect* of the defences. This will help you decide which one is most appropriate in a given scenario.

| Defence | Main points | Which crimes | Effect |
|---|---|---|---|
| Insanity | defect of reason caused by disease of the mind (internal factor) **M'Nagten** rules | All | Not guilty by reason of insanity |
| Automatism | must be a total loss of control (caused by an external factor) **Broome v Perkins 1987** | All | Acquittal |
| Intoxication – involuntary | must remove *mens rea* – **Kingston** | All crimes requiring *mens rea* | Acquittal |
| Intoxication – voluntary | **Majewski** | Specific intent crimes Basic intent crime | Reduces to basic intent crime Guilty |
| Duress | direct threat of imminent death or serious injury **Hasan** | Not murder or attempted murder **Howe** | Acquittal |
| Duress of circumstances | threat of imminent death or serious injury by circumstances | Not murder or attempted murder | Acquittal |

*Task*

Note the principle and brief facts of the following cases

*Sullivan*

*Broome v Perkins*

*Kingston*

*Majewski*

*Re A (twins case)*

*Graham*

*Hasan*

*Sharp*

**Key criticisms**

There is a problem with finding insanity in respect of people whose conditions are not normally associated with mental disorder, such as the 'diabetes' cases

The insanity defence originates from an 1843 case and should be updated because of medical advances

The stigma of an insanity verdict may also mean people who genuinely do have a mental problem do not plead the defence.

The difference between not taking insulin, and taking it but not eating properly, are small but one leads to a defence of insanity and the other to automatism

The law on both insanity and automatism is unclear, as recognised by the Law Commission in their 2012 scoping paper

Neither the 1991 Act nor the 2004 Act defines insanity

The law on intoxication is arguably unclear

Majewski seems to dispense with the requirement of mens rea. If D is drunk that is enough to prove recklessness, no other evidence is required. This favours the prosecution.

The Majewski 'rules' are not fully clear as to which crimes are specific intent and which are basic intent

Threats of duress won't help a person who is not of 'reasonable fortitude' as in Bowen

The effect of Howe puts D in a very difficult situation by insisting that even where a close family member is threatened with death D must not kill to save them. Can a person of 'reasonable fortitude' make such a choice? D may be prepared to put his/her own life at risk to save someone else but not feel capable of risking the life of someone close

## Sample examination question

'The defence of intoxication represents a satisfactory compromise between justice for an individual defendant and the demands of public policy'

Assess the accuracy of this statement. 50 marks

## Special study unit – possible connections

The case of **Re A** represents a development of the law on necessity. The CA decided that there were extreme, but limited, situations where there could be a right to choose that one innocent person could die to save the life of another. Duress of circumstances is a development of the law on both necessity and duress; arguably, these developments were necessary in order to do justice in the circumstances. Any of the cases on this development can be discussed.

The Law Commission has suggested reforms of this defence. In their 2006 report 'Murder, manslaughter and Infanticide' the Law Commission said that it is not right that duress cannot be a defence to murder in any circumstances. At one time it was being proposed that duress should be a partial defence to murder. The current recommendation is that duress is a full defence and that it should also apply to murder, both first and second degree, and to attempted murder, as long as the threat involved is of death or serious injury. For further information on reforms look at their web site at http://lawcommission.justice.gov.uk/

The *stare decisis* rule says 'treat like cases alike' and deciding whether duress applies on a case-by-case basis can lead to uncertainty. Should Parliament act to clarify the issue or have the courts succeeded in doing so? **Quayle – Hasan**

In **Heard 2007**, (see intoxication) the defence interpreted **Majewski** as saying that basic intent crimes were where *mens rea* included recklessness and specific intent crimes were where *mens rea* was intention only.  The judge preferred the prosecution's argument, which was that crimes of basic were not limited to those where recklessness sufficed and that the correct distinction was between crimes requiring 'ordinary' intent and crimes requiring 'specific' or 'purposive' intent.  The appeal to the CA involved an interpretation of the distinction from **Majewski** between basic and specific intent crimes.  The CA agreed with the trial judge that specific intent could include recklessness where the offence required *mens rea* for more than the illegal act itself, e.g., a consequence, and that basic intent could include intention where the *mens rea* was only for the act itself and nothing further.  An example was given of criminal damage endangering life where the *mens rea* is intent or recklessness not just for damage but also as to endangering life.  According to the CA's new interpretation of **Majewski** this is specific intent as the *mens rea* goes to more than a simple act and includes a consequence (endangering life).  **Majewski** was decided in the HL and although the CA can interpret the *ratio decidendi* this way this development of the law may well be challenged.

## The offences

**Chapter 13:** Common law offence of assault (assault and battery)

**Chapter 14:** Statutory offence under the **Offences against the Person Act 1861**

**s 47**, assault occasioning actual bodily harm

**Chapter 15:** Statutory offences under the **Offences against the Person Act 1861**

**s 20**, grievous bodily harm and wounding

**s 18**, grievous bodily harm and wounding with intent

The five different offences against the person contained in this study block are commonly called 'the assaults'. However, they are separate and distinct offences, with different rules on each.

### Example

Jane threatens Jenny and then pushes her. Jenny is scared and runs away. She trips and grazes her knee. Frightening Jenny is assault, pushing her is battery. Jenny grazed her knee which is actual bodily harm, **s 47**. If she is seriously hurt or cut badly it will be grievous bodily harm or wounding, **s 20**. If Jane *intended* to harm Jenny seriously, it would be grievous bodily harm or wounding with intent, **s 18**.

The offences of assault and battery come from the common law, the others from an Act of Parliament. Note the date of the Act. It is very old and much in need of reform. Reforms have been suggested but not implemented and this is a popular area for evaluation questions. At the end of the Study Block, there is a full summary of all the offences together with criticisms and proposed reforms.

### The defences

**Chapter 16:** Self-defence and the prevention of crime

**Chapter 17:** Consent

Although these two defences are also general defences, in that they apply to most offences, for examination purposes consent and self-defence are most commonly seen with the non-fatal offences against the person.

### Example

If Jane believes that she is being attacked by Jenny and she hits her, she can use the defence of self-defence.

Alternatively, if Jane and Jenny are playing cricket and Jenny is hurt when Jane hits the ball at her, then if Jane is charged with an offence she can argue the defence of consent. She will say that Jenny consented to being harmed because she agreed to play a game which could result in an injury.

*"There could be no dispute that if you touch a person's clothes while he is wearing them that is equivalent to touching him"*

*R v Thomas 1985*

By the end of this Chapter, you should be able to:

### Explain the actus reus and mens rea of assault and battery

### Explain the differences between them

### Explain how the law applies in practice by reference to cases

### Identify possible criticisms

Common assault includes two separate offences, assault and battery. It is called common assault because it comes from the common law. This means that assault and battery are not defined in any statute so the rules come from cases. The **Criminal Justice Act 1988 s 39** classifies them as summary offences (triable only in the magistrates' court) so for convenience they are charged under this section.

### Examination pointer

It is better not to say they are *offences* under **s 39 Criminal Justice Act**. They are common law offences *charged* under the **Act**. Think of common assault as an umbrella under which the two crimes of assault and battery sit. They frequently occur together. If you need to discuss both, then refer to common assault and then describe assault and battery in turn.

Assault and battery are also trespass to the person which is a civil matter, a tort. Here we are only dealing with *criminal* assault. The definitions as developed by case law are currently:

**Assault: to cause someone to apprehend immediate and unlawful personal violence**

**Battery: the unlawful application of force to another**

### Example

Fred raises his fist and threatens Simon with a punch on the nose. This is an assault because Simon 'apprehends', or fears, violence. If Fred then follows up the threat there is both an assault and a battery. You may also have actual bodily harm but we'll come to that later.

We will look at each offence in turn.

### Assault

The definition of assault is 'an act by which a person **intentionally or recklessly causes another to apprehend immediate and unlawful violence**'. This definition was used by the CA in **Ireland 1996** (discussed below) and confirmed by the HL the following year, in the twin appeals of **Ireland & Burstow 1997**.

### Actus reus

**The *actus reus* is to:**

### cause the victim to apprehend

### immediate and unlawful violence

**Cause the victim to apprehend**

Apprehend means to become aware of or look forward to. Here it is not look forward to in the positive sense but with a sense of fear. It is the effect on the victim that is important with assault. Assault is not the actual violence but the *threat* of it, so as long as V expects violence to take place that is enough.

## Example

D walks into a bank pointing a banana concealed in a bag and saying, "I have a gun. Give me the money or I'll shoot you." The cashier is very frightened and does as D says. This is an assault. The fact that there is no possibility of carrying out the threat doesn't matter. V is in fear of immediate violence.

D walks into a bank pointing a real gun and saying, "Give me the money or I'll shoot." The cashier knows him from college and she thinks he is doing it as a joke. This is unlikely to be assault. V doesn't believe that any violence is about to take place.

Whether it amounts to assault therefore depends on whether or not V thinks that violence is about to take place.

## Can words alone constitute an assault?

Early cases indicated that words would not amount to assault unless accompanied by some threatening gesture (like raising your fist). In **Meade and Belt 1823**, it was said that 'no words or singing are equivalent to an assault'. This has changed over the years and in **Wilson 1955**, the words 'get out the knives' was said to be enough for assault. Also in **Constanza 1997**, a case of stalking, the CA held that words alone could amount to an assault. Even silence is now capable of amounting to an assault. In **Smith v Chief Superintendent of Woking Police Station 1983**, a 'peeping Tom' assaulted a woman by looking at her through her bedroom window at night. He had caused her to be frightened.

## Food for thought

It is the effect on the victim that is important, thus it seems right that words – or even silence – should amount to assault if they put the victim in fear of harm. The law has arguably become more satisfactory over the years, at least on this point.

## Key case

In **Ireland**, D had repeatedly made silent telephone calls, accompanied by heavy breathing, to three women. In the appeal to the HL in 1997, Lord Steyn confirmed that words would be enough for assault, saying,

> *"The proposition that a gesture may amount to an assault, but that words can never suffice, is unrealistic and indefensible. A thing said is also a thing done. There is no reason why something said should be incapable of causing an apprehension of immediate personal violence, e.g., a man accosting a woman in a dark alley saying 'come with me or I will stab you.' I would, therefore, reject the proposition that an assault can never be committed by words".*

## Words may prevent an assault

If D accompanies the threat with words which indicate that no violence will take place then there is no assault. An example of this is seen in a very old case. In **Turbeville v Savage 1669**, D was having an argument with V and placed his hand on the hilt of his sword. This would indicate an assault. He then said 'If it were not assize time, I would not take such language from you'. There was held to be no assault. The statement was held to indicate that he would *not* assault V because it was assize time and the judges were in town.

## Example

You say to John "I would hit you if it were not your birthday." This indicates you won't do so (assuming it is his birthday!). No assault has taken place.

### immediate and unlawful violence

The threat must be of 'immediate' violence. This means if you threaten someone just as you are about to get on a train it won't be enough. You can't carry out your threat 'immediately'. The term is widely interpreted though. In **Smith v Chief Superintendent of Woking Police Station**, V was scared by D looking at her through her bedroom window at night. She was frightened of what he might do next. The CA held this was sufficient.

In **Ireland 1997**, D argued that the 'immediacy' requirement was lacking. The CA held it was satisfied because by putting himself in contact with the victims D had caused them to be in immediate fear.

### Food for thought

Is immediate fear the same thing as fear of immediate harm? The CA in **Ireland** seemed to think so. The appeal to the HL did not focus on this issue so it remains unclear. If D phones V and says, "I have planted a bomb in your house. It is set to go off in 5 minutes." there is no problem. Both the fear and the harm are immediate. However, if D says "I have planted a bomb in your house. It is set to go off in a week." then it is a different matter. V may be in immediate fear, but is not in fear of immediate harm.

On a positive note, the courts appear to be reacting to the reality of the times. In **Ireland**, the CA said, "*We must apply the law to the conditions as they are in the 20th century*".

It is now the 21st century and the law will hopefully be applied taking into account the latest methods of communication which are much more 'immediate'.

Note that in many of these cases some actual harm was also caused. This means they can come under the statutory offence of an assault occasioning actual bodily harm under **s 47 Offences Against the Persons Act 1861** as happened in **Roberts**. They are discussed here as well as the next Chapter because for **s 47** to be satisfied an assault or battery must take place first.

### Food for thought

A good argument that words should suffice is that they can sometimes be just as threatening as a gesture. As in the 'bomb' example I used earlier. Also in a society that has a sophisticated communications network the immediacy issue is more easily satisfied.

### Mens rea

In **Savage1991**, Lord Ackner said, "... the mental element of assault is an intention to cause the victim to apprehend unlawful and immediate violence or recklessness whether such an apprehension is caused". That recklessness for all assaults is **Cunningham** (subjective) recklessness was confirmed in the joint appeals of **Savage & Parmenter1992**.

### Applying the mens rea rules to assault

For **direct intent**, the prosecution must prove that it was D's aim or purpose to cause the victim to apprehend unlawful and immediate violence.

For **indirect intent**, it must be proved that it was a virtual certainty that V would apprehend immediate and unlawful violence and that D appreciated this.

For **recklessness**, it must be proved that D recognises a risk that V would apprehend immediate and unlawful violence but goes ahead and takes that risk.

### Battery

Battery is the unlawful application of force to another. As noted earlier it often follows an assault. Assault and battery therefore go together in many, but not all, cases.

### Example

In my earlier example of the punch on the nose, there would be both. Simon saw the punch coming, so he was in fear of harm. If Fred hit Simon from behind this would only be a battery. No assault would have occurred because Simon was not in fear.

### Actus reus

The *actus reus* is the unlawful application of force to another. It can be slight because the law sees people's bodies as inviolate. Lane LCJ said in **Faulkner and Talbot 1981**, that it was "any intentional touching of another person without the consent of that person and without lawful excuse. It need not necessarily be hostile, or rude, or aggressive, as some earlier cases seemed to indicate".

In **Thomas 1985**, the court said, "if you touch a person's clothes whilst he is wearing them that is equivalent to touching him".

In 2011, the TV presenter Fiona Bruce was sprayed with some aerosol string while she was filming an episode of Antiques Roadshow. The Ds were charged with common assault, specifically battery, for applying unlawful force.

### unlawful

Part of the *actus reus* is that the force must be unlawful. In **Collins v Wilcock 1984**, a police constable who took hold of a woman's arm was acting unlawfully. If there had been a lawful arrest this would not have been the case.

Consent may make the application of force lawful. This would include things like surgery and sports. Consent may be implied. Everyday jostling and most sports contacts are not battery because there is implied consent to touching. This would not be the case if unreasonable force were used. A small nudge in the cinema queue is fine, an elbow in the ribs would not be. In a game of rugby, a tackle within the rules is fine, but a punch would not be. As both *actus reus* and *mens rea* must be proved in their entirety, there is no offence if an element is missing. Consent means the 'unlawful' element of the *actus reus* is missing. Self-defence also makes a battery lawful, but again not if unreasonable force is used.

*The two defences of consent and self-defence are commonly used in the non-fatal offences against the person. However, they apply to other crimes too, so are discussed again under Defences.*

### application of force

There is a requirement that force is applied. Battery cannot be caused by an omission; there must be an act. This was confirmed in **Fagan**. D argued that not moving off the police officer's foot was an omission not an act. The court confirmed that battery could not be committed by omission, but found him guilty on the basis that there was a continuing act. The *actus reus* was the driving onto the police officer's foot and staying there.

### Direct or indirect force?

Some early cases suggest that the force had to be direct but this is unlikely to be the case now. In **DPP v K 1990**, a schoolboy put acid in a hot air drier. Later another pupil used the drier and was badly scarred by the acid. This was held to be a battery. The case raised another issue. The boy had been using the acid in an experiment in class and was merely trying to hide it. He did not have *mens rea* when he put it in the machine, but he did have *mens rea* when he failed to do anything about it. We saw above that a battery could not be committed by omission. In **DPP v K**, omitting to rectify what he had done was held to be enough though.

In **Haystead 2000**, the harm appeared to be indirect. Here, D punched his girlfriend who was holding her baby. She dropped the baby resulting in the baby hitting his head on the floor. The defendant was convicted of battery on the baby.

### Food for thought

Although in **Haystead**, it seemed to be indirect force it may just be a widening of the meaning of direct. The court held that direct could include via another person or a weapon. Thus setting a dog on someone can be seen as direct force. This is reasonable, as it is unlikely to be argued that throwing a brick at someone was not direct and there is little real difference. In civil law, indirect actions have long been held to be a battery. In **Scott v Shepherd 1773**, D threw a squib into a market place. Someone picked it up and tossed it away to avoid being harmed. A second person then did the same. The third was not so quick and was injured when the squib exploded. The court held this to be a battery by D on the third person.

### Mens rea

As with assault, the *mens rea* is intent or recklessness. Here it is as to whether force is applied.

### Task

Look back at the application of the rules on intent and recklessness to an assault. Apply the same rules for a case of battery.

### Summary

| Assault *Actus reus* | |
|---|---|
| to cause the victim to apprehend immediate and unlawful personal violence | What is the effect on the victim? |
| Words may be enough, or even silence | Wilson/Ireland |
| *Mens rea* | intent to cause the victim to apprehend immediate and unlawful personal violence or being subjectively reckless as to this |
| Battery *Actus reus* | |
| unlawful application of force to another | Collins v Wilcock |
| Can include touching V's clothes | Thomas |
| May include indirect force | DPP v K |
| *Mens rea* | intent to apply unlawful force or being subjectively reckless as to this |

**Self-test questions**

*What is the current definition of assault?*

*Can words alone constitute an assault? Use a case to support your answer.*

*What is the mens rea for assault?*

*Does a battery have to be hostile? Use a case to support your answer.*

*What two defences may make a battery lawful?*

For answers to the tasks and self-test questions, please go to my website at www.drsr.org and click the button 'Answers to tasks'. For a range of free interactive exercises, click on 'Free Exercises' and then the OCR book.

Chapter 14 Assault occasioning actual bodily harm (ABH) under s 47 of the Offences against the Person Act 1861

*"It has been recognised for many centuries that putting a person in fear may amount to an assault. The early cases predate the invention of the telephone. We must apply the law to the conditions as they are in the 20th century".*

*Swinton L.J*

By the end of this Chapter, you should be able to:

**Explain the actus reus of ABH as an assault or battery which causes harm**

**Explain the mens rea of ABH**

**Explain how the law applies in practice by reference to cases**

**Identify possible criticisms**

This offence comes under **s 47 Offences Against the Persons Act 1861**. It is commonly known as *ABH*. **S 47** provides:

*"whosoever shall be convicted on indictment of any **assault occasioning actual bodily harm** shall be liable to imprisonment for not more than five years"*

Until 1984, it was thought that the Act merely provided for a greater penalty where an assault resulted in harm being caused. It is now clear that a new offence was created (**Courtie 1984**). In fact, in **Savage**, Lord Ackner indicated that it created two offences, an assault occasioning ABH and a battery occasioning ABH.

The offence has the *actus reus* and *mens rea* of assault or battery plus the further *actus reus* of some harm being caused. Let's look at this in more detail.

**Actus reus**

There are three parts to this.

**assault – the conduct, an assault or battery**

**occasioning – a matter of causation**

**actual bodily harm – the consequence**

**Assault**

The offence is an *assault* occasioning actual bodily harm. Assault, as we saw, covers both assault and battery. This is seen in **Savage1991**.

**Key case**

In **Savage**, a girl threw a glass of beer over another girl. As she did so, she let go of the glass which broke, resulting in a cut to the other girl's wrist. The throwing of the beer was enough for a battery. Lord Ackner said, "*It is of course common ground that Mrs Savage committed an assault upon Miss Beal when she threw the contents of her glass of beer over her.*" In referring to assault, he is describing a battery, confirming that the word assault in **s 47** includes both assault and battery.

There was no proof she intended to throw the glass and she said it was an accident. However, she did intend to throw the beer. The throwing of the beer was enough for the *actus reus* of battery. She intended to do this, so there was *mens rea* too. Once battery was proved, for her to be convicted under **s 47** the prosecution merely had to show this had 'occasioned' (caused) the harm.

So, 'assault' for **s 47** requires the *actus reus* and *mens rea* of an assault or a battery. Now to 'occasioning'.

### occasioning

Occasioning means bringing about, or causing. **S 47** is a result crime so the prosecution must show that the assault or battery caused the result (actual bodily harm). D's actions must make a significant contribution to the harm and the chain of causation must not be broken.

### Task

Look back at Chapter 1 on *actus reus* and causation. Read **Roberts** to remind you of the facts. The question was whether the battery by D caused the harm. Why did the action by the victim not break the chain of causation? What type of action might do so?

In **Savage**, the HL said that once the assault was established, the only remaining question was whether the victim's conduct was the natural consequence of that assault. According to Lord Ackner,

> "the word 'occasioning' raised solely a question of causation, an objective question which does not involve inquiring into the accused's state of mind".

Occasioning therefore relates to *actus reus* not *mens rea*. There is no need to intend any harm at all.

### Examination pointer

Causation is a common issue in a problem question where a result crime like ABH is involved. If harm has occurred, you may need to discuss all three of these offences. You will certainly have to discuss two of them because **s 47** cannot happen without one of the others. You will need to define and explain assault and/or battery. Then define harm. Finally show that the assault (or battery) caused the harm. Use a case like **Roberts** or **Savage** to explain this and apply it to the facts given. If those facts remind you of a more relevant case, use that instead.

Finally, you will need to explain *mens rea*, but only as regards the assault. We'll come back to this.

### actual bodily harm

In **Miller 1954**, this was held to be any hurt or injury calculated to 'interfere with health or comfort', which could include mental discomfort. In **Chan-Fook 1994**, the CA qualified this a little. Psychiatric injury was enough but not "mere emotions" such as fear, distress or panic. Really trivial or insignificant harm is excluded. Some type of identifiable medical condition will be needed, but it is clear that harm is not confined to physical injury.

In **DPP v Ross Smith 2006**, the QBD held that cutting someone's hair without consent amounted to assault occasioning actual bodily harm. At trial, the magistrate had accepted that as the victim had suffered no physical or psychological harm the offence was not proved. The QBD disagreed. Referring to **Chan-Fook** and **Burstow**, it was held that 'harm' included hurt or damage and 'actual' meant merely that it was not trivial harm. 'Bodily' harm applied to all parts of the body, of which hair was a part, and her hair had been cut so there was 'bodily harm'. The court also held that pain was not a necessary requirement of actual bodily harm.

**Key case**

In **Ireland 1996**, silent 'phone calls which caused psychiatric harm came under **s 47**. D's argument was that there was no assault because there was no fear of 'immediate' harm. If there was no assault, there could be no assault occasioning actual bodily harm. The argument failed as the court found sufficient 'immediacy' in a telephone call. The CA also relied on **Chan-Fook** to confirm that psychiatric harm was enough for 'bodily harm'. The opening quote came from the CA and was approved in the HL.

*Mens rea*

The *mens rea* of assault is intent or recklessness to cause assault or unlawful force (**Venna 1976**).

D need not intend, or be reckless as to, any harm, only the assault or battery. This was held to be the case by the CA in **Roberts 1971**. D argued that he did not intend to cause harm and nor was he reckless. He was found guilty because he had the *mens rea* and the *actus reus* for the battery, plus harm had been caused. This was enough for **s 47**. Despite this seemingly clear principle of law, there was conflict in several cases over the next 20 years.

**Key case**

The issue was finally put beyond doubt by the HL in the joint appeals of **Savage & Parmenter 1992**. These two cases had been decided differently in the lower courts. The principle of **Roberts** had been followed in **Savage** but not in **Parmenter**.

In **Savage & Parmenter**, the HL held **Roberts** to be the correct law. The throwing of the beer with intent to do so was enough for a battery. The question for the court was whether a further mental state had to be established in relation to the bodily harm element of the **s 47** offence. Lord Ackner said, "*Clearly the section, by its terms, expressly imposes no such requirement*".

This means that if D has *mens rea* for the assault and additionally harm occurs, it can amount to the more serious charge under **s 47**. Think about it as an equation:

Assault (AR + MR of assault or battery) + occasions (AR, causation) + harm (AR consequence) = **s 47**

**Example**

Sandra shouts threateningly at Tara. Tara is scared that Sandra will hit her. She jumps back and hits her head causing severe bruising. This will be enough for a charge under **s 47**. There is the *actus reus* of an assault (Tara is in fear of immediate violence) plus *mens rea* (Sandra intends to frighten her) and this assault occasioned (caused – jumping back and falling is foreseeable, as in **Roberts**) actual bodily harm (severe bruising).

So, the *mens rea* for **s 47** is intent or subjective recklessness as to the assault only, not the harm. The prosecution will have to show one of the following:

**Direct intent: causing fear of violence or the application of force is D's aim or purpose.**

**Indirect intent: D appreciates that it is virtually certain that the V will fear violence, or D appreciates that the application of force is virtually certain.**

**Subjective recklessness: D is aware of the risk of V being in fear, or is aware of the risk of force being applied, and goes ahead anyway.**

## Food for thought

One problem with **s 47** is that the *mens rea* does not match the *actus reus*. For the *actus reus* of **s 47** you need ABH to have occurred, the *mens rea* is only for assault or battery though (**Roberts**, **Savage**). This is confusing, and arguably unfair. Should D be guilty of causing ABH where there was only intent to scare someone? On the other hand, should D get away with harming someone when the attempt to scare them caused harm?

## Summary of s 47

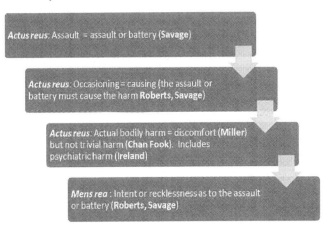

*Actus reus*: Assault = assault or battery (**Savage**)

*Actus reus*: Occasioning = causing (the assault or battery must cause the harm **Roberts, Savage**)

*Actus reus*: Actual bodily harm = discomfort (**Miller**) but not trivial harm (**Chan Fook**). Includes psychiatric harm (**Ireland**)

*Mens rea*: Intent or recklessness as to the assault or battery (**Roberts, Savage**)

## Self-test questions

*From which case did the opening quote come?*

*What are the three parts to the actus reus?*

*For which part of this is mens rea needed?*

*According to **Roberts**, what sort of action by V could break the chain of causation?*

*In which case did the HL finally confirm that the principle in **Roberts** was correct?*

For answers to the tasks and self-test questions, please go to my website at www.drsr.org and click the button 'Answers to tasks'. For a range of free interactive exercises, click on 'Free Exercises' and then the OCR book.

Chapter 15 Grievous bodily harm (GBH) and wounding under s 20 and s 18 of the Offences against the Person Act 1861

*"In the context of a criminal act therefore the words 'cause' and 'inflict' may be taken to be interchangeable"*

*Lord Hope*

By the end of this Chapter, you should be able to:

> **Explain the actus reus of wounding and GBH in s 20 and s 18**
>
> **Explain the difference in the mens rea between the two sections**
>
> **Explain how the law applies in practice by reference to cases**
>
> **Identify possible criticisms and explain the proposed reforms for all the offences in this Study Block – see Study Block summary**

**Section 20** makes it an offence to:

> *"unlawfully and maliciously wound or inflict any grievous bodily harm upon any other person, either with or without any weapon or instrument"*

**Section 18** makes it an offence to:

> *"unlawfully and maliciously by any means whatsoever wound or cause any grievous bodily harm to any person with intent to do some grievous bodily harm to any person"*

These two offences are commonly called malicious wounding (**s 20**) and wounding with intent (**s 18**). However, there are actually two separate offences under each section.

**unlawfully and maliciously wounding**

**unlawfully and maliciously inflicting / causing grievous bodily harm**

There is very little difference in the *actus reus*; each needs **either** a wound **or** serious injury. We will deal with the two sections together for *actus reus* and then look at the different *mens rea* for each.

*Actus reus for s 18 and s 20*

There are four matters to consider.

> **unlawfully**
>
> **wound**
>
> **inflict / cause**
>
> **grievous bodily harm**

We'll take these in turn. I have left out 'malicious' for the moment as this has been treated as relating to *mens rea*.

**Unlawfully**

If the act is done lawfully, no offence has occurred. Thus if D has acted in self-defence this makes it lawful, so part of the *actus reus* is missing. Consent may also make it lawful.

In **Clarence 1888**, D, knowing he had a sexually transmitted disease, had sex with his wife. She caught the disease. This amounted to grievous bodily harm. D's conviction was quashed on the basis that the sex was by consent and it made no difference that the wife did not know about the disease.

This is more limited now. In **Brown 1994**, the House of Lords decided that consent of the victim could no longer be a defence if serious harm was *intended*. In **Dica 2004**, D had consensual sex with two women knowing he was HIV positive. They both became infected with HIV and he was convicted under **s 20** with recklessly inflicting grievous bodily harm. On appeal, the CA confirmed the point in **Brown** that consent was not a defence to *intentional* harm. However, as the charge was *recklessly* inflicting grievous bodily harm, they held that the issue of consent should not have been withdrawn from the jury. A retrial was ordered.

*Consent is discussed further in defences.*

### Wound

### Key case

In **C v Eisenhower 1983**, a wound was defined as being 'any puncture of the skin'. The case involved a child firing an air gun. The pellet hit V in the eye but did not break the skin. It was held that internal bleeding caused by the rupture of an internal organ was not a wound. Therefore, something that does not break the skin, such as an abrasion, bruise or burn would not amount to a wound.

### Inflict and cause – is there a difference?

The *actus reus* of **s 20** is to unlawfully and maliciously wound or *'inflict'* grievous bodily harm. The *actus reus* of **s 18** is to unlawfully and maliciously wound or *'cause'* grievous bodily harm. In **Clarence**, the word 'inflict' was held to mean that a prior assault was required, as for **s 47**. Other cases seem to have ignored this requirement. In **Wilson 1984**, the HL held that a person could be charged under **s 20** without an assault. They relied on the Australian case of **Salisbury 1976** where it was said that 'inflict' does not imply assault is needed. However it was said that the word 'inflict' did mean that *direct* application of force was needed. It was therefore narrower than the word 'cause'.

### Food for thought

This uncertainty has been clarified. Both **Salisbury** and **Wilson** were approved by the HL in **Ireland** & **Burstow**. In the CA Lord Bingham had said it would be *"an affront to common sense"* to distinguish between the two offences in this way. The HL confirmed that liability for GBH could occur without the application of direct or indirect force, and rejected the argument that 'inflict' was narrower than 'cause'. Lord Hope made the statement in the opening quote. **Clarence** was referred to as a "troublesome authority". In **Dica**, the CA again confirmed that there was no requirement of assault for a charge under **s 20**.

A factor worth noting (as it was by the HL) is that the **1861 Act** consolidated several different Acts. Therefore, the difference in the two sections is not as significant as it would be had they been written at the same time.

One criticism is that if there is no requirement of assault in **s 20** then it is hard to justify convicting D of *assault* occasioning actual bodily harm as an alternative, as was confirmed again in **Savage and Parmenter**.

### Grievous bodily harm

This is commonly called GBH. In **Smith 1961**, grievous was interpreted by the HL to mean 'really serious'. In **Saunders 1985**, the CA held that the word 'really' was unnecessary. Thus, GBH includes *any* serious harm. In **Burstow 1996**, a campaign of harassment by D, which led to V suffering severe depressive illness, was charged under **s 20**. In the joint appeals to the HL in **Ireland & Burstow 1997**, the HL confirmed that psychiatric harm could come under **s 47, s 18** or **s 20**.

Serious harm is usually required, but note should be taken of **Bollom 2004**. A baby suffered bruising to several parts of her body and her mother's partner was charged with GBH. Although the CA substituted the conviction for one of ABH, it was made clear that bruising could amount to GBH if the victim was a young child. This means the age of the victim may be relevant in deciding the appropriate charge. Presumably, this argument could also be applied to an old or vulnerable person.

A wound may occur without GBH. Conversely, GBH may occur without a wound.

### Example

Let's reconsider two cases we saw when looking at **s 47**.

In **Savage**, the glass broke and cut the other girl. This is technically a wound as the skin has been broken. She could have been charged with wounding under **s 20**. It would not be 'serious' harm though so no charge of inflicting GBH would succeed.

In the joint appeals of **Ireland & Burstow**, the HL said psychiatric harm could amount to GBH. This type of harm could not be a wound though.

### Examination pointer

Look for clues in the scenario. If it refers to a cut then discuss wounding under either **s 18** or **s 20**. If it is only a small cut you could discuss **s 47**. If a serious internal injury is mentioned then discuss GBH. In all cases, the prosecution must establish a chain of causation. D's act must make a *significant contribution* to the wound or harm (see Chapter 1).

**S 20** refers to 'with or without any weapon or instrument'. **S 18** refers to 'by any means whatsoever'. Remember these offences came from different Acts and were not written at the same time. It doesn't matter *how* D inflicts or causes the harm. However, the use of a weapon may help in establishing intent to cause serious harm, and so point you at **s 18**.

### Mens rea

It is important to be able to identify the different *mens rea* in **s 18** and **s 20**. There are two differences: the type of *mens rea* and the type of harm that the *mens rea* relates to.

Both sections contain the word 'maliciously'. This does not mean spite or ill will, as we might view the word. As regards **s 20**, the CA interpreted it in **Cunningham 1957** as meaning intent or subjective recklessness (see Chapter 2). For **s 18**, it would appear that the word maliciously is unnecessary. In **Mowatt**, the judge said, "*In s 18 the word 'maliciously' adds nothing*".

### Mens rea for s 20

As noted above this is intent or subjective recklessness. However, D need not intend or recognise the risk of serious harm. Intending or seeing the risk (*mens rea*) of *some* harm is enough as long as the result (*actus reus*) is serious harm. This was confirmed by the CA in **Mowatt 1968** and later approved by the HL in **Savage & Parmenter 1992**.

### Key case

In **Parmenter** D threw his baby into the air and caused GBH when he caught it. His argument that he lacked *mens rea* succeeded. He had not seen the risk of *any* injury (he'd done it before several times with older children) so he was not guilty.

It is only necessary to prove that D foresaw some harm *might* occur. It is not necessary to prove that D foresaw that some harm *would* occur. This point was confirmed in **DPP v A 2000**. Here a 13-year-old boy shot his friend whilst they were playing with two air pistols. His argument that he lacked *mens rea* was rejected. The case is similar to **Eisenhower**.

In **Jones v First-Tier Tribunal 2011**, the CA held that for a charge of GBH there was no need to prove that the action was hostile. D had run in front of a lorry and the driver was injured. D argued he had no *mens rea* as he had only intended to harm himself, not anyone else. The CA held that it was foreseeable that harm could be caused to the driver of the lorry; therefore, the *mens rea* of recklessness could be proved for the **s 20** offence. In **Jones v FTT 2013**, the SC allowed D's appeal and reinstated the tribunal's decision that there was no *mens rea*. The SC felt that the CA had decided that anyone running into a busy road must have at least seen the risk of some harm and referring to **Parmenter** held this was sufficient *mens rea* for **s 20**. However, the SC said that the question of whether D himself foresaw harm was a matter for the tribunal and not an appeal court.

### Food for thought

S 18 and s 20 involve *either* GBH *or* wounding. The first has been interpreted as 'really serious' harm (**Smith**), however wounding has been interpreted as an 'open cut' (**Eisenhower**), which could be quite trivial. The prosecution failed to prove D had inflicted a wound in **Eisenhower** because there was no open cut and thus no 'wound'. This case highlights the need to get the charge right. A charge of GBH could have succeeded. Another issue is that, as for **s 47**, the *mens rea* does not match the *actus reus*. For **s 20**, you need serious harm to have occurred, but the *mens rea* is only for some harm (**Mowatt**).

### Application of mens rea for s 20

> **Direct intent: It is D's aim to cause some harm**
>
> **Indirect intent: Some harm is a virtual certainty and D appreciates this.**
>
> **Subjective recklessness: D recognises the risk of *some harm* and goes ahead anyway.**

### *Mens rea for s 18*

The *mens rea* for **s 18** is specific intent, i.e., intent only. It was confirmed in **Belfon**, where D had slashed someone with a razor, that recklessness was not enough, there must be intent to cause serious harm. **S 18** says *"with intent to do some grievous bodily harm"*. It was confirmed in **Parmenter** that for **s 18** D must intend *serious harm*. This is the vital difference and makes **s 18** much more serious, leading to a possible maximum life sentence. **S 20** carries a maximum of 5 years.

A further difference with **s 18** *mens rea* is that it includes intent to resist or prevent a lawful arrest. The problem with this is that it is added as an alternative to intent to cause GBH, so has been interpreted as meaning that if the situation is resisting or preventing an arrest, intent is only needed for that, not the harm. This is seen in **Morrison 1989** where D dived through a window resisting arrest and a police officer was badly cut. The CA upheld his conviction and held that it was enough that he intended resisting arrest. Regarding GBH, the word 'malicious' suggested that intent OR recklessness was enough, and he had been reckless.

## Application of mens rea for s 18

Direct intent: It is D's aim or purpose to cause grievous bodily harm

Indirect intent: *Grievous bodily harm* is a virtual certainty and D appreciates this

## Which charge?

It was confirmed in **Savage** that a jury could bring in **s 20** as an alternative verdict when someone is charged under **s 18** and **s 47** as an alternative to **s 20**.

If not, the conviction may be changed on appeal.

In **Bollom 2004**, the conviction for GBH under **s 20** was reduced by the CA to ABH under **s 47**.

Alternatively, D may put in a plea before or during the trial.

In **Topp 2011**, (unreported) a woman bit her boyfriend's testicles. He needed several stitches and she was charged with wounding with intent under **s 18**. Prior to the trial, she pleaded guilty to **s 20**, arguing she did not intend serious harm. The prosecution accepted the alternative plea.

Sometimes both charges are brought so the prosecution can be more confident of getting a conviction.

In **Hargreaves 2010**, D was in a taxi with her boyfriend and another man, all of whom had been drinking. She was in the back and was having an argument with her boyfriend, who was sitting in the front. He turned towards her and she kicked out at him, ramming a stiletto heel through his eye and into his brain. She was charged with both grievous bodily harm with intent under **s 18**, and an alternative charge of inflicting grievous bodily harm under **s 20**. (She said that she had kicked out at him as she believed he was going to attack her and pleaded self-defence. The defence succeeded and she was acquitted of both offences.)

## Examination pointer

All this means you may need to discuss all three statutory offences. Explain the *actus reus* of either GBH or wounding as appropriate, using cases in support. Note carefully the difference in the *mens rea* as this may help you to decide which section is most appropriate. Thus if you go for **s 18**, explain and apply the law (with cases) but then say that if the prosecution can't prove intent to cause GBH then D may be convicted of **s 20** instead. If you go for **s 20**, you can then discuss **s 47** if you feel the harm may not be serious enough.

## Food for thought

If **s 18** requires serious harm in both *actus reus* and *mens rea*, then arguably so should **s 20**. There is still a difference in the *mens rea* because **s 18** requires intent to be proved.

Another issue is sentencing. The maximum sentences for **s 20** and **s 18** are very different. The maximum for **s 20** is the same as **s 47**, i.e., 5 years. This seems strange. Life for **s 18** can be justified in that intent seriously to injure is also the *mens rea* for murder. Which charge is brought will depend on the chance factor of whether the victim dies or not. The same sentence for **s 47** and **s 20** is harder to justify. In **Parmenter**, the CA. noted there was an overlap between **s 47** and **s 20** but indicated that **s 20** was a more serious offence. The Law Commission proposes a maximum of 5 years for **s 47**, as now, but a maximum 7 years for **s 20**. This seems more realistic – but the reforms may be a long way off becoming reality.

A further recommendation by the Law Commission is that **s 18** would be 'intentional serious injury' and **s 20** would be 'reckless serious injury'. This would clear up the problem of the *mens rea*. It is arguably unfair to charge someone with GBH when the *mens rea* was only for some harm. A final criticism of the current law is that there are two different offences in each section. This makes four offences in all, which is unnecessarily complicated

## Problems and reforms

We have seen some of the problems, but as these, and the proposed reforms, apply to all these non-fatal offences they are discussed further in the Study Block summary.

## Summary

| Actus reus | |
|---|---|
| Inflict or cause | Mean the same thing (Ireland) |
| Wound | Open cut (Eisenhower) |
| Grievous bodily harm | Serious harm (Smith/Saunders) |
| **Mens rea** | |
| S 20 Intent or recklessness | To cause some harm (Mowatt) |
| S 18 Intent only | To cause serious harm (Parmenter) |

## Self-test questions

*How has 'wound' been interpreted?*

*How has 'grievous bodily harm' been interpreted?*

*Which cases can you use to support your answers to the above questions?*

*What is the difference in the mens rea between s 20 and s 18?*

*What are the maximum sentences for **s 20** and **s 18** respectively?*

For answers to the tasks and self-test questions, please go to my website at www.drsr.org and click the button 'Answers to tasks'. For a range of free interactive exercises, click on 'Free Exercises' and then the OCR book.

"... a person defending himself cannot weigh to a nicety the exact measure of his necessary defensive action"

The Privy Council in **Palmer 1971**

By the end of this Chapter, you should be able to:

*Explain the defences of self-defence and prevention of crime*

*Identify the principles on which these defences rely and how they overlap*

*Refer to appropriate case examples*

The law allows a defence where D is doing something that would otherwise be an offence, but is acting to protect certain public and/or private interests. The term 'public and private defence' covers prevention of crime (public defence), self-defence, defence of another and defence of property (private defences). If successful, these defences result in an acquittal.

### Prevention of crime

This is public defence. It is a statutory defence found in **s 3(1)** of the **Criminal Law Act 1967**, which provides that a person:

> "... may use **such force as is reasonable in the circumstances** in the prevention of crime, or in effecting or assisting in the lawful arrest of offenders or suspected offenders or of persons unlawfully at large".

The main point is that the defence is only available if the force used is *reasonable in the circumstances*.

### Example

I see a man grab a woman and try to snatch her handbag. I pull him away and cause bruising. I can use **s3** as a defence if charged with battery. I was using 'reasonable' force to prevent a crime.

### Self-defence

This is private defence. It is a common law defence developed by the courts. However many of the matters which have arisen are now covered by **s 76** of the **Criminal Justice and Immigration Act 2008**. Although usually referred to as self-defence, it covers force used in defence of another. In my example, I am also defending the woman, so could use self-defence as well as prevention of crime.

As seen in my example, the defences overlap, so the principles developed by the courts are essentially the same. In **Hitchins 2011**, the CA held that there was no difference between self-defence under the common law and **s 3**. **S 76** applies to both and is "intended to clarify the operation of the existing defences" in particular, as to whether the degree of force used was reasonable in the circumstances.

There are two main questions to consider:

**Did D honestly believe the action was justified? (What D thought; a subjective question)**

**Was the degree of force reasonable in the circumstances? (What a reasonable person would do; an objective question)**

The burden is on the prosecution to satisfy the jury that D was *not* acting in self-defence. They will have to convince the jury that in the circumstances, the action was *not* justified, or that *unreasonable* force was used.

### Examination pointer

As with consent, self-defence is usually seen with the non-fatal offences against the person. For example, battery is the *unlawful* application of force. If D acted in self-defence and did not use excessive force, then the 'unlawful' part of the *actus reus* is missing. However, self-defence can apply to murder. The main issue would be whether killing someone was using excessive force. This will be a question for the jury based on the circumstances, or the circumstances as D believed them to be. If the person was armed and dangerous, that circumstance may justify extreme force. Note that if the defence succeeds D is acquitted.

### Did D honestly believe the action was justified?

This subjective question is whether the particular D believed that the action which made up the offence was justified.

**S 76(7)** confirms the opening quote from **Palmer 1971**, stating that D *"may not be able to weigh to a nicety the exact measure of any necessary action"* and that if D only did what was *"honestly and instinctively"* thought to be necessary this would be strong evidence that only reasonable action was taken.

This means excessive force may be acceptable if D 'honestly and instinctively' thought it necessary in the circumstances. However, **s 76(6)** provides that the degree of force is not to be regarded as reasonable if it was disproportionate in the circumstances as D believed them to be. The force should not be disproportionate, but this is considered in the circumstances as D believes them to be; it is a subjective test. If D mistakenly believes someone is being attacked or threatened, then self-defence may be relied on, even if there was no actual threat. This was seen in **Williams (Gladstone) 1987**. A man saw a woman being robbed by a youth and struggled with him. D came on the scene and believed the youth to be under attack. He punched the man and was charged with actual bodily harm. His defence succeeded. The court held that he was to be judged on the facts *as he saw them*.

### Was the degree of force reasonable in the circumstances?

This second question is objective and a matter for the jury to decide based on the circumstances of the case, and the nature of the threat. Early cases indicated that in order for the defence to succeed, D should show there was no possibility of retreat. However, in **McInnes 1971**, the CA said that a person is not obliged to retreat from a threat in order to rely on the defence, but that this may be evidence for the jury when considering whether force was necessary, and if so whether it was reasonable. As we saw above, **s 76(6)** provides that the degree of force is not to be regarded as reasonable if it was disproportionate. So D does not have to retreat, but if leaving the scene is an easy option then it may mean any force used isn't seen as reasonable.

There must however, be a perceived threat. In **Malnik v DPP 1989**, D had armed himself with a martial arts weapon and gone to visit a man whom he believed had stolen some cars. He was arrested when approaching the house. He argued that the man was known to be violent, so having the weapon to protect himself was justified. The court held that the defence was not available because there had been no imminent threat; he had put himself in danger by going to the house. Again, in **Burns 2010**, there was an easy alternative. A prostitute agreed to go with D in his car but later changed her mind and wanted to return to where he had picked her up. He tried to remove her forcibly from the car and she suffered cuts and bruises. The court held that he had used unreasonable force, which was therefore unlawful and a battery. It resulted in harm, so was ABH. The CA upheld his conviction and held the use of force was unjustified; he could have regained possession of the car simply by driving her back.

*Example*

I disturb a burglar in my house and, feeling rather brave, hit him over the head with a china vase. While he lies unconscious at my feet, I kick him in the ribs a few times to punish him for daring to enter my house. The first action may be self-defence. The second is not. There is no threat and I am merely exacting revenge.

In **Martin 2001**, the court confirmed that the test is objective and up to the jury to decide.

*Key case*

In **Martin 2001**, the jury rejected a plea of self-defence by a farmer who shot and killed a 16-year old burglar and seriously injured another. According to evidence, they were retreating and posing no threat, and the jury felt that using a pump-action shotgun was excessive force in the circumstances. In the CA, Woolf LCJ confirmed that the farmer was entitled to use reasonable force to protect himself and his home, but that the jury were *"surely correct in coming to their judgment that Mr Martin was not acting reasonably"*

Referring to the subjective and objective questions, he went on to say,

*"As to the first issue, what Mr Martin believed, the jury heard his evidence and they could only reject that evidence, if they were satisfied it was untrue. As to the second issue, as to what is a reasonable amount of force, obviously opinions can differ ... it was for the jury, as the representative of the public, to decide the amount of force which it would be reasonable and the amount of force which it would be unreasonable to use in the circumstances"*

**S 76** states that the degree of force used by D was not 'reasonable in the circumstances' if it was disproportionate.

*Mistaken use of force*

Mistake is commonly seen along with self-defence in relation to the non-fatal offences against the person. It is where D uses self-defence mistakenly believing it is necessary in the circumstances.

*Example*

A man approaches me to ask directions. I mistakenly believe I am about to be attacked and hit him over the head with my umbrella. If I am charged with battery or actual bodily harm, the jury must decide if hitting him with an umbrella was justified in the circumstances that I believed, i.e., that I was being attacked.

Other than the above provision on disproportionate force, **s 76** states that what is reasonable is decided by reference "to the circumstances *as D believed them to be*", so there is a subjective element. If D is mistaken the jury must consider the circumstances that D believed, not the actual circumstances.

In **Williams (Gladstone) 1987**, above, D successfully argued self-defence based on his mistaken belief that his actions were justified because he believed he was defending the youth. In

**Martin 2001**, the defence failed because using a weapon was seen as unreasonable force, however Woolf LCJ confirmed that

*"In judging whether the defendant had only used reasonable force, the jury has to take into account all the circumstances, including the situation as the defendant honestly believes it to be at the time, when he was defending himself. It does not matter if the defendant was mistaken in his belief as long as his belief was genuine".*

In **Hargreaves 2010** (see GBH), D said that she had kicked out at her boyfriend as she believed he was going to attack her. This amounted to self-defence, because a mistaken belief can be relied on as long as genuinely held; she was not guilty of grievous bodily harm.

These cases, along with **s 76**, show that D may use mistake to justify the use of force even if it is not reasonable. The defence can succeed as long as D genuinely believes that force is justified in the circumstances.

### Examination pointer

There are two ways to approach self-defence. Reasonable force can, for example, make a battery lawful, eliminating part of the *actus reus,* so there is no offence. Alternatively, reasonable force means self-defence can be used as a defence to a battery charge. Either approach is acceptable.

If a mistake is used to justify self-defence, you will need to discuss **Williams** as confirmed by **Martin** and by **s 76**, i.e., that the mistake must be genuine but does not have to be reasonable.

### Self-defence and intoxication

Although a mistake need not be reasonable as long as it is genuine, an intoxicated mistake will not provide a defence. This is the case even though the mistake may have been honestly made.

In **O'Grady 1987**, D hit his friend over the head in the mistaken belief that the friend was trying to kill him. Both of them were drunk at the time. He was convicted of manslaughter and appealed. The CA rejected his appeal and said he could not rely on a drunken mistake to justify his actions. It was not fully clear whether this would apply to specific intent crimes such as murder, but in **Hatton 2005**, the CA said the rule applied whether the charge was murder or manslaughter. **S 76 (5)** confirms that D cannot rely on a mistaken belief caused by voluntary intoxication. Therefore, D can use the defence based on an unreasonable mistake, but not a drunken one.

### Food for thought

The courts are reluctant to allow intoxicated mistake to support the defence for public policy reasons. In **O'Grady**, the CA said, *"Reason recoils from the conclusion that in such circumstances a defendant is entitled to leave the court without a stain on his character".*

It is arguable that policy issues are a matter for an elected government and Parliament, not the courts. A related problem is that, if successful, the defence leads to an acquittal, "without a stain on his character". On the plus side, it can be said that **s 76** has clarified some of the uncertainties.

### Task

*Discuss what defence(s) Amy should use in the following situations, using a case to support this and explaining whether it is likely to be successful and, if so, the effect it will have.*

1. Amy is walking down the street one dark and rainy night when a young man steps out of a doorway right in front of her. Being a paranoid sort of person, she thinks she is being attacked and strikes out in alarm, cutting his cheek. In fact, he was just coming from his own house.

2. Walking home from the pub in a drunken haze Amy sees what she thinks is a man with a weapon coming towards her. She picks up a brick and hits him over the head, causing severe concussion and a nasty cut. It turns out he is from the local radio and is interviewing people on the streets for their views on violence at closing time.

3. Amy is walking down the street when she sees someone whom she believes is assaulting a young man. She intervenes and attacks him but he promptly arrests her. It turns out he is a policeman in plain clothes.

### Examination pointer

You may need to explain and apply the rules on self-defence and mistake when assessing whether the force was justified. Explain that force must be reasonable but if it is then self-defence can, for example, make a battery lawful, therefore taking away part of the *actus reus*. If the facts indicate that D is acting under a mistake discuss the additional rules, i.e., that the mistake must be genuine but does not have to be reasonable. Finally if D is intoxicated use O'Grady to explain why the defence will fail

### *Summary of key issues*

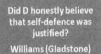
Did D honestly believe that self-defence was justified?

Williams (Gladstone)

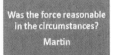
Was the force reasonable in the circumstances?

Martin

D is judged on the facts as they are believed to be, even if that belief is mistaken

Williams (Gladstone)/s 76

D cannot rely on a drunken mistake

O' Grady/Hatton/s 76

### *Self-test questions*

> What are the two main questions for the jury?
>
> Why was self-defence rejected by the jury in **Martin**?
>
> Can you rely on a mistaken belief to justify using force?
>
> What was decided in **Hatton** and confirmed by s 76?
>
> What is the result of a successful plea of self-defence?

For answers to the tasks and self-test questions, please go to my website at www.drsr.org and click the button 'Answers to tasks'. For a range of free interactive exercises, click on 'Free Exercises' and then the OCR book.

*"We think that it can be taken as a starting point that it is an essential element of an assault that the act is done contrary to the will and without the consent of the victim"*

*Lord Lane CJ*

By the end of this Chapter, you should be able to:

### Explain the defence of consent

### Discuss some of the issues relating to this defence

### Apply it to the different non-fatal offences

### Refer to appropriate case examples

This defence is mainly relevant to non-fatal offences against the person. There are limits on how far an individual is free to consent to being harmed. Consent is never a defence to some offences, e.g., murder. Thus, we saw in Chapter 1 that Diane Pretty was unable to get immunity from prosecution for her husband if he helped her to die. For the non-fatal offences, the courts will look at the nature and degree of harm consented to, as well as whether harm was intended. Consent can also be either express or implied.

## Example

A woman is dying and in pain. She asks her doctor to give her an injection to help her die. Even though she has clearly consented, her consent is not available as a defence to a murder charge if the doctor agrees to give her the injection.

A player is injured by an opponent's tackle during a game of rugby. The defence can be used to a charge of battery or actual bodily harm, and probably to grievous bodily harm. This consent is implied in such games.

In **Leach 1969**, a man asked to be crucified on Hampstead Heath. He survived and the people who had nailed him to the cross were charged under **s18 Offences against the Person Act**. Their defence that he consented failed. The degree of harm and the fact that the act carried no social benefit influenced this decision.

Consent can provide a defence to common assault. In **A-G's Reference (No 6 of 1980) 1981**, Lord Lane CJ made the comment in the opening quote, that lack of consent was an essential element of an assault. The case is important as the CA gave guidelines on the types of activities where there would be implied consent to an assault.

The following case gives a guide to which activities a person may consent to, expressly or by implication.

## Key case

In **A-G's Reference (No 6 of 1980) 1981**, a fight between two youths resulted in one of them suffering a bloody nose. The other was charged with actual bodily harm. The CA gave a list circumstances which would be lawful even if harm occurred. These were "properly conducted games and sports, lawful chastisement or correction, reasonable surgical interference, dangerous exhibitions, etc." In these circumstances, consent is implied.

It had been argued by the Attorney General that the consent defence should fail because the fight had occurred in public. The CA held that it made no difference whether it occurred in public or not. The issue was that they intended harm.

One influence on the issue of whether consent is an available defence is public policy. The CA said it was not in the public interest that people should cause each other actual bodily harm for no good reason. As in **Leach**, there was no social benefit to the activity.

Another influence on the courts appears to be a moral one. A leading case on consent to physical harm is **Brown 1994**.

### Key case

In **Brown**, consenting homosexuals engaged in sado-masochistic behaviour in a private home. Injuries were caused and they were charged under **s 47** and **s 20 Offences Against the Person Act**. They were convicted even though they all consented. The case went to the HL. The decision to uphold their convictions was only by a 3-2 majority. One reason appears to be the extent of the harm caused. Another was that the harm was intentional. The case raised moral issues too. Lord Templeman said, "... pleasure derived from the infliction of pain is an evil thing". The two dissenting judges may have agreed but Lord Mustill thought that this was no reason to bring such behaviour within the criminal law. Lord Slynn thought the issue was whether the act was done in public or not. As it was in private, the law should not interfere.

### Food for thought

In **Brown**, Lord Slynn thought the issue was whether the act was done in public or not. This had already been rejected in **A.G.'s Reference (No 6 of 1980)**. There the CA held that the issue was whether D intended harm. Which argument do you prefer? Should private actions be within the law regardless of whether harm was intended?

Let's look at some of the different types of activity mentioned in **A.G.'s Reference (No 6 of 1980)**.

### *Properly conducted games and sports*

Sport is seen as having a social benefit. In **Coney 1882**, it was held that a blow in sports such as boxing with gloves or wrestling would not amount to an assault, but a fistfight would. Such fighting is not socially acceptable so the consent defence is likely to fail, as in **A-G's Reference (No 6 of 1980)**. Where D's conduct is not within the rules of the game, the position was unclear. In **Billingshurst 1978**, consent was accepted even though the injury suffered was serious and D was acting outside the rules of rugby, but in several later cases, it failed. The position was clarified in **Barnes 2004**.

### Key case

In **Barnes 2004**, D had been found guilty of grievous bodily harm after a late tackle in a football match. The conviction was quashed and the CA held that criminal cases should be reserved for times when the conduct was *"sufficiently grave to be categorised as criminal"*. People taking part in sport consented to the risk of injury. It now seems that the defence can be used in all but extreme sporting cases.

Case law has long viewed 'manly sports' and 'manly diversions' as lawful activities. The question is how far this includes activities that are arguably not 'sport'.

In **Jones 1988**, a group of boys tossed two other boys 10 feet into the air resulting in a ruptured spleen and a broken arm. This was construed as 'rough horseplay' and the defence allowed. In **Aitken 1992**, drunken RAF officers doused a fellow officer with white spirit and set fire to him. They were found not guilty of grievous bodily harm because it was assumed that the victim consented to "rough and undisciplined horseplay".

**Food for thought**

These situations could be construed as violent bullying but the defence of consent was allowed. Do you think this goes too far? How far do you think the victims truly consented?

Lack of intent to cause injury seems to have influenced the decision in **Jones**. As the *mens rea* for **s20** includes recklessness this is also something that you could discuss as less than satisfactory. The Ds must surely have recognised the risk that throwing someone 10 feet in the air could cause 'some harm'.

It can be argued that it is inconsistent to allow consent in cases like **Aitken** and not in cases like **Brown**. However, it appears from these cases that consent is a defence to reckless harm, but not to intentional harm. Do you think Parliament should legislate on the issue of consent?

### Lawful chastisement

Corporal punishment in schools has been illegal since 1986 but this did not extend to parents smacking their own children. In **A v UK 1998,** a stepfather successfully used the defence of lawful chastisement to a charge of actual bodily harm. He had beaten the child with a stick over a period of time. However, the case went to the **European Court of Human Rights** which held that this violated **Article 3** of the **Convention** prohibiting torture and inhuman and degrading treatment.

In **Williams 2005**, it was claimed that the ban on corporal punishment in schools did not apply if parents had expressly given permission to the school to chastise their children. The HL rejected this argument and held that under the **Education Act 1996** corporal punishment was illegal whether the parents had consented or not.

Under the **Children Act 2004 s 58**, smacking is illegal even by a parent, if it causes bruising or cuts. What is now referred to as 'reasonable punishment' is, however, still a defence to common assault and this has been criticised in a Council of Europe report released in 2005. Following a consultation in late 2007, the government decided not to amend the law.

### Reasonable surgical interference

Most surgical treatment would amount to a battery if carried out without the patient's consent. It is generally accepted that consent must be real. Thus, consent by a child or consent induced by fraud may not be valid. In **Burrell and Harmer 1967**, a 12- and 13-year-old were not deemed to have consented to actual bodily harm caused by tattooing.

In **Richardson 1999**, a dentist who had been suspended carried out treatment on several people, one of whom complained to the police. The prosecution argued that consent to the treatment was not real because the patients did not know the full facts. The CA rejected this argument and held that they had consented to the treatment, and this was enough.

In **Tabassum 2000**, D had persuaded several women to allow him to measure their breasts. He told them that it was for producing a database for doctors. The women consented to him doing this and were fully aware of the nature of the action he planned to take. However, they said that they only consented because they thought that D was a doctor with medical training. The CA agreed with the trial judge that consent to a medical examination was not the same as consent to indecent behaviour. The act consented to was not the act done and the defence failed.

In **Wilson 1996**, a husband branded his initials on his wife's buttocks. It was done at her request but she needed medical attention and he was charged with ABH. The CA held that the defence of consent was available.

## Task

Compare the different approaches in **Brown** and **Wilson**. Consider whether consenting individuals should be permitted to make their own decisions about their private behaviour without fear of prosecution? Alternatively, should the law be more protective of the victim? Write a paragraph on your thoughts and file it for essay practice.

### Consent and sex

In **Clarence 1888**, a man who infected his wife with a sexual disease was charged under **s20**. She did not know he had the disease. The court held that she had consented to sexual intercourse so the case was dismissed.

## Food for thought

Is consent to sex the same as consent to a disease? Hardly. A different view can be seen in more recent cases. The law now requires that consent is not just to the act, but to the 'quality' of the act.

In **Dica 2004**, D had consensual sex with two women knowing that he was HIV positive, and they both became infected with HIV. He was convicted of GBH under **s 20** and appealed. The CA referred to both **Clarence** and **Brown**. They said that on the point that consent to sexual intercourse was the same as consent to the risk of a consequential disease; **Clarence** was no longer good law. The question was whether there was consent to the risk of harm, not just consent to sex. They added that since **Brown**, D could no longer use consent to a charge of grievous bodily harm if such harm was intentional. However, in **Dica** the prosecution had not alleged intent so the defence should have been left to the jury. A retrial was ordered and in 2005, he was convicted of GBH.

## Food for thought

Is this decision a sign of a change of heart by the judiciary? Some academics interpreted **Brown** as rejecting the defence of consent based on the amount of harm. Others argued it was based on whether the harm was intended. The judgement itself is complicated and the reasoning somewhat obscure. In **Dica**, the CA appeared to agree that **Brown** was based on intention, saying that the defence would fail where grievous harm was intentional but could succeed if it was inflicted recklessly. However, they added that the victim must consent to the risk of harm, not just the activity itself. This means a case like **Clarence** could be decided differently today.

## Task

Do you think that the Vs truly consented in **Richardson**, **Jones** and **Aitken**? There seemed to be no real consent to any kind of harm. Is the idea that the victim must be consenting to the harm, not just the act itself, a better interpretation of consent? Look back at these cases and compare to **Dica**. Write a paragraph with your views of the decisions.

## Examination pointer

Much of the above can be used in an essay on the problems of the non-fatal offences generally. It also relates to law and morals.

**Task**

**Note which case matches the comment and keep for revision.**

*Leach 1969*

*A.G.'s Reference (No 6 of 1980) 1981*

*Brown 1994*

*Billingshurst 1978*

*Richardson 1999*

*Wilson 1996*

**Principles**

*the injury suffered during a game of rugby was serious*

*a husband branded his initials on his wife's buttocks*

*a dentist who had been suspended carried out treatment on several people*

*a man asked to be crucified on Hampstead Heath*

*the CA gave a list circumstances which would be lawful even if harm occurred*

*consenting homosexuals engaged in sado-masochistic behaviour*

**Reforms**

Reforms have not been very forthcoming by the courts, other than the decision in Dica to reject the defence in cases of intentional sexual diseases, which was a much needed reform because the law had come from the outdated case of Clarence. There is understandably a reluctance to be seen to interfere too much in people's personal freedoms, and there could be conflict with parts of the European Convention on Human Rights. However, if judges do not wish to be too creative then Parliament should act. It is anyway more appropriate for an elected Parliament to decide such policy issues.

The Law Commission's 2000 report on consent, although confined to sexual offences, aimed at producing a definition that would also be consistent with other offences. This report recommends that consent should be defined as "a subsisting, free and genuine agreement to the act in question" which could be express or implied, and 'evidenced by words or conduct, whether present or past'. It seems that it would be better for juries to have a clearer definition such as this as the law is unlikely to produce justice unless it is unambiguous and applicable to everyone in the same way. It would be beneficial if this definition were to be extended to consent as a defence for all offences, in particular the non-fatal offences. An agreement to the risk of serious harm would mean the defence could be used in a case such as Brown, the 'act in question' being GBH. However the defence would fail in Richardson as the consent was not a "free and genuine agreement to the act in question".

If the proposed reforms were taken up there would be an improvement in how the defence of consent is applied.

**Summary**

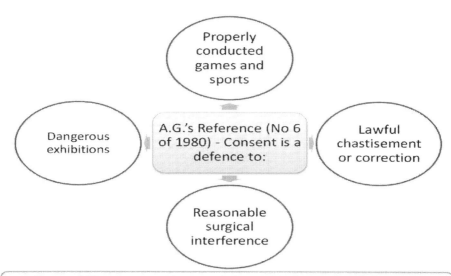

Brown / Dica – consent is not a defence to grievous bodily harm or wounding if done with intent

## The effect of consent

| | |
|---|---|
| Murder | Cannot use the defence of consent |
| Assault | Can make an assault lawful e.g. in sports |
| Battery | Can make a battery lawful e.g. in sports |
| Assault occasioning actual bodily harm **s47 Offences against the Person Act** | As above, it may make the assault lawful but not if harm was intended: **A.G.'s Reference (No 6 of 1980)** |
| Wounding or grievous bodily harm under **s20 Offences against the Person Act** | Can be a defence if D acted recklessly but not if harm was intended: **Brown/Dica** |
| Wounding or grievous bodily harm with intent under **s18 Offences against the Person Act** | Cannot use the defence of consent: **Brown/Dica** |

**Self-test questions**

*What point is made in **Brown** regarding consent to intentional grievous bodily harm?*

*State two of the activities where consent is implied as stated in **A.G.'s Reference***

*Name one of the cases involving 'rough horseplay' where the defence was allowed*

*Why was the conviction quashed in **Barnes 2004**?*

*From which case did the opening quote come?*

**Note in particular the *mens rea* for each offence**

**Assault**

*Actus reus*: to cause the victim to apprehend *immediate* and unlawful personal violence – **Ireland**

*Mens rea*: intent or subjective recklessness to cause fear of harm – **Savage**

**Battery**

*Actus reus*: unlawful application of force to another – **Collins v Wilcock**

*Mens rea*: intent or subjective recklessness to apply force – **Venna**

**Assault occasioning actual bodily harm under s47 OAPA 1861**

*Actus reus*: An assault (or battery) which causes harm – **Chan Fook**

*Mens rea*: intent or subjective recklessness for the assault or battery only – **Savage**

**Malicious Wounding under s 20 OAPA 1861**

*Actus reus*: unlawful and malicious wounding or inflicting grievous bodily harm – **C v Eisenhower / Saunders**

*Mens rea*: intent or subjective recklessness to inflict *some* harm – **Mowatt**

**Wounding with intent under s 18 OAPA 1861**

*Actus reus*: unlawful and malicious wounding or causing grievous bodily harm **C v Eisenhower / Saunders**

*Mens rea* – intent (only) to cause grievous bodily harm – **Parmenter**

**Task**

Match the principle to the case

*Cases*

   *Wilson 1955*

   *Ireland 1996*

   *C v Eisenhower 1984*

   *Miller 1954*

   *Haystead 2000*

   *Smith 1961*

   *Chan-Fook 1994*

*Principles*

   *Silence may be enough for an assault*

   *Grievous means really serious harm*

   *Words may be enough for an assault*

   *Actual bodily harm is anything that causes personal discomfort*

*Mere emotions such as fear, distress or panic are not enough for actual bodily harm*

*Wound means an open cut*

*A battery can be via another person*

**Key criticisms**

We have seen many problems whilst looking at the individual offences, and it is in clear the **Offences Against the Person Act 1861** is in need of reform. There are also more general issues:

**Language:** the **Act** is very complicated and was written in 1861, so much of the language is obscure. Lawyers and juries have struggled to understand the complexities of the different offences. The courts also have difficulty interpreting words such as 'occasioning', 'actual bodily harm', 'grievous' and 'maliciously' as they are not used in the same sense today. This can result in conflicting case law and injustice. The word 'maliciously' has been interpreted as meaning recklessly (**Parmenter**). However it appears in **s 18** as well as **s 20** and the *mens rea* for **s 18** is intent only. In **Parmenter**, the judge had difficulty explaining 'maliciously' to the jury. He said that it meant that it was enough that D *should have foreseen* that some harm might occur. This sounds very like objective rather than subjective recklessness. In fact, on appeal, this was said to be a misdirection. It highlights the fact that these words need to be clearly explained.

**Common law:** assault and battery are outside the **Act**. Clarity would require all the offences to be together in one place. However, an alternative argument is that the common law can keep them up to date. This happened in **Ireland,** where it was recognised that an assault could be via a telephone.

Proposals for reform have been produced and Bills put before Parliament over a long period of time, but to date Parliament has not found time to debate the issues – see below under proposed reforms

**Task**

Look back at the **Food for thought** boxes in this study block. Write some notes on these with case examples. Add your own thoughts. Then read through the reforms. Ask yourself whether the proposed reforms would solve any of the problems you have identified.

Keep these notes for revision and as a guide to the exam question below.

So, there are plenty of problems. What is being done about them?

**Proposed reforms**

The Law Commission has been considering codification of the criminal law for some time. This was a huge task and so it was decided it would be better to work on a series of self-contained bills to deal with different parts of the criminal law. In 1993 the Commission produced a report (**No 218**) and draft Bill on the non-fatal offences against the person. This never received parliamentary time but in 1998 the government produced its own Bill incorporating most of the recommended changes, but again little happened. Now the Commission is about to readdress the issue and issued a consultation paper in 2014. They note on their site (have a look at 'On-going projects' in criminal law under 'Our Work') that the Act is outdated and uses archaic language. They particularly refer to the lack of a clear hierarchy, noting s20 is seen as more serious than s47 but has the same maximum sentence; and to the problem caused by the different words of 'cause' and 'inflict' in s18 and 20.  The intention is to restructure the law and modernise and simplify the language.

No Bill has yet received parliamentary time, something you can add to your critique.  The table below shows the proposals from the 1998 Bill, The offences are redefined and in all of them the *mens rea* matches the *actus reus*.

| Name of proposed offence | Explanation of proposed offence | Current offence |
| --- | --- | --- |
| Intentional serious injury | Clause 1: intentionally causing serious injury | S 18 |
| Reckless serious injury | Clause 2: recklessly causing serious injury | S 20 |
| Intentional or reckless injury | Clause 3: intentionally or recklessly causing injury | S 47 |
| Assault | Clause 4: intentionally or recklessly applying force to or causing an impact on the body of another; or intentionally or recklessly causing another to believe force is imminent | Common assault (assault and battery) |

In each case the word 'cause' is used.  The Bill also defines injury to include both physical and psychiatric harm.  It excludes any harm caused by disease except for Clause 1.  This is in line with **Dica.**

The Law Commission project commencing in 2015 following their consultation is likely to result in something very similar, although we cannot be sure at this stage.  One difference is that in their 2014 paper they suggest an offence of causing minor injuries and thus again separating assault and battery.

The Commission notes that the Act is widely recognised as being outdated and that it uses archaic language.  It also says that the structure of the Act is unsatisfactory; because there is no clear hierarchy of offences and the differences between sections 18, 20 and 47 are not clearly spelt out.

The following is a quote from their site in 2012.

> *"Section 20 (maliciously wounding or inflicting grievous bodily harm) is seen as more serious than section 47 (assault occasioning actual bodily harm) but the maximum penalty (five years) is the same.  Furthermore the actus reus for sections 18 (intentionally wounding or causing grievous bodily harm) and 20 appear to be the same apart from the distinction between "causing" and "inflicting", which is notoriously difficult to draw.*

*This project will therefore aim to restructure the law on offences against the person, probably by creating a structured hierarchy of offences, as well as modernising and simplifying the language by which these offences are defined".*

**Summary of the related defences**

| Defence | Main points | Which crimes | Effect |
|---|---|---|---|
| Consent | must be consent to the harm **Dica** | Not intentional GBH / wounding or murder | Acquittal |
| Self-defence | force must be reasonable **Martin** | All | Acquittal |
| Mistake | must be genuine but need not be reasonable **Williams (Gladstone)** | All | Acquittal |

As for defences, there are also a few criticisms which can be considered

**It can be argued that it is inconsistent to allow consent in cases like Aitken and not in cases like Brown**

**The judgement in Brown is complicated and the reasoning somewhat obscure**

**The 'patients' did not truly consent in Richardson but the defence was allowed**

**Sample examination question**

Discuss the different non-fatal offences against the person and how far reform of these offences is necessary. 50 marks

**Special study unit – possible connections**

Where you are asked to discuss developments in the law there is a lot of material within this study block to provide a base. The *Food for thought* sections can help you find ideas for an evaluation of developments and particular cases, whether in relation to the various assaults or the defences. The **Law Commission's** role in law-making can be discussed in relation to the reform of the law on the non-fatal offences generally. It has been a long time since the **Commission** suggested reforms. Parliament has not yet enacted them, this raises a question as to how effective the **Commission**'s role is.

The use of the rules of **precedent** can be discussed. **Clarence** was *followed* until recently when it was said to be bad law by the CA. It was not *overruled* because the CA cannot use the **1966 Practice Statement** to overrule a decision of the HL. Earlier cases were *distinguished* and the law developed in **Ireland** (developing the law on assault to meet changes in technology), and in **Brown** (developing the law on consent to meet social needs). In relation to the interpretation of statute law, the approach of the courts to the **Offences against the Person Act 1861** has been mixed. In **Eisenhower**, the word wound was taken very *literally* and the outcome does not necessarily conform to what Parliament intended. A more *purposive* approach can be seen in **Ireland** where actual bodily harm in **s 47** was interpreted to include psychiatric harm. Arguably, Parliament would have intended that harm could include such harm, had it had the medical knowledge that is now available on psychiatric injury.

In **Ross Smith 2006**, the QBD held that cutting someone's hair without consent amounted to an offence under the **Offences against the Person Act 1861** of assault occasioning actual bodily harm even though the victim had suffered no physical or psychological harm. Referring to **Chan-Fook** and **Burstow**, the QBD interpreted 'harm' to include hurt or damage and 'actual' to mean merely that it was not trivial harm. Also 'bodily' harm applied to all parts of the body, of which hair was a part, and pain was not a necessary requirement of actual bodily harm.

As well as discussing the developments in general and the key criticisms above, the use of the rules of **precedent** can be referred to. Earlier cases were *distinguished* and the law developed in **Dica**. **Clarence** was regarded as bad law. Consent to sex may no longer be true consent.

In relation to the interpretation of statute law, the HL refused to allow consent to intentional grievous bodily harm in **Brown**. There were different reasons behind the decisions and the *ratio decidendi* was not fully clear. This case also shows the difficulty of interpreting an Act that is very old, (the **Offences against the Person Act 1861**).

These are just a few ideas to show how the substantive law studied in this block relates to the more general issue of development of the law, and to highlight some cases which could be discussed critically.

**Chapter 18**: Theft – *actus reus*

**Chapter 19**: Theft – *mens rea*

**Chapter 20**: Robbery

**Chapter 21**: Burglary

This Study Block covers the main three property offences. Theft is a big area so I have split it into two parts. The first two Chapters will cover *actus reus* and *mens rea* respectively. Once you have done theft however, you will find that you have almost all you need for robbery and much of what you need for burglary, which are covered in the following two Chapters.

The terms 'theft', 'robbery' and 'burglary' are used rather indiscriminately in newspaper reports which can be confusing. Simply put, theft covers what most people would think of as stealing, like taking property belonging to someone else without their consent. The offences of robbery and burglary are theft with an added ingredient. Robbery is theft using force, or a threat of force. Burglary is theft from a building.

*Example*

> **I steal a bicycle from outside the railway station. This is theft.**
>
> **I tell the owner I will beat him up if he doesn't give me the bike. This is robbery.**
>
> **I take the bike from someone's back yard. This is burglary.**

We will look at the different ways a theft may be committed. Although my example is valid, theft is wider than just taking something and can include e.g., merely using something belonging to someone else. Robbery is fairly straightforward but you need to understand what amounts to 'force' so we will discuss this in more detail in the third chapter.

The offence of burglary also includes more than theft from a building. Damaging property can amount to burglary, e.g., so we will also look at the wider issues of this offence in the final chapter of this Study Block.

"... in a prosecution for theft it is unnecessary to prove that the taking is without the owner's consent ..."

*Lord Steyn*

By the end of this Chapter, you should be able to:

**Explain the actus reus of theft**

**Explain how the law applies in practice by reference to cases**

**Identify possible criticisms**

As you can see from the quote, theft is wider than just taking something without permission. It is defined in the **Theft Act 1968 s 1(1)** which says a person is guilty of theft:

*'if he dishonestly appropriates property belonging to another with the intention of permanently depriving the other of it'*

The offence of theft comes under **s 1**. The following sections then explain each part of the *actus reus* and the *mens rea* in the definition. You will need to learn these too.

*Task*

There are 3 parts to the *actus reus* and 2 to the *mens rea*. Read the definition again and try to identify each of them before going on.

*Examination pointer*

Giving sections of **Acts** will enhance your answer. One way to remember them is to note that they are in order. **S 1** is the offence itself and then 'dishonestly' **s 2**, 'appropriates' **s 3**, 'property' **s 4**, 'belonging to another' **s 5**, 'with the intention of permanently depriving the other of it' **s 6**. Subsection 1 of each of these explains each term. Further subsections may then add to this.

So you could say "D may be charged with theft under **s 1(1)** of the **Theft Act 1968**. The *actus reus* is the appropriation of property belonging to another. It could be argued here that the items are not property. This is further defined under **s 4(1)** which states ..."

We'll look at each part of the *actus reus* and then the *mens rea*. Did you spot which was which?

**The actus reus is**

    **appropriates s 3 (conduct)**

    **property s 4 (circumstance)**

    **belonging to another s 5 (circumstance)**

**The mens rea is a bit more difficult, it involves**

    **dishonesty s 2 and**

    **the intention of permanently depriving the other of it s 6**

In this Chapter, we will look at each part of the *actus reus*.

## Appropriation s 3(1)

This term covers many more types of conduct than 'take'. It is defined in **s 3** as

*'any assumption by a person of the rights of an owner'*.

Assumption here means take over e.g., you 'assume' someone's identity if you pretend to be them. For theft, you assume someone's right in property.

The best way to approach this is to consider what rights an owner has in the first place. If you own something, you have a right to do what you like with it. So you can use it, alter it, damage it, destroy it, lend it, sell it, give it away etc. If someone else does any of these things with it then they may well have *appropriated* it because they have 'assumed' your rights.

At one time, it was thought that you could not appropriate something if you had authorisation from the owner, i.e., consent. This caused problems – and much case law.

In **Lawrence 1971**, the HL held there could still be an appropriation even if the owner consented. They found a taxi driver guilty of theft after he took more money than the correct fare (about £7 instead of 55p) from a foreign student. The student had offered him his wallet after he said £1 wasn't enough. He argued it could not be theft because the student gave him the wallet. The House disagreed. The decision was not without its critics. There is an offence under **s 15** of the **Act** of 'obtaining property by deception' which would have covered this type of conduct. Why then, it has been argued, did the House need to interpret **s 3** so widely? The next case appeared to complicate matters further.

In **Morris 1984,** Ds switched labels on goods in a supermarket with intent to pay the lower price. The question was, had an appropriation taken place? The CA held that appropriation took place when D assumed *any* of the rights of the owner, so it occurred as soon as the goods were removed from the shelf with intent to pay the lower price. It could therefore be appropriation even before they switched labels. The HL's interpretation was narrower. Although Lord Roskill said that **s 3** meant interference with *any* of the rights of the owner, he later made clear that there must be 'an *adverse* interference' with those rights'. Thus appropriation only took place when D did something unauthorised, in this case, switching labels. In the case of some-one swapping labels for a joke, Lord Roskill said that they would have 'appropriated', but would not have the *mens rea* of dishonesty or intent to permanently deprive and so would not be guilty of theft.

### Food for thought

This seems to contradict **Lawrence**, which allowed for an appropriation even with the owner's consent or authorisation. In **Morris,** Lord Roskill said appropriation *wouldn't* occur if the owner had expressly or impliedly consented – and goods are removed from a supermarket shelf with the owner's consent. The House did not need to decide on the issue because both D's had done something 'adverse' by switching labels, the owner did not authorise label switching. The student consented in **Lawrence,** so which case do you think is to be preferred? Another matter for discussion is the difficulty for juries; the practical joker example shows how far appropriation (*actus reus*) and dishonesty (*mens rea*) are linked.

So, according to **Morris**, it can be theft even if you don't take anything. *Mens rea* may be harder to prove before D gets to the check out, but if, as in **Morris**, you intend to pay less than you should, then you intend to permanently deprive the owner of the difference in price. This is also likely to be seen as dishonest. The HL considered the matter again in the next case.

### Key case

In **Gomez 1993**, D was the assistant manager of a shop. He was asked by an acquaintance to obtain some goods in exchange for two stolen cheques. Knowing that the cheques were stolen, D got the shop manager to authorise the sale of the goods to the acquaintance. The CA allowed his appeal against a conviction for theft because the manager had consented. On the basis of **Morris**, there was no appropriation and so no theft. The prosecution appealed to the HL. The appeal raised the question of whether – and how – the earlier two cases could be reconciled. The House decided to revert to **Lawrence**. They held that it was a clear decision that an act could be an appropriation even if done with consent. They declared **Morris** to be incorrect on this point. Lord Keith said that although a customer putting items into a shopping basket is not a thief, the customer has appropriated those items.

So has **Gomez** made the issue certain? Maybe not. In **Galasso 1993,** the same year, the CA seemed to view **Gomez** as not going as far as Lord Keith suggested. Later cases were not always consistent. A narrow interpretation of **Gomez** was seen in **Mazo 1996**. The CA accepted that an appropriation could take place with the owner's consent, but only if that consent had been induced by deception or fraud. In this case, although there was evidence that V did not have full mental capacity, it was held that a gift of a number of cheques she had made to D, her maid, was valid, there was insufficient evidence of any deception. There was therefore no appropriation and D's appeal against her conviction for theft succeeded. However, the next case shows a wider interpretation.

**Key case**

In **Hinks 1998**, the CA again held that appropriation did not depend on whether there was consent, and said that consent was only relevant to the issue of dishonesty. Here, a man of limited intelligence had been persuaded to give Mrs Hinks, who claimed to be his 'carer', £60,000 over a period of a few months. The CA upheld the conviction for theft. Her appeal was rejected by the HL. Lord Steyn made the point in the opening quote, confirming the *ratio decidendi* of **Lawrence**, and continuing that it went 'to the heart of' the present case. Thus, even a gift could amount to an appropriation. It should be noted that the HL decision was only a 3-2 majority and Lords Hutton and Hobhouse argued strongly that there was no appropriation.

In **Briggs 2004**, the CA considered another case where V had been deceived into parting with money. The D was dealing with the purchase of a house on behalf of elderly relatives. The relatives gave authority for money for the purchase to be transferred to the seller's solicitor. They believed they were getting title to the property but in fact, title was transferred to D. Their consent to the transfer was therefore induced by fraud. D argued that property was not appropriated where, by fraud, an owner was induced into parting with it. The CA agreed. They noted that if there could be an appropriation in such cases there would be little need for many of the deception offences.

**Food for thought**

It can be argued that the interpretation of appropriation in **Gomez** and **Hinks** was too wide. As the CA pointed out in **Briggs**, it means that many of the deception offences would be redundant. It is unlikely that Parliament would have legislated on these if they had intended appropriation to include situations where V is deceived into parting with something. Maybe the minority argument in **Hinks** was correct. However, a case like **Mazo**, where there was not enough evidence of deception and no appropriation, would come under neither offence. A prosecution against **Briggs** would probably have succeeded had D been charged with one of the deception offences.

**Hinks** makes clear that consent is not relevant to appropriation, but is to dishonesty. Thus, the fact that V has consented may be relevant to whether D was dishonest. Otherwise, you could be guilty of theft of a genuine gift. Lord Keith intimated this in **Gomez** when he referred to Lord Roskill's joker in **Morris**. There may be appropriation in such cases, but if it isn't done dishonestly and with intent to permanently deprive then *mens rea* won't be proved. We will look at *mens rea* in the next chapter.

**Examination pointer**

It follows from **Gomez** that where consent is obtained by deception the charge may be theft under **s 1**. As the matter is not fully clear, you may need to refer to, e.g., **Briggs** to support the alternative argument that there is no appropriation. Then go on to look at *mens rea*, even if there is an appropriation a prosecution may fail on this issue.

If you come by something innocently but then deal with it dishonestly this can be theft. As we saw, **s 3(1)** defines appropriation as being *'any assumption by a person of the rights of an owner'* it continues *'and this includes, where he has come by the property (innocently or not) without stealing it, any later assumption of a right to it by keeping or dealing with it as owner.'* This would apply if you picked up a mobile phone by mistake, but after getting home decided to keep it.

**S 1(2)** provides *"it is immaterial whether the appropriation is made with a view to gain or is made for the thief's own benefit"*. This means taking and destroying something is still appropriation. Taking something and giving it away would also come within this section.

**Examination pointer**

A problem question will usually involve one or two particular issue e.g., it may be arguable whether there is an 'appropriation' or whether the property 'belongs to another'. As I pointed out earlier, **s 1** defines theft. The other sections merely expand on each part of the definition. They aren't offences in themselves. So you should avoid statements like "D will be guilty of appropriation under **s 3**". All 5 elements have to be proved. If they are then D will be guilty of theft under **s 1**. If any one of them can't be proved, D is not guilty of theft.

**Task**

You pick up a watch in a jeweller's intending to steal it. You see a shop assistant looking over at you and put it back. Are you guilty of theft? Think about this as you read this Chapter. We'll come back to it.

### *Property s 4(1)*

Property includes,

> *"money and all other property, real or personal, including things in action and other intangible property"*

Real property relates to land; personal would be anything else. Tangible property is something you can touch like a book or a car. Intangible means things you can't touch such as the right to the balance in a bank account or the copyright on a song. These are called 'things in action' because they are rights which can only be enforced by a court action, e.g., by suing someone for stealing the lyrics of a song and making a record. The section goes on to say that (with a few exceptions) land can't normally be stolen. Just about everything else can be though.

In **Kelly 1998**, an artist was given access to the Royal College of Surgeons to draw specimens. He took some body parts and when accused of theft argued it was not 'property'. You can't own someone's body.  The CA held it was theft and that parts of a body could come within **s 4** if they had been treated in some way e.g., by preserving them for medical purposes.

In **Marshall 1998,** Ds acquired underground tickets from travellers and then sold them.  On appeal, they argued the tickets were not property belonging to another.  The CA held that there was appropriation of property (the tickets themselves) belonging to London Underground (who 'owned' them).

In **Oxford v Moss 1978,** an examination paper was taken by a university student prior to the exam.  This was not theft of the paper, as he intended to return it.  Knowledge of what was on the paper was appropriated, but this was held not to be property.

So, you can steal most things including money and rights.  However **s 4(3)** excludes wild plants (unless taken for "reward or sale or other commercial purpose") and **s 4(4)** excludes wild creatures (unless they have been tamed or kept in captivity).

### Example

Whilst exercising his rights of access to open land under the **Countryside and Rights of Way Act 2000**, Chris picks some wild mushrooms and then sells them to the local restaurant.  He also takes home a rabbit to show his kids.  The first is theft because he has taken them for "reward or sale or other commercial purpose".  The second isn't unless the rabbit had been someone's pet.  In that case, it would also be theft.

### Examination pointer

Watch for references to the subsections in a problem question.  In my example above you would need to pick up on the fact that although **s 4(1)** includes most things, according to **s 4(3)** you can't normally steal wild plants.  Then go on to say it may be 'property' in this case because selling them would be for "reward or sale or other commercial purpose" under **s 4(3)**.  As regards the rabbit, this would not be theft if it is wild, but if 'tamed' it can be, **s 4(4)**.  Don't worry too much if you can't remember the numbers of all the subsections though – no-one's perfect!

### *Belonging to another s 5(1)*

This is also wide and is not confined to property actually owned by another, having possession or control of it can suffice.  **S 5(1)** states,

> *'Property shall be regarded as belonging to any person having possession or control of it, or having in it any proprietary right or interest ...'*

### Example

You lend a coat to a friend, Sue, for the evening.  Whilst she is dancing, someone takes it.  They have appropriated property belonging to you, as you owned it.  They have also appropriated property 'belonging to' Sue as she had possession at the time.

You can have control of property without knowing of its existence.  Thus such property can be stolen.  In **Woodman 1974**, the owner of a disused business premises sold a load of scrap metal.  He didn't know the buyers had left some behind.  D went onto the property and took some of the remaining scrap.  He was convicted of theft.  The owners of the premises no longer owned the metal, as they had sold it, but they did have 'control' of it.

There is a difference between something which is lost and something which is abandoned.  The first belongs to someone so keeping it could be theft, the second does not so can't be.

### Example

You have some old books which you don't want anymore. You leave them at college hoping someone may find them useful. You have abandoned them so they cannot then be stolen.

In **Hibbert & McKiernan 1948**, it was held that taking lost golf balls on a golf course was theft. They had been lost, not abandoned.

In **Rickets 2010**, the court considered whether goods left in bags outside a charity shop were 'property belonging to another'. D had argued that they had been abandoned and therefore did not constitute 'property belonging to another'. The court held that if goods were left outside a charity shop then it could be assumed that it was the owner's intention to donate them as a gift to the shop. Therefore, they were not abandoned, but remained the property of the person who had left them until taken in by the charity. Removing the goods before this time could therefore amount to theft. A second point arose as regards control. Some property was also taken from a bin outside another charity shop and the question again was whether it 'belonged to another' The court held that it did, the bin was in close proximity to the charity shop, it could therefore be inferred that the bin was under the control of the charity shop.

It is even possible to steal your own property if someone else has a right to it. **S5** says 'having in it any proprietary right or interest ...' This is illustrated by **Turner 1971**, where a garage had a right to hold D's car until their bill was paid. Turner was thus guilty of theft when he took it back without paying the repair bill.

### Examination pointer

Look out for situations where someone else has possession or control of the property, or where it is debateable whether something has been abandoned and be prepared to discuss these points. Note also that the definition is 'belonging to *another*'. It doesn't say you have to appropriate it from a *particular* person.

Problems occurred where in contract law title to property had already passed, e.g., in **Edwards v Ddin 1976**, D obtained petrol at a self-service station and *then* decided to leave without paying. At the time he appropriated the petrol he had no *mens rea*, when he formed the *mens rea* there was no *actus reus* as title had passed when the petrol entered the tank so it was not 'property belonging to another'. This situation has now been dealt with under **s 3 TA1978**, with the offence of 'making off without payment', which would also apply to leaving a restaurant without paying for a meal if you originally intended to pay. If you intended not to pay from the start it could be theft as you would have the *mens rea* (intent) at the time of the *actus reus* (consuming the food).

### Obligation to deal with the property in a certain way

> *S 5(3)* provides, '*Where a person receives property from or on account of another, and is under an obligation to the other to retain and deal with that property or its proceeds in a particular way, the property or proceeds shall be regarded (as against him) as belonging to the other'*.

### Example

Your mother gives you £20 and asks you to do the shopping tomorrow. You *received* property, the £20. You are *obliged* to *retain* it until tomorrow, and to *deal with* it by doing the shopping. You may have been given the £20, but under **s 5(3)** it *belongs* to your mother.

In **Davidge and Burnett 1984**, D was given money by her flatmates to pay bills. She spent it on Christmas presents. She was found guilty of theft as she had an obligation to deal with it in a certain way (pay the bills) and had not done so.

In **Hallam & Blackburn 1995**, investment advisers were convicted of theft when they did not invest sums entrusted to them. However, there must be an obligation to deal with it in a particular way and thus there was no conviction in **Hall 1973**. A travel agent paid deposits for flights into his firm's account and was later unable to repay the money. He was not guilty of theft as there had been no special arrangements for the deposits to be used in a particular way.

**Property received by mistake**

**S 5(4)** provides,

> 'Where a person gets property by another's mistake, and is under an obligation to make restoration (in whole or in part) of the property or its proceeds or of the value thereof, then to the extent of that obligation the property or proceeds shall be regarded (as against him) as belonging to the person entitled to restoration, and an intention not to make restoration shall be regarded accordingly as an intention to deprive that person of the property or proceeds'

Put simply – and it needs to be – this means that if you are given something by mistake (and so have an obligation to give it back), keeping it can be theft. It would cover overpayments of wages as in **AG's Reference No 1 of 1983** where D knew she'd been overpaid and simply left the money in her account. The same applies if you buy goods from a shop and are given too much change by mistake. Essentially the excess belongs to the shop so you are obliged to give it back. Keeping it is theft of that amount.

**Task**

**Look at the following situations. Decide if the *actus reus* of theft has occurred and explain the significance of any particular sections in each case**.

Sam gets home from college to find she has picked up the wrong coat by mistake. She decides to keep it.

Peter buys a book to read on his journey home and thinks it is such rubbish he leaves it on the train in disgust. Susan picks it up and takes it home.

Simon pays a local builder £100 to buy sand to build a patio. The builder buys himself a second-hand dishwasher instead.

Mary buys a CD and gives a £20 note. She is given change from a £50 note and keeps it.

**Summary of theft: S1 Theft Act 1968**

*Actus reus*

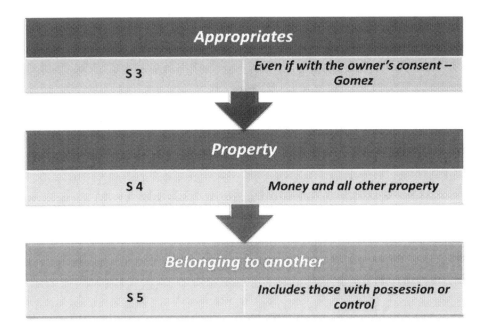

*Mens rea* (see next chapter) is dishonesty **s 2** and intent to permanently deprive **s 6**

So you may be found guilty of theft in the task concerning the watch. The *actus reus* is the appropriation (by picking it up – **Gomez**) of property (the watch) belonging to another (the shop). You also have *mens rea*, you intended to permanently deprive the shop and your actions were dishonest. (We'll look at *mens rea* next.)

Self-test questions

*When can wild plants or animals be classed as property?*

*Did **Gomez** follow **Morris or Lawrence** on the issue of consent?*

*From which case did the opening quote come?*

*What was appropriated in **Hinks**?*

*What are the 2 parts to the mens rea of theft??*

For answers to the tasks and self-test questions, please go to my website at www.drsr.org and click the button 'Answers to tasks'. For a range of free interactive exercises, click on 'Free Exercises' and then the OCR book.

"We can see no reason why, when in a jury box, they should require the help of a judge to tell them what amounts to dishonesty"

*The CA in **Feely 1971** on the role of a jury*

By the end of this Chapter, you should be able to:

**Explain both the actus reus and mens rea of theft**

**Explain how the law applies in practice by reference to cases**

**Identify possible criticisms**

We saw that theft is defined in the **Theft Act 1968 s1(1)** which says that a person is guilty of theft if,

'he **dishonestly** appropriates property belonging to another with the **intention of permanently depriving the other** of it'

You learnt that 'appropriates' 'property' and 'belonging to another' relate to the *actus reus*. 'Dishonesty' and 'intent to permanently deprive' relate to *mens rea*. Every one of these elements must be proved, or the prosecution will fail.

In **Gomez**, the distinction was made between an honest shopper and a thief. A person who takes an item off a supermarket shelf appropriates it. Only the fact that a shopper means to pay the right price stops them being a thief. This is because they are not being dishonest. They have no *mens rea*. In **Madely 1990**, Richard Madely was found not guilty of theft when he absentmindedly forgot to pay for some goods. The prosecution could not prove *mens rea* because he lacked any intention to permanently deprive.

### Dishonesty

The **Act** does not define dishonesty but it does provide three specific situations where the person is *not* deemed dishonest:

**S 2(1)(a)** provides that a person's appropriation of property belonging to another is not to be regarded as dishonest if 'he appropriates the property **in the belief that he has in law the right to deprive the other of it**, on behalf of himself or a third person.'

**S 2(1)(b)** provides that it is not dishonest if a person 'appropriates the property **in the belief that he would have the other's consent** if the other knew of the appropriation and the circumstances of it'.

**S 2(1)(c)** provides that a person is not dishonest if 'he appropriates the property **in the belief that the person to whom the property belongs cannot be discovered** by taking reasonable steps'.

The belief does not have to be reasonable, just *honestly held*. It is subjective, so it is *D's* belief that is important. However, D will need to persuade a jury that it was honestly held. The less reasonable it is, the harder it will be to convince a jury of this.

### Example

You're having coffee with a friend. She goes to the loo leaving her coffee and her handbag on the table. You wait for a while, but need to leave to catch your bus. You drink her coffee and take £50 from her bag (some friend). Can you rely on **s 2(b)**? You'll need to convince a jury that you believe she would have consented in the circumstances. This may not be hard in relation to the coffee; after all it was going cold. It will be a lot harder to convince the jury that you believed your friend would consent to taking the £50 though.

In **Small 1987**, D had taken a car which had been left for over a week with the keys in the ignition. Two issues arose. He argued it had been abandoned and so he believed he had a right to take it – **s 2(1)(a)**. The CA quashed his conviction and made clear that the issue under **s 2** is whether a belief is *honestly* held, not whether it is reasonable. The second issue was not pursued, but if the car *was* abandoned then it did not 'belong to another'. Thus, there would be no *actus reus* and no need to look at dishonesty at all.

### Example

You take a bicycle which belongs to a friend. You could argue under **s 2(1)(a)** that the friend owed you money so you believed you had a legal right to it. Alternatively you could argue under **s 2(1)(b)** that you believed the friend would have consented in the circumstances. Under **s 2(1)(c)** you could argue that you thought the friend had left the country and so couldn't be traced by taking reasonable steps.

In a case such as **Small s 2(1)(c)** could also have been argued. Though with a car it would be harder to convince a jury he honestly believed he couldn't trace the owner as cars must be registered.

Note that **s 2** relates to *mens rea* not *actus reus*. So a *belief* that you had a legal right to something is enough, even if you are wrong. Similarly if the other person doesn't consent but you believed they would this will suffice. Lastly, a belief you could not trace the owner by taking reasonable steps would be sufficient. You do not actually have to *take* reasonable steps to find the owner.

### Examination pointer

Watch for the above points, especially for **(c)**. It is a common mistake in examinations for candidates to say that as no steps were taken D was dishonest.

### The Ghosh test

In addition to **s 2**, which merely shows when D is *not* dishonest, (and despite the opening quote) the courts have developed a test for dishonesty. It comes from the case of **Ghosh 1982**.

### Key case

In **Ghosh**, a surgeon claimed fees for operations he had not performed. The question was whether the prosecution had proved that he had acted dishonestly. The CA laid down what is now known as the 'Ghosh test'.

Lord Lane said that the jury must determine whether *"according to the ordinary standards of reasonable and honest people what was done was dishonest. If it was not dishonest by those standards, that is the end of the matter and the prosecution fails. If it was dishonest by those standards then the jury must consider whether the defendant himself must have realised that what he was doing was by those standards dishonest"*.

This means that there are two questions for the jury

> **Was D's act dishonest by the ordinary standards of reasonable and honest people? If not, stop here, if so, ask the second question:**

**Did D realise the act would be regarded as dishonest by such people?**

If the jury can answer 'yes' to both parts D is dishonest.

As is often the case, it is a two-fold test with both a subjective and objective element. The first, 'objective' test, is what reasonable and honest people would have thought about D's actions. The jury will look at what D did and ask themselves whether they think that action was dishonest. The second, 'subjective' test, is what D believed reasonable and honest people would think. Here the jury will have to decide what *D* was thinking in relation to that action. This is harder.

### Food for thought

Does the **Ghosh** test make things clear for a jury? Is it too wide? In this sort of case, where D claims fees for operations he has not performed, the question is probably not a difficult one for the jury to answer. It may be harder where D's actions have some 'do-good' element. Might a jury decide on moral rather than legal grounds? Writers often refer to the 'Robin Hood' type scenario. If D (Robin) takes from the rich and gives to the poor the Jury may not consider this conduct dishonest. The problem is that members of the jury will probably differ on what they regard as dishonest. This could result in different verdicts, depending on the composition of the jury. A jury with several people on it who believe in animal rights may not regard removing animals from a laboratory as dishonest, for example. The answer to the first question would therefore be 'no'. Whatever D thinks is then irrelevant because once the first is answered in the negative there is no need to consider the second question. Motive is not normally relevant in criminal law (except in sentencing) but it may matter to a jury.

Let's reverse the facts in the Robin Hood case. This time Robin steals from the poor and gives to the rich. Now would the jury think it dishonest? Quite likely. Morally this may be OK, but legally it means that the same facts can lead to a conviction or acquittal depending not only on motive, but also on who the victim is. Arguably, taking from one person should not be any different to taking from another.

The CA noted the lack of clarity in the law and attempted to put it right in **Ghosh**. It is by no means certain that they have done so. The second part of the test is only partly subjective. It is what D (subjective) thinks ordinary people (objective) would regard as dishonest. It is hard for the jury to know what D thought reasonable people *would* regard as dishonest. D's own circumstances and upbringing would be reflected in the subjective part of the test. D may have some very odd ideas about what is regarded as dishonest. So, it isn't only a hard question for the jury to answer, the test is complicated in itself. However, for the moment we are stuck with it.

We saw in Part A that **s 1(2)** provides "*it is immaterial whether the appropriation is made with a view to gain or is made for the thief's own benefit*". This touches on dishonesty as well as appropriation. It means that the Robin Hood argument should fail even though Robin isn't gaining a benefit.

### Examination pointer

When discussing the *mens rea* of theft you may need to look at both **s 2** and **Ghosh**. Look for clues in the scenario set, e.g., any reference to being owed money should point you to **s 2(1)(a)**, taking from a friend or colleague to **s 2 (1)(b)**, something found to **s 2(1)(c)**. Reference to D's age or mental capacity requires you to discuss that it is what D *believes* that is important, not what is *reasonable*. If these don't apply, or may not succeed, then explain and apply the **Ghosh** test.

**Task**

Look at the following situations. State which belief under **s 2(1)** you can argue and whether you think you'll convince the jury you honestly held that belief.

> **You find a football in your garden and keep it**
>
> **You take some money from a friend's bag in an emergency**
>
> **You find a £2 coin in the street and keep it**
>
> **You find a handbag containing a wallet and credit cards in the street and keep it**

Note that under **s 2(2)** the fact that you are willing to pay for the property does not mean you are acting honestly. At first glance, you may think it unfair to find D guilty of theft in such a case but compare the following two situations.

> **D takes a bottle of milk from a neighbour's doorstep and leaves more than enough money to replace it**
>
> **D is a very rich employer and really likes a vintage car belonging to an employee. One day D takes the car and leaves double what it is worth**

In the first situation, you may think it is unfair to find D guilty, but if it weren't for **s 2(2)** the employer wouldn't be guilty either. Anyone could take anything they wanted as long as they could pay for it. Also in the first case D could use the **s 2(1)(b)** defence.

**Summary of Dishonesty**

**Does** s 2(1)(a) **apply? Belief in a right to the property**

**Does** s 2(1)(b) **apply? Belief in consent**

**Does** s 2(1)(c) **apply? Belief that the owner can't be found**

**If the answer is 'Yes', D is not dishonest**

**If the answer is 'No', apply the Ghosh test**

*Intention to permanently deprive*

**S 6(1)** provides that this will exist where D's *'intention is to treat the property as his own to dispose of regardless of the other's rights'*.

In **Raphael and another 2008**, D had taken the victim's car by force (robbery) and had then demanded payment for it to be returned. The CA noted that **s 6(1)** included an intention to 'treat the thing as his own to dispose of regardless of the other's rights' and said *"it is hard to find a better example of such an intention"* than an offer to return the property to the owner in return for a sum of money. The return of the property was subject to a condition that was inconsistent with the rights of the owner, i.e., the demand for payment.

It will also exist where property is borrowed *'for a period and in circumstances making it equivalent to an outright taking or disposal'*. This means it is not usually theft if you mean to return the item. This would apply to borrowing but could be different if you have used it and so reduced its value.

### Example

You borrow a month's season ticket intending to return it later. You use it for three weeks and are charged with theft. You can argue that you had no intention to permanently deprive the owner of it. This argument is likely to fail. The use of it for this period will make it 'equivalent to an outright taking' and so come within **s 6**.

In **Lloyd 1985,** D borrowed some films from the cinema where he worked and copied them. The CA held **s 6** would apply if D used something so that "all the goodness or virtue is gone". On the facts this was not the case so there was no liability. This narrow interpretation of **s 6** has been seen as rather too generous to D and later cases have shown a significant widening of it.

In **Velumyl 1989**, D took money from his employer's safe intending to return it. The CA held that this was sufficient, as he had treated the money as his own. It was also made clear that as he would be unable to replace the exact notes taken he had intended to deprive the owner of those notes. D's best hope in a case like this is to convince the jury that the intention to put them back showed the conduct was not dishonest.

The broader approach is seen again in **Lavender 1994** and **Marshall 1998**.

In **Lavender**, D took some doors from his flat which belonged to the council. He hung them in his girlfriend's flat which belonged to the same council. Arguably, he hadn't intended to permanently deprive the council of the doors as he merely moved them around. The court held D had treated the doors as his own to dispose of regardless of the other's rights.

In **Marshall**, the CA held that acquiring underground tickets from travellers and then selling them was within the scope of **s 6**. The Ds had treated the tickets as their own to dispose of regardless of London Underground's rights.

### Food for thought

It can be argued that the **Lloyd** approach is too narrow but the wider approach in these later cases can also be criticised. It means that D is liable even where there does not appear to be any intent to permanently deprive.

Another case which illustrates **s 6** is **Cahill 1993**. Very early one morning D took a pile of newspapers from a newsagent's doorstep on his way home. He was very drunk at the time and couldn't fully explain what he intended to do with them. His conviction was quashed because the judge's direction to the jury only went as far as *'to treat the property as his own'* and did not add *'to dispose of regardless of the other's rights'*. Had the direction been given correctly he may have been found to have *mens rea*. Much would depend on where he dumped them, close by or not. The newspapers would be worthless after the end of the day. If they didn't find their way back to the shop then 'all the goodness or virtue' would be gone.

### Examination pointer

If given a scenario like **Velumyl** you could argue that D may not be dishonest under **s 2**. Suggest D may have believed that the owner would have consented (perhaps borrowing from the employer had been allowed before). Or D believed they had a right to it (perhaps they were owed wages). Alternatively rely on the **Ghosh** test. The jury may consider that by intending to return the money, D was not dishonest by ordinary standards.

A final point:

In **Small 1987**, D had taken a car. It may be hard to prove intention to permanently deprive in such a case because a car is easily traceable. (It was for this reason that a separate offence of taking without consent was later added to the **Theft Act**.) You should look for clues in the type of property that has been taken.

## Task

Consider the following situations and decide if **s 6** is satisfied:

> *Dave takes Steve's tickets for that night's pop concert and returns them the next day.*

> *Frank takes £10 from his mother's purse and puts it in his pocket. His sister sees him and says she will tell if he doesn't return it. He puts it back.*

> *Ellie borrows a book from a friend and reads it. She then throws it away.*

## Recap

Let's look back at the Task where you took a watch and put it back.

You appropriated (by picking it up) property (the watch) belonging to another (the shop). You have the *actus reus* for theft. Do you have *mens rea*? It may be difficult to find evidence but you know you acted dishonestly. You know 'ordinary reasonable people' would regard the fact that you only put it back because someone was watching as dishonest. You can argue that you didn't keep it so haven't permanently deprived anyone. This actually doesn't matter. It is *intent* to do so that makes it theft. Intent relates to *mens rea* (what you think) not *actus reus* (your actual conduct). Again, it will be hard to prove, but yes, technically you have committed theft. As has Frank in the above task, although he may be able to argue under **s 2(1)(b)**, that he believed his mother would have consented in the circumstances.

**Summary – here's the *actus reus* again**

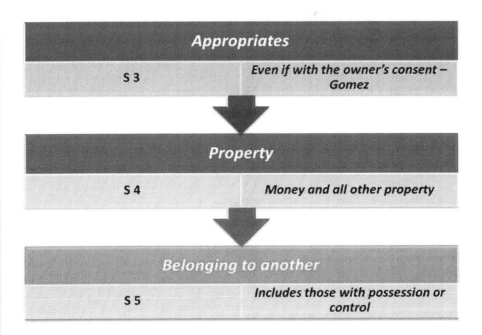

163

**Summary of mens rea**

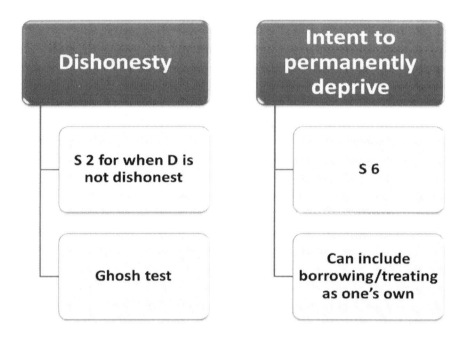

**Self-test questions**

*What are the 3 statutory beliefs in s 2?*

*Do these beliefs have to be reasonable?*

*What is the Ghosh test?*

*When can borrowing amount to intent to permanently deprive?*

*Can you state all the section numbers dealing with each part of the actus reus and mens rea?*

For answers to the tasks and self-test questions, please go to my website at www.drsr.org and click the button 'Answers to tasks'. For a range of free interactive exercises, click on 'Free Exercises' and then the OCR book.

"What is a robbery, ladies and gentlemen? Well, in very crude terms, it is a theft that has been carried out through violence."

*R v West 1999*

By the end of this Chapter, you should be able to:

**Explain the actus reus and mens rea of theft and what turns it into robbery**

**Explain how the law applies in practice by reference to cases**

**Identify possible criticisms**

Robbery is essentially a type of aggravated theft. **S 8** of the **Theft Act 1968** makes it a more serious offence if D uses force (or the threat of force) in order to steal. **S (8)(1)** provides:

"*A person is guilty of robbery if he steals, and immediately before or at the time of doing so, and in order to do so, he uses force on any person or puts or seeks to put any person in fear of being then and there subjected to force*".

It is an indictable offence and carries a maximum life sentence.

Let's look at each part of this offence to clarify what is needed. It's easier than it might look.

**Actus reus**

There are several parts to this.

**steals**

**immediately before or at the time of doing so**

**in order to do so**

**uses force on any person or puts or seeks to put any person in fear**

**Steals**

Robbery involves a theft PLUS the force element. It is therefore necessary to prove all the *actus reus* and *mens rea* elements for theft before considering whether there may be a robbery. An example we looked at with theft is **Raphael 2008**. D had appropriated property (the car) which belonged to another (the owner). He had acted dishonestly and intended to permanently deprive the owner of it (by treating it as his own regardless of the other's rights). He had therefore committed theft. When he took the car, he had hit the man with an iron bar. This turned the theft into robbery.

As you have to prove theft, it follows that you can also use the defences to theft. This means that the **s 2(1)** defences will apply here too. Thus in **Robinson 1977** D threatened V with a knife in order to get money he was owed. He believed he had a legal right to the money (even though he knew he had no right to use a knife to get it) so had a defence under **s 2(1)**. If there is no theft then there can be no robbery.

**Task**

Look back at the *actus reus* and *mens rea* of theft. Be sure you can explain:

Appropriation – property – belonging to another

Dishonesty – intention to permanently deprive

If all these can be proved *and* there is the additional element of force, it may be a robbery.

## Immediately before or at the time of doing so

The use (or threat) of force must be before or during the theft. This seems to suggest that the use of force once the appropriation has taken place would not be enough to make it robbery. This is not interpreted too strictly by the courts.

## Key case

In **Hale 1979,** the Ds entered the victim's house and one went upstairs and stole some items from a jewellery box. The other was downstairs tying up V. The CA declined to quash their convictions for robbery even though the appropriation may have already taken place. The appropriation was seen as a continuing act. Therefore, it was open to the jury to conclude that it continued whilst the victim was tied up.

In **Lockley 1995**, the court confirmed the point in **Hale 1979** that appropriation was a continuing act. Force on a shopkeeper *after* the D's took some beer could amount to robbery. Remember **Fagan** and continuing acts? No? Then have a look at Chapter 1 again.

## Examination pointer

A common mistake is for candidates to go straight on to the robbery issues, but you need a theft to have occurred, so if you see a potential case of robbery in an exam question take it step by step. Firstly, consider whether there is appropriation of property belonging to another. Then consider whether it was dishonestly appropriated with the intention of permanently depriving someone of it. If so, you have theft. Go on to consider if there are any additional elements which may turn the theft into an offence of robbery, as in **Raphael**.

## In order to do so

So we can see that the appropriation may continue whilst D is removing the goods from the premises. If force is used, or threatened, this may amount to robbery. However, the force or the threat of force must be 'in order to' steal. This means it must be applied with the purpose of facilitating the theft. If the jury are satisfied that D stole something, yet the force or threat of it was not applied in order to steal, they cannot convict under **s 8(1)**. Using force to get away is not 'in order to steal'. It may be theft, but not robbery.

## Uses force on any person or puts or seeks to put any person in fear

The word force is not separately defined in the Act. In **Dawson and James 1978**, the CA said that since it was an ordinary word it was for the jury to determine its meaning. In **West 1999**, the judge made the comment in the opening quote. He then continued, *"What does that mean? What it means, ladies and gentlemen, is; if you are in the supermarket and someone puts their hand into your basket and takes your purse out, a pickpocket, that is theft. It has been stolen from you. If you are outside in the street, and you are approached by someone who held a knife at your throat and then took your purse out of your bag, you will have been robbed, because immediately before or during the course of the theft, you were subject to violence or a threat of violence."* The indication here is that violence is needed, as was the case in **Raphael**. However, it is clear from several cases that the use of force can be small. Snatching a bag from someone's grasp was held to be robbery in **Corcoran v Anderton 1980**. Similarly, in **Clouden 1987**, wrenching a shopping basket from someone's grasp amounted to robbery.

A second point arose in **Corcoran**. The two D's had tried to take the handbag by force. It fell from one D's hands and they ran off without it. The court held that the theft was complete when D snatched the handbag from her grasp. This means that a robbery can occur without anything being taken. This isn't as daft as it seems. You can commit theft without taking something. In **Gomez**, it was said that taking something from a supermarket shelf was appropriation. If done dishonestly it could be theft even though you haven't left the shop, if done with force it can be robbery.

**Example**

You are in a shop. You put an item in your pocket intending to avoid paying for it. You have appropriated property belonging to the shopkeeper. This would be seen as dishonest in the eyes of 'ordinary' people. You would also be intending to permanently deprive the owner of it. This is theft. If you threaten another shopper to "keep quiet or else" when you take it, then you have used the threat of force in order to steal. This is robbery. In both cases, the crime has been committed even if you drop the item in your hurry to get away

Note that the force or threat can be on 'any person'. As in my example, it need not be on the victim of the theft. If you wanted to gain entrance to a casino at night to steal the profits, then knocking out a security guard would suffice. So might tying up and blindfolding someone whose house overlooks the casino. This would depend on why you did it. If it was to prevent them seeing you and raising the alarm it would be robbery. If it was just to prevent them seeing you and pointing you out at a later date it would not. The difference is that in the first case it is *in order to* steal (without being stopped because the alarm has been raised). In the second it is just to avoid being recognised and doesn't help with the theft.

**Task**

Look back at theft to remind yourself of all the parts to the *actus reus* and *mens rea*. Apply these to **Clouden**. You should end up by establishing theft. Keep your workings; we'll come back to this.

**Food for thought**

The use of force can be really minor yet the maximum sentence for robbery is life imprisonment. Consider whether this is just. Prior to the Act, the Criminal Law Revision Committee had said that snatching a bag from an unresisting owner would not suffice. **Corcoran** and **Clouden** show that the courts have interpreted the requirement for force very widely. If a person tries to prevent D from taking a bag and there is a struggle then robbery appears an appropriate charge. If, however, there is no resistance then theft would seem to cover it.

**Being then and there subjected to force**

This means that it must be a threat of immediate force. As with the 'immediately before or at the time' element there is no set time limit. It will be a matter for the jury to decide based on all the circumstances. If the force is used just before or just after (**Hale**) then it may be robbery. However, if D threatens force in a week's time if the security guard doesn't look the other way tonight, it is unlikely to be robbery.

In **R v DPP; B v DPP 2007**, some boys pushed another boy around and took his mobile phone and other items. They were charged with robbery under **s 8**. V said he had not felt particularly scared and the D's argued that as he was not frightened there was no robbery. The court interpreted the Act and held that it was the intention of D rather than the fortitude of V that was important. If this were not the case, guilt would be dependent on how brave, or not, the victim was. This was not what Parliament would have intended and not what the Act implied. They had intended to scare him and some force had been used so their convictions were upheld.

### Mens rea

Firstly, because robbery requires that a theft took place, the prosecution will need to prove the *mens rea* for the theft. This is dishonesty and intention to permanently deprive. We saw above that this also means D can use the **s 2** arguments to show lack of *mens rea* in relation to dishonesty. In **Robinson 1977**, D had a defence under **s 2(1)** because he believed he had a legal right to the money.

### Task

Find the notes you made in the last task on **Clouden**. Now add the additional *actus reus* and *mens rea* for robbery. OK? Now you should be able to tackle an exam question.

As regards the robbery itself, accidentally using force or causing fear in a victim is unlikely to be robbery. Robbery requires force 'in order to' steal and accidentally using force would not meet this requirement. Thus, the force or threat of it must be intentional or reckless. As we saw in Chapter 2 all recklessness is now subjective or **Cunningham** recklessness, so D must recognise the risk of force or of putting someone in fear of it.

### Examination pointer

You may have a scenario which appears to be a robbery because there is evidence of force. Go through all the elements of theft and then **s 8**. If you then fail to prove robbery on one of the above issues say that although D is unlikely to be convicted of robbery a theft conviction would be possible. The overlap between theft, robbery and burglary means you may need to discuss more than one. Look out for clues as to *how* (force may make it robbery) and *where* (if in a building it may be burglary) it happens.

### Summary

**actus reus**

- steals
- uses force
- or puts someone in fear
- immediately before or at the time

**mens rea**

- as for theft
- dishonesty
- intent to permanently deprive
- s 2 defences may apply

**Self-test questions**

*What turns theft into robbery?*

*What are the five elements to theft?*

*How was appropriation treated in **Hale**?*

*What amounted to force in **Corcoran**?*

*What is the mens rea for robbery?*

For answers to the tasks and self-test questions, please go to my website at www.drsr.org and click the button 'Answers to tasks'. For a range of free interactive exercises, click on 'Free Exercises' and then the OCR book.

"When you invite a person into your house to use the staircase you do not invite him to slide down the bannisters"

*Scrutton LJ*

By the end of this Chapter, you should be able to:

**Explain the actus reus and mens rea of burglary**

**Identify the connection with theft and what turns it into burglary**

**Explain how the law applies in practice by reference to cases**

**Identify possible criticisms**

A common view of a burglar is someone sneaking out of a bedroom window late at night with a bag of stolen goodies. This is quite right. Such a person is likely to be a burglar. However, there is – as usual – more to the offence than this.

There are several ways to commit burglary. These come under the **Theft Act 1968 s 9(1)** which has 2 sub-sections.

Under **s9(1) Theft Act 1968** a person is guilty of burglary if:

**(a)** '*he enters any building or part of a building as a trespasser and with intent to commit any such offence as is mentioned in subsection (2) below; or*

**(b)** *having entered any building or part of a building as a trespasser he steals or attempts to steal anything in the building or that part of it or inflicts or attempts to inflict on any person therein any grievous bodily harm.*'

**S 9(2) Theft Act 1968** provides: '*The offences referred to in subsection (1)(a) above are offences of stealing anything in the building or part of the building in question, of inflicting on any person therein any grievous bodily harm and of doing unlawful damage to the building or anything therein.*'

(NB the original **s 9(2)** included rape but this was removed in 2004).

**Actus reus**

Much of the *actus reus* is the same for burglary under both (a) and (b). They differ only in the secondary offences, known as the 'ulterior' offences. Under (a), these are theft, grievous bodily harm, or criminal damage. Under (b) they are theft or grievous bodily harm. The main difference between the two is that for (a) D will be guilty without actually committing the ulterior offence. It is enough that the intention to do so is there. In (b) D must commit or attempt either theft or grievous bodily harm (but needn't have intended to do so at the time of entry, we'll come back to this with *mens rea*).

Let's look at the common elements first.

**enters**

Both types of burglary require entry as a trespasser. At common law, this included entry by any part of D's body or even an instrument used to remove property. This wide definition seems to have been rejected in **Collins 1972** where the court said entry had to be both 'effective and substantial'.

**Key case**

In **Collins,** D had had a few drinks. He climbed a ladder to a girl's bedroom and saw her lying naked in bed. He descended, took off his clothes (apart from his socks!), climbed the ladder again and sat on her window sill. She awoke and saw him. The story might have ended there had the girl not also had a few. She thought it was her boyfriend paying a night visit and got up and encouraged him in. They then had sex. At some point, she decided that it might not be her boyfriend. She turned on the light to find that she was right. She slapped him and told him to get out. He was charged with burglary under **s 9(1)(a)**. This meant the prosecution had to prove he entered as a trespasser with intent to rape (which was part of this section until 2004). He argued that he was outside when the girl asked him in so he didn't enter as a trespasser.

His conviction was quashed because the jury had not been properly directed. The CA held that the jury must be satisfied that entry was both "effective and substantial". Edmund Davies LJ said it was not enough that there was trespass at civil law. D had to have known, or at least been reckless as to the fact, that he was trespassing. On these rather unusual facts this was not clear. Had he still been on the ladder when she encouraged him it would not be entry as a trespasser. If he was in the room intending to have sex before this invitation it would be. Sitting on the window sill made it unclear whether he had 'entered' before or after he had been invited. Edmund Davies LJ said *"The point is a narrow one, as narrow maybe as the window sill which is crucial to this case"*.

Later, in **Brown 1985**, the CA said the word 'substantial' was unnecessary. Entry was proved even if D had not fully entered the building. Here D had the top half of his body inside a broken shop window. He argued that there was no entry and so no *actus reus*. His appeal against conviction was rejected.

The CA again considered the issue of entry in **Ryan 1996**. Here D had only his arm and head through a window. Unfortunately for him, he got stuck and had to be rescued by the fire brigade. Again, D's appeal was on the basis that entry was not proved. Again, it was rejected.

**Food for thought**

Even without the requirement of 'substantial', this type of entry hardly seems to be effective. He wasn't in any position to take anything. Will different juries have different ideas of what amounts to 'effective' entry? Should there be more certainty as to what amounts to 'entry'. Consider whether judges are using too much discretion and thus making the law uncertain.

**building or part of a building**

Note that **s 9** refers to part of a building. This means you may have permission to be in a building – and so not be a trespasser – but not to be in a particular part of it. If you enter that part, you will be entering 'part of a building' as a trespasser. You may therefore be charged with burglary if the rest of the *actus reus* and *mens rea* can be proved. A customer in a shop can commit burglary by going somewhere where customers are not permitted to go. A conviction was obtained in **Walkington 1979**, where D was in a department store and then went behind a counter where he opened a till. The court held that the counter area was a 'part of the building' and he did not have permission to be in that part of the building so had entered it as a trespasser.

In **Stevens v Gourley 1859**, Byles J defined a building as *"a structure of considerable size and intended to be permanent or at least endure for a considerable time"*.

**S 9(4)** adds that a building includes a vehicle or vessel that is inhabited. Thus, a camper van would be included. It does not have to be inhabited at the time of the burglary.

**Food for thought**

It is unclear what will amount to a 'building'. Two similar cases had different results. In **B & S v Leathley 1979**, a freezer container which had been in the same place for 3 years and was likely to remain there was found to be a building. In **Norfolk Constabulary v Seekings & Gould 1986**, a trailer with electricity and shutters used as a temporary store was not. This seems to be a fine distinction. The main difference seems to be that in the first, the wheels had been removed and in the second, they were still attached to the chassis. It can be argued that the jury has a difficult job in deciding whether something is a building without a clearer direction from the judge.

**as a trespasser**

Trespass is going somewhere without, or in excess of, permission. Look back at **Collins**. Note that D must be a trespasser at the time of entry.

**Example**

Susan is invited to a party. She has an argument with the host and is told to go. On her way out she steals a coat. She can't be convicted of burglary under either subsection because she did not enter as a trespasser. Now consider the difference if she had been told to go and then gone into a bedroom and stolen some jewellery. She has entered this part of the building (the bedroom) as a trespasser (she no longer has permission to be there) and can be charged with burglary.

As I said above **s 9** refers to part of a building so if you have permission to be in one part you can still be a trespasser in another part.

**Example**

In a pub, you are allowed in the bar but not the living quarters. If you went into the living quarters with intent to steal this would be burglary.

Although permission will usually mean there is no trespass it may still be burglary if D goes beyond that permission. In **R v Jones & Smith 1976**, D had left home but had permission to enter his father's house whenever he liked (his father said at the trial "*Christopher would not be a trespasser in the house at any time*"). He came one day with a friend and stole the television. The CA upheld his conviction for burglary. He had gone beyond the permission granted when he stole the television. As he entered with this in mind, he had entered as a trespasser. The opening quote was referred to with approval in this case although it actually came from a civil case. The same could apply to shops where you have permission to be there, but if you enter with intent to steal you have entered as a trespasser.

In **Walkington**, he had argued that he had not entered the shop as a trespasser. The court held that the counter area was a 'part of the building' where customers were excluded. He entered this part as a trespasser.

In **Laing 1995**, D was found hiding in the storeroom of a shop after closing time. His conviction was quashed because at the time he entered the shop it could not be proved he was a trespasser.

**Food for thought**

Compare **Walkington** and **Laing.** Why do you think the court did not treat the storeroom as 'part of a building' in **Laing**? It may be that it was because he had not entered the storeroom with intent to steal. He entered it as a trespasser but not with intent to steal from the storeroom, but from the shop itself.

Another difficulty with the *mens rea* for burglary is that it will be hard to prove what was in D's mind at the time of entry. Not all burglars carry a bag marked 'Swag'!

## Examination pointer

Burglary and theft may come up in the same question so look carefully at the given facts. In my example above, you would discuss burglary and conclude Susan could not be convicted of burglary as regards the coat. She could be charged with theft so you would go on to explain and apply the law on this.

### *Mens rea*

Both types of burglary require entry as a trespasser. Trespass is a civil law concept but for the criminal law, it requires *mens rea*. This is intent or subjective recklessness. You have *mens rea* if you knew or recognised the possibility that you were entering without, or in excess of, permission. This was confirmed in **Collins 1972**. Edmund Davies LJ said there could be no conviction for burglary *"unless the person entering does so knowing that he is a trespasser and nevertheless deliberately enters, or, at the very least, is reckless whether or not he is entering the premises of another without the other party's consent"*

## Task

Martin is asked by a householder to fit a kitchen. While working in the house he asks to go to the toilet. Once upstairs he sees the bedroom door open and decides to steal some jewellery. Has he committed burglary and if so which subsection would it come under? Will it make a difference if he doesn't actually take the jewellery?

## Summary of the common elements

**Entry as a trespasser**

**To a building or part of one**

**With mens rea of intent or recklessness**

Once it is proved that D entered a building (or part of one) as a trespasser (knowing this, or being reckless as to it) the *actus reus* and *mens rea* for the ulterior offence(s) must be considered.

## Actus reus and mens rea of the ulterior offence

In (a) only *mens rea* is needed. D will be guilty even if none of the ulterior offences is actually committed or attempted. It is enough that the intention to do one of them is there.

During the riots in the UK in August 2011 there were many looters, and potential looters, who were charged with burglary under **s 9(1)(a)**. As long as D entered a building as a trespasser with intent to steal, a charge of burglary will be appropriate even if nothing is actually taken. In one particular example an estate agent and two 22-year-old students were charged under **s 9(1)(a)** when they were found in PC World outside opening hours. Similarly a youth worker was charged with theft and burglary (entering with intent to steal) when found in possession of a £300 television in Comet. Remember though that the *mens rea* must exist at the time of entry.

**Task**

Look back at **Collins** again. At that time rape was included in **s 9(1)(a)**. At what point did he intend to commit this ulterior offence? If the court had found that he did enter as a trespasser do you think the prosecution would have been able to prove intent for a conviction under **s 9(1)(a)**?

In (b) D must commit or attempt one of the two ulterior offences (so will need both *actus reus* and *mens rea* for the ulterior offence), but needn't have intended to do so when entering.

In **R v Downer 2009**, the CA confirmed that in order to find out what constituted a burglary, it was essential to have regard to the two types of burglary described in (a) and (b) of **s 9(1)** of the **Theft Act**. The Ds had been arrested while still at the flat they were attempting to steal from, they had therefore committed an offence under **s 9(1)(b)**, i.e., having entered the flat as trespassers, they committed or attempted to commit theft.

**Food for thought**

Is the law on burglary too complicated? In **s 9(1)(a)** there must be intent to commit the ulterior offence at the time of entry, but there is no need actually to commit it. For (b) there is no need to prove intent but the ulterior offence must be attempted or committed. There are 3 ulterior offences in (a) and 2 in (b). It also seems odd to many people that you can be convicted of burglary without actually taking anything. Finally the inclusion of GBH in both subsections seems inappropriate in a property offence.

**Summary of the key issues**

> **Entry as a trespasser**
>
> **To a building or part of one**
>
> **With mens rea of intent or recklessness as to the trespass**

*Plus*

> **At the time of entry D has the mens rea of intent to steal, commit GBH or criminal damage for (a) but no further actus reus is needed.**
>
> **No intent at the time of entry is needed for (b) but actus reus and mens rea of theft or GBH (or attempt) are needed.**

Finally, intent to steal only if there is something worth having is enough. You don't need to intend to steal something specific. The CA in **AG's Reference Nos 1 & 2 1979** considered **Husseyn 1977** (a theft case) and held that conditional attempt could be enough as long as the indictment related to theft of unspecified items. In **Husseyn**, the D's had broken into a van containing a holdall with sub-aqua equipment in it. Their appeal against conviction for attempted theft was successful. The indictment had stated intent to steal sub-aqua equipment and as they did not know it was there, they could not be found to have intended to steal it. In **AG's Reference Nos 1 & 2 1979**, the CA did not overrule **Husseyn** but said it only applied where the indictment stated intent to steal something specific.

**Example**

Dave enters a building intending to steal something only if there is anything of value inside. There isn't anything worth having so Dave leaves empty-handed. This is enough for Dave to be charged with burglary under **s9(1)(a)** – as long as the charge is correctly worded. With intent to steal 'some or all of the contents' would suffice.

Burglary is an either-way offence, tried in either the magistrates' court or the Crown court, unless there is intent to commit GBH in which case it is indictable and can only be tried in the Crown court. The maximum sentence is 10 years or 14 if it is a 'dwelling', e.g., a private house.

## Task

Look at the following examples and decide if Paul can be charged with burglary. Look carefully at the *actus reus* and *mens rea* and the differences between burglary under (a) and (b). Ask yourself whether he entered with intent or whether he committed the *actus reus* of an ulterior offence. Then decide which subsection these would come under.

Paul comes into your house without permission as he is cold and wants to sleep. He notices a nice clock and takes it.

He again enters because he is cold and wants to sleep but smashes up some furniture to make a fire.

He goes to the house intending to steal but once inside gets scared and runs away.

## Summary

| Actus reus | | | S 9(1)(a) and (b) | Mens rea | |
|---|---|---|---|---|---|
| Entry | to a building or part of one | as a trespasser | | Intent or subjective recklessness as regards the trespass | |
| **S 9(1)(a)** | | | | **S 9(1)(b)** | |
| Actus reus | Mens rea | | | Actus reus | Mens rea |
| No further *actus reus* needed | Intent (to steal, commit GBH or commit criminal damage) | | | Steals or commits GBH | *Mens rea* for theft or GBH |
| | At the time of entry | | | | At the time of the ulterior offence |

## Examination pointer

If you see that a theft has occurred, look for clues which may indicate it is more than theft. If force is used it could be robbery. If it took place in a building, it could be burglary. Keep an open mind and discuss all the possibilities – as long as they are sensible and relevant to the question.

**Self-test questions**

*What are the 3 common elements for burglary under both subsections?*

*What is the mens rea for the above?*

*What are the 3 ulterior offences for s 9(1)(a)?*

*What are the 2 ulterior offences for s 9(1)(b)?*

*At what time does mens rea have to exist?*

For answers to the tasks and self-test questions, please go to my website at www.drsr.org and click the button 'Answers to tasks'. For a range of free interactive exercises, click on 'Free Exercises' and then the OCR book.

| Theft s1 Theft Act 1968 | | |
|---|---|---|
| s3 | *actus reus* | appropriation |
| s4 | | property |
| s5 | | belonging to another |
| s2 | *mens rea* | dishonesty |
| s6 | | intent to permanently deprive |
| Robbery s8 | *actus reus* | Theft PLUS force or the threat of it in order to steal |
| | *mens rea* | As for theft |
| Burglary | *actus reus* for both types of burglary | entry to a building or part of one as a trespasser |
| s 9(1)(a) | *mens rea* – no further *actus reus* needed | with intent to steal, inflict GBH or cause unlawful damage |
| s 9(1)(b) | *actus reus* – no further *mens rea* needed | steals or inflicts GBH, or attempts to do so |

**Task**

Note the principle and brief facts for the cases below

> *Gomez*
>
> *Woodman*
>
> *Ghosh*
>
> *Clouden*
>
> *Hale*
>
> *Collins*
>
> *Jones & Smith*

**Key criticisms**

> Conflicting cases on appropriation have left the law on theft uncertain
>
> D can be guilty of theft without actually taking anything
>
> The Ghosh test is difficult for juries
>
> D can be guilty of theft of wild plants and animals if e.g., they are used commercially
>
> The distinction between something lost and something abandoned may not be clear
>
> The force for robbery can be minor yet the maximum sentence is life imprisonment
>
> For burglary what is, and is not, a building remains unclear

## The burglary offences are unnecessarily complex

### Sample examination question

Discuss whether the law relating to dishonesty and appropriation in theft is now in a satisfactory state. 50 marks

### Special study unit – possible connections

Where you are asked to discuss developments in the law there is a lot of material within this study block to provide a base. The *Food for thought* sections can help you develop ideas for an evaluation of developments and the key criticisms will help you discuss particular cases critically.

The use of the rules of **precedent** can be discussed. Earlier cases were *distinguished* and the law developed in **Morris**. **Gomez** then overruled **Morris** on the issue of consent. In **Briggs** the CA didn't overrule **Gomez** but interpreted 'appropriation' more narrowly and noted that it was unlikely that Parliament would have created separate deception offences if they had intended appropriation to include situations where V is deceived into parting with something.

In relation to the interpretation of statute law, consider how far the intentions of Parliament when passing the **Theft Act** have been satisfied by judicial interpretation. The issues of appropriation and dishonesty in theft (**Gomez** etc. and **Ghosh**), and the use of force in robbery, as well as the flexible interpretation of 'at the time' seen in **Hale,** are all matters which can be discussed. A comparison of the literal and purposive approaches could be applied to these cases, and others. For example **Corcoran** and **Clouden** show that the courts have interpreted the requirement for force very widely. Prior to the Act the Criminal Law Revision Committee had said that snatching a bag from an unresisting owner would not suffice so it appears the intention of Parliament was narrower. In relation to burglary the issue of entry as a trespasser has caused some conflicting case law, so **Collins, Brown** and **Ryan** can be discussed in relation to the interpretation of **s 9(1)**. The interpretation of what will amount to a 'building' is seen in **B & S v Leathley** and **Norfolk Constabulary v Seekings & Gould.**

In **R v DPP; B v DPP 2007**, the court interpreted the **Theft Act** by looking at the intention of Parliament (a purposive approach)and held that it was the intention of D rather than the fortitude of V that was important. If this were not the case, guilt would be dependent on how brave, or not, the victim was. The court held that this was not what Parliament would have intended and not what the Act implied.

These are just a few ideas to show how the substantive law studied in this block relates to the more general issue of development of the law, and to highlight some cases which could be discussed critically.

Before looking at the questions, refer back to the section in the introduction headed 'Examinations'. This gives further information, e.g., how many questions you must answer in each paper. Note the marks available. The questions in the first two sections of the paper are worth 50 marks. The questions in the last section are only worth 20 marks. You should be careful to plan your time accordingly. You will have two hours to answer all three questions for a total of 120 marks. This paper represents 30% of the full course, i.e., 60% of the A2 part. (*The Special Study paper is 20% of the course, i.e., 40% of the A2*).

The marks are given for A01, A02 and A03 as follows:

**Section A:** 50 marks 25 for A01, 20 for A02 and 5 for A03

**Section B:** 50 marks 25 for A01, 20 for A02 and 5 for A03

**Section C**: 20 marks (5 per 'dilemma') all A02

The guides which follow each question provide a comprehensive range of what you could cover. Note, though, that other cases may have been heard since this was written. Although you are not expected to know the changes which occurred during the twelve months prior to the examination, an up-to-date knowledge will always enhance an answer. Also note that the guide may include cases you are not familiar with. This is because there may be several possible cases on a particular area; you are not expected to cite them all but you should refer to at least 8 cases for Level 5 marks in Sections A and B. Any cases which establish a precedent or indicate a development in the law are highlighted throughout this book as '**Key Cases**'. These are the 'must-know' cases. Other cases are important too because they highlight different issues. The more you know, the easier it will be for you to select a relevant case to fit the particular question. Section C does not require a specific number of cases and maximum marks are possible without any, though it may be easier to gain such marks if you use a relevant case because this shows you have recognised the issue and appropriate principle. The main point with these short scenarios is to use the appropriate law and logical reasoning to reach a firm and confident conclusion. It is entirely acceptable to use bullet points in your answers for Section C.

**Examination pointer**

When using a case in support you need to do more than merely refer to it, you need to develop it a little. This can be achieved in just a few words by reference to any *relevant* facts or to the principle (*ratio decidendi*) as appropriate.

**All questions are from the January 2013 papers**

*Note that only A01 and A02 are discussed as A03 will depend on these. E.g., for Level 5 A03 you need to get the equivalent of Level 5 for the other two added together (between 37 and 50 marks).*

*Section A: Essay Question*

The current law on involuntary manslaughter attracts criticism and needs to be reformed urgently.

Discuss the extent to which this statement is accurate.

50 marks

The following guide is just that: a guide. You do not need to include everything but this gives you a range of material to choose from. You should pick out those points that make most sense to you so that you can discuss them confidently. The sample answer and comments should help you to see what you need. However, remember that you should refer to at least 8 cases for Level 5 marks.

**Assessment Objective 1 (up to 25 marks)**

Explain that involuntary manslaughter has the *actus reus* of murder, the unlawful killing of a human being, but without the same level of *mens rea*

Define unlawful act/constructive manslaughter

There must be an unlawful act, which must be criminal – **Lamb**

The act must be dangerous, an objective test – **Church**

It must be an act not an omission – **Khan**

There must be a risk of physical harm – **Church/Dawson**

The unlawful act must cause death – **Cato/Dalby/Kennedy**

Explain the *mens rea* is that for the unlawful act

There is no need to foresee a risk of death, or even harm – **Nedrick**

Define gross negligence manslaughter – **Adomako/Misra**

There must be a duty of care – **Khan and Khan/Wacker/Evans**

There must be breach of duty – **Wacker/Warner/Wood and Hodgson**

There must be a risk of death – **Misra**

The death must have occurred as a result of the breach of duty – **Adomako** (thus the usual causation rules apply)

The breach must be sufficiently gross to be deemed criminal by the jury – **Adomako/Misra**

Define reckless manslaughter:

Explain that the *mens rea* is subjective recklessness – **Lidar**

**Assessment Objective 2 (up to 20 marks)**

Discuss some or all of the following issues:

Involuntary manslaughter covers a huge range of situations

The objective test as regards what is dangerous for unlawful act manslaughter means there can be liability even if D does not foresee a risk of harm; it is enough that a reasonable person would do so – **Church**

The unlawful act can be quite minor but it is a serious crime carrying a possible life sentence

There is no special *mens rea* for this type of manslaughter. It is the *mens rea* for the unlawful act

Gross negligence manslaughter is based on the civil duty of care which seems wrong in a serious criminal case

The overlap is between unlawful act manslaughter and gross negligence manslaughter is not always clear – **Khan/Willoughby**

The uncertainty can lead to confusion for juries and could result in different decisions based on similar facts

In 1996, the Law Commission suggested that involuntary manslaughter should be abolished: 'Legislating the Criminal Code: Involuntary Manslaughter (Report 237)'.

In 2006, the Law Commission suggested that the law on manslaughter should be amended: 'Murder, Manslaughter and Infanticide'

This suggests uncertainty not only in the law but also in the proposals for reform

With the later proposals, the offence of gross negligence manslaughter would remain unchanged so the problems would remain

However, unlawful act manslaughter would require a higher level of *mens rea* which seems more just

Reckless manslaughter appeared to have been abolished but was accepted in **Lidar**, again leading to uncertainty in the law

*You could include some of the following from the 'Food for thought' sections in Chapters 8 & 9 to develop these points.*

### Food for thought 1

Both **Church** and **Dawson** show that for an act to be deemed dangerous, there must be a risk of physical harm. It appears that this does not include psychiatric harm. In many other areas of law, physical harm has been extended to include psychiatric. It can be argued that 'dangerous' should include an act which could cause psychiatric harm. **Dawson** can be criticised on the basis that a robbery with imitation firearms could be construed as dangerous. The reaction of a victim to such a robbery could be unpredictable. Someone might decide to 'have a go' and this would certainly be dangerous, whether the guns were real or not.

### Food for thought 2

Whether the unlawful act is dangerous is an objective test, based on what a reasonable person would see as dangerous. It is not relevant that D didn't see it as dangerous. For such a serious offence it can be argued that a subjective test should be used.

### Food for thought 3

The Law Commission has criticised the fact that the *mens rea* for this type of manslaughter may be for some quite different offence. Manslaughter is a very serious offence but the *mens rea* may be for a minor crime, such as criminal damage. Arguably, manslaughter should have a *mens rea* of its own and D should at least be subjectively reckless about causing death or serious injury.

### Food for thought 4

In **Adomako**, the CA had set out a list of what type of conduct might be deemed sufficiently negligent. The HL rejected this on the basis that it could confuse juries who might think that only those situations would suffice. The HL thought it better to leave it to the jury to decide on the facts whether the conduct was sufficiently bad to be deemed criminal. It is therefore not at all clear what exactly does amount to criminal negligence. It is hard for a jury to decide what was sufficiently negligent if the law is not clear.

## Food for thought 5

Although on the facts, the conviction in **Willoughby** was upheld, it does highlight the difficulties. The overlap is not always clear. If the judge has trouble identifying whether it is gross negligence or unlawful act manslaughter, then arguably the law is still too uncertain, as argued in **Misra**. It is also unclear whether the civil test for duty is enough. It would seem so, but if it is, then another criticism is that it should not be. The functions of the criminal and civil law are very different.

You could also consider how far the law should impose a duty on a drug dealer to his client. Although the CA declined to find there was a duty in **Khan**, there could arguably have been a common law duty, as in **Stone and Dobinson**. The decision may be one of policy rather than law. Taking on responsibility for an invalid is sufficient, responsibility for a prostitute to whom D had supplied drugs is not. This is another area that needs clarification.

## Food for thought 6

In such a serious crime it is less than satisfactory that there is still confusion about whether reckless manslaughter exists, and if it does, whether the test is subjective or objective. Since **Gemmell & Richards** overruled **Caldwell** on recklessness as the *mens rea* for criminal damage it would appear that the HL prefers the subjective test. Arguably it is time the matter was addressed, either by the HL or by Parliament.

## Food for thought 7

Having such a serious crime relying on the common law for its development is questionable. The courts themselves have indicated it is the role of Parliament to create the law on such a major issue. The public have long called for change. The Law Commission proposals are no longer new. All these problems and calls for reform make this area a popular essay question. Another problem in relation to both types of involuntary manslaughter is that they cover such a wide range. The level of fault involved can vary enormously from something just short of intent to the virtually accidental. Justice requires greater clarity in the law. Even where changes have been proposed and accepted, the reforms have been not only been slow but arguably far too limited.

## Reforms

Use the section headed **Reforms** in Chapter 9 and the Task on the Law Commission proposals to develop this part of your answer.

## Conclusion

Finally, you need to add a conclusion briefly referring to your discussion and to the question as regards whether reforms are urgent.

### Section B: Problem question

Jonty and Patrick are professional jockeys riding in a race in which the prize money is £100,000. Before they get on their horses, Jonty goes up behind Patrick and hits him hard across the back of his head, making Patrick's head bleed. Patrick swears at Jonty and then says, "I'll make you sorry pal, that prize is mine!"

At the starting gate Jonty kicks Patrick. This makes Patrick's horse rear up and Patrick is thrown off, spraining his wrist. An official sees what Jonty has done and disqualifies him from the race. Jonty jumps off his horse and runs over to the official, grabs his jacket, and says, "If the TV cameras weren't here I'd beat you up!" Jonty runs back to where Patrick is sat on the ground and stamps on Patrick's ankle, breaking it.

Discuss the potential liability of Jonty and Patrick for non-fatal offences against the person, including any relevant defences.

50 marks

Again, remember that you should refer to at least 8 *relevant* cases for Level 5 marks.

**Assessment Objective 1 – Knowledge**

Explain assault and battery – common law but charged under **s 39 Criminal Justice Act 1988**.

Define assault as intentionally or recklessly causing another to apprehend immediate and unlawful violence – **Ireland/Constanza** (words are enough)

Note words can negate an assault – **Turbeville v Savage**.

Define battery as intentionally or recklessly inflicting unlawful force – **Collins v Wilcock/Thomas** (touching clothes is enough).

For both, the *mens rea* is intention or subjective recklessness as to the assault or battery.

Define assault occasioning actual bodily harm under **s 47 Offences against the Person Act 1861 (OAPA)**

Explain the three *actus reus* elements:

*An assault = assault or battery*

*Occasioning = causing*

*Actual bodily harm = something which interferes with health or comfort/is not trivial – Miller/Chan Fook*

Explain that *mens rea* is intention or recklessness but this is only needed for the assault or battery – **Roberts/Savage**.

Define unlawful and malicious wounding or inflicting/causing grievous bodily harm under **s 20 and s 18 OAPA**

*Explain the actus reus is the same for both. Either a wound or grievous bodily harm*

*Explain a wound must break all layers of the skin – Eisenhower*

*Explain grievous means really serious or merely serious harm – Smith/Saunders*

*Explain the mens rea for s 20 is intention or subjective recklessness but only for some harm not necessarily serious harm – Parmenter*

*Explain the mens rea for s 18 is intention only and must be for serious harm or with intent to resist arrest – Morrison*

Define the defence of consent

*Explain consent can be a full defence leading to acquittal usually only if within the rules of the game – Billingshurst*

***Even if outside the rules, the action must be sufficiently grave for the defence to fail –
Barnes***

## Assessment Objective 2 – Application

There are five different acts so it is best to take each separately. However, if any of the law applies more than once you can refer back.

### Jonty hitting Patrick across the back of the head

Explain this could be a wound under **s 18** or **s 20** because it bleeds which means all the layers of skin are broken – **Eisenhower**

Explain he hit him "hard" so there could be intention to cause serious harm making it **s 18** – **Mowatt**

Explain that even if it was hard to prove intention to cause serious harm he clearly intended at least some harm so **s 20** is satisfied – **Parmenter**

If the harm is not serious enough for **s 18** or **s 20** then **s 47** is certainly satisfied as there is more than trivial harm

Explain the act is nothing to do with the sport so the defence of consent is not available

Conclude Jonty is guilty of at least **s 47** and possibly **s 20** or **s 18**. The latter is possible as he hit him 'hard' and on the head

### Patrick swearing at and threatening Jonty

Explain assault can be by words alone – **Constanza**

Explain MR is intent or recklessness, i.e., if Patrick recognises a risk that Jonty would apprehend immediate and unlawful violence but goes ahead and takes that risk this is enough

This could be argued either way as it may be common behaviour among jockeys to swear

If so, it can be argued either that Patrick had no *mens rea* or that Jonty consented to the assault

The 'I'll make you sorry' seems more than this however and indicates Patrick has intention or at least subjective recklessness to cause Jonty to fear violence

Conclude that Patrick is likely to be guilty of assault

### Jonty kicking Patrick

Explain any touching can be battery (**Thomas**) and he clearly intends to do this so Jonty has the AR and MR of battery

Explain a sprained wrist would interfere with his comfort (**Miller**) and be more than trivial harm (**Chan-Fook**) so **s 47** is possible

Explain Jonty only needs MR for the initial battery not the harm – **Roberts/Savage**

As he intended the kick this is enough

Refer to the above discussion of consent (that the act is nothing to do with the sport so the defence of consent is not available)

Conclude he is guilty of **s 47** ABH

### Jonty grabbing the official by his jacket

Refer to the above that touching clothes is enough for battery (**Thomas**) and words is enough for assault (**Constanza**)

Explain that words can also negate an assault – **Turbeville v Savage**

As he says "If the TV cameras weren't here" this will apply as it suggests he will not beat him up because the cameras are there

Conclude that this means he is unlikely to be guilty of assault

**Jonty breaking Patrick's ankle**

Explain this is 'serious harm' – **Saunders**, so **s 20** or **s 18** apply

He clearly intends to harm him as he "runs back" to do it

The question is whether he intends some harm or serious harm

As he stamps on Patrick's ankle when Patrick is sitting down he may have sufficient MR for **s 18**

Conclude that if it can be proved he intended serious harm it will be **s 18** but if not he will certainly be guilty under **s 20** as he clearly intended some harm

*Section C: Dilemma question*

Marianna and Evgeny are students in the same accounting class. Every week Evgeny struggles to get his accounts right and Marianna always laughs at him. Marianna's behaviour makes Evgeny feel so depressed that his doctor sends him for counselling. Evgeny decides to punish Marianna for laughing at him. The next time Evgeny struggles with his accounts Marianna laughs at him again. When the class ends Evgeny grabs Marianna and punches her in the head several times. Marianna dies of a brain haemorrhage (internal bleeding).

Evaluate the accuracy of **each** of the four statements A, B, C and D individually, as they apply to the facts in the above scenario.

**Statement A:** Evgeny will not succeed with the defence of loss of self-control because he does not attack Marianna immediately.

**Statement B**: Evgeny will not succeed with a defence of loss of self-control because Marianna only laughs at him.

**Statement C**: Evgeny will succeed with a defence of loss of self-control because his actions were understandable for someone in his situation.

**Statement D**: Evgeny will succeed with a defence of diminished responsibility.

**Assessment Objective 2 – Reasoning and application**

**Statement A:**

Reason that there must be a loss of control

Reason that Evgeny loses control when he punches Marianna 'several times'

Reason that since the **Coroners and Justice Act** the loss of control need no longer be 'sudden'

Reason that though Evgeny waits until the end of the class the defence can still succeed

Conclude that the statement is inaccurate

(*Note that although you need to reach a firm conclusion there may be 2 possible answers. As long as you have been logical, and your conclusion is supported by your reasoning, either one will be fine. E.g., if you have argued that there is an element of revenge in the way Evgeny attacks Marianna, then the defence fails as revenge is specifically excluded under the* **Coroners and Justice Act**. *You can therefore conclude that the statement is accurate)*

**Statement B:**

Reason that a qualifying trigger for loss of control can be fear of serious violence or things done or said

Reason that laughing at Evgeny is something done

Reason that the things done or said must constitute circumstances of an extremely grave character and cause the defendant to have a justifiable sense of being seriously wronged

Reason that Marianna because only laughed at Evgeny this is not enough to be a qualifying trigger

Conclude that the statement is accurate

**Statement C:**

Reason that for loss of control D is compared to a normal person of the same age and sex and with a normal degree of tolerance and self-restraint

Reason that Evgeny is depressed and having counselling so may not have a normal degree of tolerance or self-restraint

Reason that the defence only succeeds if a 'normal person' would have reacted in the same or a similar way in D's circumstances

Reason that a normal person would not have punched Marianna in the head several times for being laughed at

Conclude that statement is inaccurate

**Statement D:**

Reason that for diminished responsibility D must have an abnormality of mental functioning arising from a recognised medical condition

Reason that depression is likely to be a recognised medical condition especially as he is sent for counselling

Reason that the abnormality of mental functioning must substantially impair his ability to understand the nature of his conduct, form a rational judgement or exercise self-control

Reason that Evgeny's ability to form a rational judgement or exercise self-control is substantially impaired because he punches Marianna several times

Conclude that the statement is accurate

*(Note that an alternative conclusion is again possible here. You could argue that Evgeny's ability to form a rational judgement or exercise self-control is not substantially impaired because depression is too minor. You would then conclude that the statement is inaccurate.)*

### Middle level answers for the essay and problem questions and how to improve them

*As you read the answers make a few notes as to how you think they could be improved in light of the above. There is a comment at the end of each on how to develop the answer to achieve the highest level so you can check this against your notes.*

**Essay question**

Involuntary manslaughter is the unlawful killing of a human being, but does not have the same level of *mens rea* as murder. There are two types, constructive manslaughter and gross negligence manslaughter. For the first there must be an unlawful act (which is why it is also called unlawful act manslaughter). This has to be a criminal rather than a civil act as seen in Lamb where there was not a criminal act so he was not guilty of manslaughter. However, although the act must be criminal manslaughter covers a lot of situations. The act could be quite minor like an assault or criminal damage. This seems wrong for such a serious crime. It must also be an act not an omission – Khan.

There must be a risk of harm. This has been confirmed in several cases including Church and Dawson. Both these cases show that there must be a risk of physical harm. This could be a criticism of the law because it does not include psychiatric harm. In many other areas of law, like the non-fatal offences against the person, harm includes psychiatric harm.

Another criticism of the law is that the *mens rea* is only for the unlawful act, as with the wide range of acts discussed above this seems wrong as it means someone can be guilty of a serious crime when they only intended to cause criminal damage or a minor assault. The Law Commission has criticised this so it shows the law is in need of reform.

The other type of manslaughter is gross negligence manslaughter. For this there must be a duty of care, breach of duty, a risk of death and the death must have occurred as a result of the breach of duty. These rules were set in Adomako and confirmed in Misra. The duty is the same as the civil duty of care. This is another criticism as it seems wrong in a serious criminal case.

There is no Act of Parliament covering either type of manslaughter and it can be said that having the law on such a serious crime being made by judges is wrong. It can also be said that there should only be one type so that the law is clearer. The overlap is between unlawful act manslaughter and gross negligence manslaughter is not always clear and it seemed wrong that in Khan neither applied because there was no duty and no unlawful act. They could easily have saved the girl's life just be calling an ambulance so should have been liable for her death.

Overall it is clear the law needs reforming.

**Comment**

*For Level 5 you need to have 8 cases, 6 of which are developed. Here there are only 6 cases and not enough development. Taking each paragraph in turn we can see where the answer can be improved on.*

*In the first paragraph **Khan** could be developed, so add the following; this brings in another three cases and expands on all of them, as well as **Khan** itself.*

The CA declined to find there was a duty in **Khan**, but there could arguably have been a common law duty, as in **Stone and Dobinson**, where they owed a voluntary duty of responsibility to his sister and were guilty of manslaughter. The decision in **Khan** can be seen as one of policy rather than law and this seems wrong, policy is a matter for Parliament rather than judges. That taking on responsibility for an invalid was sufficient in **Stone and Dobinson**, but responsibility for a prostitute to whom D had supplied drugs was not in **Khan** seems unjust. There is also an argument that there could be a duty based on the fact that, as stated in **Miller**, a duty is owed where D creates a dangerous situation. In **Evans**, the CA held that if a person created, or contributed to, a situation which was life threatening then a duty to take

187

reasonable steps to save that life would arise. This is not so different to **Khan** but the outcome was very different as she was guilty of manslaughter where the Khans were not. This can be criticised as another area that needs clarification and reform.

*A good point is made regarding psychiatric harm but a little more development of at least one of the cases and more evaluation would help here. In addition, there is no discussion of the fact that the act must be dangerous and this is what the risk of harm is relevant to. Add the following to the end of the second paragraph.*

The risk of harm shows that the unlawful act is dangerous, which is another element of the *actus reus*. It is an objective test based on what a reasonable person would see as dangerous as decided in **Church**. This can be criticised because it means there can be liability even if D does not foresee a risk of harm. For such a serious offence, it can be argued that a subjective test should be used. It may be fair to use an objective test in a case like **Church**, where D was guilty of manslaughter after throwing someone into a river, because not only would reasonable people see that such an act risks harm but D himself must have realised this. It would not seem so fair if D was someone very young or of limited intelligence, because they might not see the risk of harm even though reasonable people would. On the other hand, **Dawson** can be criticised because a robbery with imitation firearms could be construed as dangerous but the court decided it wasn't. The victim of a robbery might not know the firearms are imitation and their reaction could be unpredictable, so this type of act seems dangerous. If the law is unpredictable, it cannot achieve justice.

*The candidate refers briefly to the Law Commission but again this needs developing. Add the following to the end of the third paragraph.*

Arguably, manslaughter should have a *mens rea* of its own and D should at least be subjectively reckless about causing death or serious injury. In their report 'Murder, manslaughter and infanticide 2006' the Law Commission suggested that the law should be amended so that unlawful act manslaughter would involve killings caused by a criminal act where D intended to cause injury or foresaw a serious risk of causing some injury. If the suggested reforms were implemented this would go some way to solving this problem. However, although the Law Commission suggested abolishing manslaughter and replacing it with new offences back in 1996, their later report only suggests amending the law and does little to change anything on gross negligence manslaughter, so not only would the problems remain in this area, their change of approach itself indicates uncertainty.

*Finally, a conclusion is needed, briefly referring to the issues discussed and to the question as regards whether reforms are urgent. Here is an example.*

### Conclusion

As shown above there are many criticisms of the law on manslaughter and it has long been in need of clarification and reform. The Law Commission produced proposals for reform in 1996 but the government has concentrated on voluntary manslaughter reform and nothing has happened with involuntary manslaughter. The 2006 proposals from the Law Commission would require a higher level of *mens rea* for unlawful act manslaughter which seems more just, but gross negligence manslaughter would be unchanged so the problems would remain. Much needs to be done to meet the criticisms and I agree with the quote that the law is in need of urgent reform.

*Note that you can achieve Level 5 without reckless manslaughter.*

*A couple of other 'Food for thought' points which could be included instead are:*

In **Adomako**, the CA had set out a list of what type of conduct might be deemed sufficiently negligent. The HL rejected this on the basis that it could confuse juries who might think that only those situations would suffice. The HL thought it better to leave it to the jury to decide on the facts whether the conduct was sufficiently bad to be deemed criminal. It is therefore not at all clear what exactly does amount to criminal negligence. It is hard for a jury to decide what was sufficiently negligent if the law is not clear.

Although on the facts, the conviction in **Willoughby** was upheld, it does highlight the difficulties. The overlap is not always clear. If the judge has trouble identifying whether it is gross negligence or unlawful act manslaughter, then arguably the law is still too uncertain, as argued in **Misra**. It is also unclear whether the civil test for duty is enough. It would seem so, but if it is, then another criticism is that it should not be. The functions of the criminal and civil law are very different.

## Problem question

There are several different non-fatal offences here so I shall explain them and then apply them to the different situations.

Assault is intentionally or recklessly causing another to apprehend immediate and unlawful violence, this definition was confirmed by the HL in Ireland. Battery is intentionally or recklessly inflicting unlawful force, it can be slight and even include touching clothes as stated in Thomas.

ABH comes under s 47 Offences against the Person Act 1861 (OAPA) and requires either an assault or battery which then causes harm. Harm means something which interferes with health or comfort as stated in Miller. It can be psychiatric as long as it is not trivial – Chan Fook.

The two more serious offences come under s 20 and s 18 OAPA. These are unlawful wounding and causing grievous bodily harm. The actus reus for both is either a wound or grievous bodily harm. A wound must break all layers of the skin – Eisenhower and grievous bodily harm means serious harm – Saunders. The *mens rea* for s 20 is intention or subjective recklessness but only for some harm not necessarily serious harm – Parmenter. The *mens rea* for s 18 is intention to cause serious harm.

The only appropriate defence is consent. This often applies in sporting situations but maybe not when it is outside the rules of the game as stated in Billingshurst.

When Jonty hits Patrick this could be a wound under s 18 or 20 because it bleeds. Even if the harm is not seen as serious enough there is more than trivial harm so a charge of ABH will succeed.

When Patrick swears at Jonty he commits an assault. Patrick seems to intend for Jonty to fear violence because he says 'I'll make you sorry'

Jonty kicking Patrick can be either battery or ABH. If touching clothes can be battery kicking someone certainly is. He clearly intends to kick Patrick so has both the AR and MR of battery. It is likely to be ABH however, as described above, because a sprained wrist clearly interferes with his comfort.

When Jonty breaks Patrick's ankle he has caused serious harm so the AR of grievous bodily harm under both s 20 and s 18 is satisfied. He clearly intends to harm him as he runs back to do it and then stamps on him. The difference between the two sections lies in what sort of harm he intended, if he intended serious harm it will be s 18 but if it can only be proved that he intended some harm it will be s 20, as stated in Parmenter.

## Comment

It is fine to explain the various non-fatal offences and the defence first and then apply them separately. However, if you do it this way be sure you *use* the law you have explained when applying it. The explanations above are good so for A01 the candidate would be in the highest level. It is the lack of reference to the specific law and the actual scenario which has brought this answer down, because there is insufficient application for high A02 marks. One final point: it is fine to use abbreviations like ABH, but these should be written in full the first time, i.e., the first mention should say assault occasioning actual bodily harm (ABH).

More is needed as regards Jonty hitting Patrick as follows:

Reference back to the definitions of 'wound' and 'ABH'

Reference to the scenario, i.e., that he hit him 'hard' and on the 'back of the head', suggesting an intention to cause serious harm and so **s 18**. It certainly shows intent to cause at least some harm so **s 20** is satisfied

Reference back to the defence of consent

Conclusion that the act is nothing to do with the sport and is sufficiently grave (**Barnes**) so the defence will fail

Similarly, with the assault a reference back to the explanation that it can be by words alone will make it clearer that the candidate is using the *relevant* law.

For the kick the discussion of battery is fine, as is the AR of ABH, but an important point with **s 47** is that *mens rea* is only needed for the assault or battery. Reference to **Roberts/Savage** is needed and a conclusion that as he intended the kick (a battery) and caused harm (a sprain) **s 47** is satisfied as to both AR and MR.

The candidate has missed one of the situations altogether, when Jonty grabs the official and threatens him, which constitutes both a battery and an assault. The following is needed:

Reference back to **Thomas** as regards touching clothes being enough for battery, and application to the scenario (grabbing the jacket)

Reference back to **Ireland** or **Constanza** to the effect that words can amount to an assault

Explanation and application of the decision in **Turbeville v Savage** that words can negate an assault.

A conclusion that because he says "If the TV cameras weren't here" this means he will not beat him up so there is no assault.

Finally, Jonty breaking Patrick's ankle is dealt with very well with reference to the relevant parts of the AR & MR and to the scenario. Had all five scenarios been dealt with in a similar way this would be a Level 5 answer.

**Introduction**

This Study Block covers the Special Study Units. We will look at the requirements that apply in general, rather than to specific areas, as the selected topic of substantive law is now changed each academic year, and the actual questions change at each examination session (of which there is only one from 2014, in June). So this Chapter is a general guide on to how to approach the Special Study paper. You will be given a booklet (the source material) which contains materials such as extracts from judgments or Acts of Parliament, and academic articles on specific areas of law (the substantive law). Copies of these booklets will be provided for all students, by the examination board. This pre-released copy of the special study booklet can't be taken into the examination – you will probably have written lots of notes on it. However, a clean copy will be issued in the examination, along with the question paper.

The special study paper requires a critical approach, not just repeating knowledge. Knowledge is still important but it is what you do with it that matters. You need to show that you understand the significance of the overarching theme in developing the particular area of law being studied and the significance of individual cases. You also need to do this in a critical way and in the context of the role of judges and the development of the law.

You will be expected to understand and explain how the law has developed in the particular area of study. All subject areas will have been dealt with thoroughly in their respective Chapters. Here is a short summary of what you should do when you get the source material.

> *Read the source material thoroughly*
>
> *Make sure you understand the particular theme*
>
> *Make notes on the issues and the particular cases discussed*
>
> *Look at the food for thought sections in the chapters which cover the relevant area of study and the key criticisms in each study block summary*
>
> *Read the mark scheme carefully (but note that this is not prescriptive, you may add other material or use other cases to support what you say)*

For more information on the examination, see the next chapter and the introduction to this book.

For current examples of the source materials, question papers and mark schemes go to the OCR website www.ocr.org.uk

*"the role of judges, precedent and the application of statutory materials and development of the law."*

OCR explaining the overall theme for the Special Study Units

By the end of this Chapter, you should be able to:

**Recognise the link between the substantive law and the legal process**

**Show how the law is developed through precedent and statutory interpretation**

**Identify other influences on law reform, such as the Law Commission and the Human Rights Act**

The special study Units are based on materials contained in a special study booklet. Copies of these will be sent to centres at the beginning of the course. Each booklet contains material on a specific area (or areas) of the law, the 'source material'. This will include things like extracts from judgments and Acts of Parliament, together with academic articles. This material will indicate the area of substantive law to be tested. You will need to have a good understanding of the relevant area and be able discuss judicial and statutory developments. You will also need to analyse and select the appropriate law in order to apply it. The paper contains three questions and you *must answer all of them*. For this reason, you should never be tempted to try to spot what questions you might be asked. It is very dangerous, even in papers where you have a choice.

The Special Study paper represents 20% of the full course, i.e., 40% of the A2 part.

You will have plenty of time to become familiar with the 'source material'. Make sure you get to know any cases discussed well, and recognise any particular legal issues surrounding that case, and any relevant Acts. You may not know what the questions will be, but if you know the material well you shouldn't go wrong. The examiner will be looking to see if you have grasped the finer details of the cases and are able to discuss the issues addressed in a logical and coherent way. The main thing is to realise that there is no new material to learn here. What you need to do is relate what you already know to the wider issues of how, and possibly why, the law has developed, and to specific legal issues and problems raised by a particular situation.

For the Special Study paper, only 32.5% of the marks are available for AO1 but AO2 is worth 57.5% of the marks. This recognises the fact that the area of study is narrower and that the source material booklet provides a great deal of support to candidates, so the emphasis is on how you use the material rather than on your knowledge. The remaining 10% of the mark is for AO3.

There will be **three** questions; two essays and a problem question in three parts. *You must answer all three*.

Time management is important as the questions carry different marks, as follows.

*Question 1 = 16 marks (12 AO2 and 4 AO3)*

*Question 2 = 34 marks (16 AO1, 14 AO2 and 4 AO3)*

*Question 3 = 30 marks (10 for each part of the question) (10 AO1 and 20 AO2)*

You should therefore aim to apportion your time accordingly. If you plan on 15 minutes for the first question and around 30 minutes for each of the other two, you should have up to 15 minutes left for reading through and adding to your answers if needed.

The essays will test how well you can evaluate the issues. The first essay is purely evaluative (there is no A01 mark for this). You may need to discuss, e.g., how a case represents a development in the area of law under discussion and any problems surrounding it.

To gain maximum marks you need to be able to explain in detail the key critical point of the case and two other analytical points, both in the context of the question and of the overarching theme. You will also need to discuss any development by reference to an appropriate linked case. You could prepare for a discussion of the development by looking at the time-line to see where the case fits in and what came before or after it.

**Examination pointer**

When answering the first question try to pick out the key words such as 'significance' or 'importance' and use them in your answer. Also be sure to explain where the case fits in the development of the law, by reference to earlier and/or later cases on the critical point raised.

The second essay question is based on a quote from the source material and requires a mix of knowledge and evaluation. You may need to explain the law and then discuss some of the criticisms and/or developments of it in the context of the role of judges, precedent, statutory interpretation and how these affect the development of the law. A high level of analysis of the discussion indicated in the question is required for maximum marks, as well as reference to eight linked cases of which six need to be well developed. These can include cases in the source material but you should bring in one or two others to show you have done your research.

**Examination pointer**

When answering the second question you should provide a critical discussion with a balanced argument and reasoned conclusion. The quote used in the question is there to help you identify the theme so use this as a base for your analysis and refer to it in a brief introduction to show you have identified the theme. Reference to the source material is important but this can be purely a line reference, the main thing is to ensure it is relevant to the question asked.

The third question will have three very short scenarios raising specific issues. They are often based on decided cases, perhaps with a slight difference which you are expected to notice. So be logical, state the relevant law accurately, then apply it to the given facts and finally reach a conclusion based on that application.

As each scenario will usually only focus on one issue (unlike G153) you will need to be selective. You will be expected to identify the issues and pick out the relevant law to apply to the facts in order to resolve these issues. You can refer to information given in previous answers, but will not be credited a second time for repeating it. So if you have discussed the actual law earlier, refer to that and then apply it to the facts.

**Example**

Don is being charged with causing actual bodily harm. The injury he caused occurred during a rugby match when he made a late tackle and caused another player to fracture his wrist.

The issue here is whether Don can rely on the defence of consent. You might have already explained this defence in an earlier question. If so, say "Don may rely on the defence of consent, as discussed above. Here the injury occurred within a sporting context so he may succeed." Then expand a little on the *relevant* issues using the *relevant* cases in support of your statement (e.g., that it was 'a properly conducted sport' and occurred 'during' the match (**AG's Reference** and **Billingshurst**)), then consider whether the injury was intended, the amount of harm caused and whether the conduct was sufficiently grave – **Brown** and **Barnes**). Then conclude that although it was a "late tackle" it was during the game and unlikely to be seen as sufficiently grave (**Barnes**) so Don is likely to succeed with this defence. You are not just stating the law you have already discussed but are *using* it in order to apply it appropriately and come to a conclusion based on that application.

For maximum marks, you should identify the critical point at issue, include two or three points of application with a case for each point and reach a logical conclusion, as in my example.

### Examination pointer

Unlike G153, these are short individual problem scenarios based on the source material so the structure is virtually created by the question. You should identify the key facts then define the appropriate law accurately (using definitions from judicial decisions or statutory provisions). Then apply the law sensibly to the facts and reach a sustainable conclusions based on your application. Note that OCR requires you to have at least '50% commitment'. This means that your conclusion should be positive so you need to apply the relevant law the best you can in order to reach a firm conclusion one way or the other. If you have doubts, e.g., there may be an issue with conflicting case law, explain the issue and use the appropriate case to support your conclusion that 'on balance it is likely that the prosecution/defence will succeed/fail'. As long as the case you use supports your conclusion, you will gain the marks.

Once you have identified the area of law and started to become familiar with the source material you can prepare to analyse the cases and any developments in the law. Use the food for thought, summaries and any diagrams showing the legal developments in the relevant Chapters and the key criticisms and Special Study connections, including any proposals for reform, in the Study Block summaries. Also look back at the tasks in the relevant area, especially where you were asked for arguments for and against a particular point, these will help you to produce a balanced argument. The focus is on A02 so you need to show that you can critically analyse and evaluate the material for the essays and apply the law in a logical and coherent way for the problem scenarios. You will be credited for your own ideas, in fact these are welcomed, as long as you keep to the relevant issue and support what you say, e.g., by reference to a linked case and/or to whether justice has been achieved.

### Summary of the first steps

*The development of the law*

Although the subject matter changes each time, there are ways to approach the overarching theme which will not change. When you have the source materials consider them in the light of the following:

*Whether the law under discussion is judge-created or statutory or a mixture of both*

*Whether the law achieves justice*

*Whether the law has been consistent or subject to change*

*Whether the law has changed due to social/technological changes or because an earlier case was seen as wrong*

*Whether the law has developed:*

*By following the rules of precedent*

*By use of mechanisms such as the Practice Statement to avoid following precedent*

*By interpretation of a statute by judges*

*Whether development of the law has been restricted by judges (literal rule, stare decisis)*

*Whether public policy has been taken into account (the public interest)*

*Whether any interpretation of a statute has been effective/achieved justice*

*Whether any developments made by judges have been followed by parliamentary reforms*

*Whether the law is still in need of reform*

What follows will expand on these issues so that you can then apply them to the particular subject matter for the current year.

Before going on, do the task and keep this for reference for when you go on to look at the source material for your area of study. I am only going to outline the rules here as you should already know them, but you will need to refresh your memory.

**Task**

Look back at your notes on the English legal system and process. Draw a diagram showing the main rules of precedent and how these may be avoided (Practice Statement, distinguishing etc.). Then add a case on each. Keep this as a base on which to build some ideas about how far judges are developing the law.

### Judicial development

Judges may develop the law in several ways. These relate to the rules of precedent and statutory interpretation. Let's take a brief look at how these can be used to change and develop the law in line with social and technological changes.

### Precedent

The main rule of precedent is *stare decisis*. This means judges should follow what went before and treat like cases alike. Precedents set in the higher courts must be followed in all the courts below. Although Privy Council decisions are not *strictly binding* because it is outside the court hierarchy, they are made by Law Lords so can be highly *persuasive*. In relation to the then defence of provocation, in **Holley** the Privy Council rejected **Smith** and said D was to be judged against a person having "*ordinary powers of self-control*". This decision was followed in **James; Karini 2008** by the CA. The **Coroners and Justice Act 2009** has now put **Holley** into statutory form in the new defence of loss of control, which refers to a person with "*a normal degree of tolerance and self-restraint*". This shows that development of the law by judges may later be reflected in an Act of Parliament.

There are many ways to avoid following a precedent which allow for development of the law.

Overruling earlier cases by a higher court or use of the **1966 Practice Statement** by the HL or SC are obvious examples of how judges may change the law on a particular area. The **Practice Statement** allowed the HL to overrule its own earlier decisions if '*it appears right to do so*'. This gives a wide discretion and allows an old law to be changed and a new one created, an example being **Gemmell & Richards**. In **Edwards v Environment Agency 2011**, the SC confirmed that it had all the powers previously invested in the HL. So the powers given under the **1966 Practice Statement** have passed to the SC. The **Young** rules allow the CA to overrule its own earlier decisions in certain circumstances, but these are limited, so lead to fewer major developments. Lord Denning wanted the use of the **Practice Statement** to extend to the CA, but he was criticised by many other judges for this view.

Distinguishing gives a wide discretion and allows for development of the law where the material facts are different. Which facts are material may depend on the judge's view so whilst this allows for flexibility, it could also lead to uncertainty in the law. Professor Goodhard said, "*It is by his choice of material facts that the judge creates law*".

One problem with precedent is that the *ratio decidendi* can be difficult to find, especially if the judgment is complex or the reasoning obscure. In the appellate courts, decisions are based on the majority view, so there are several judgments and the reasons for the decision may differ. Judges may agree what the decision *is* but not *why*, thus producing conflicting *ratios*. This allows the later judge to choose which to follow, again allowing for flexibility but with consequential uncertainty. In **Brown**, it can be argued that the *ratio* was either that a person cannot consent to **serious harm** or that a person cannot consent to **intentional** harm.

## Task

Take another look at your notes on the English legal system and process. Now draw a diagram showing the main approaches to interpretation, with a case on each. Don't forget to add the extrinsic (external) and intrinsic (internal) aids to interpretation. Again keep this as a base on which to build some ideas about how far judges are developing the law and whether, in doing so, the intention (or supposed intention) of Parliament is being fulfilled.

## Statutory interpretation

The **literal approach** would indicate that judges are restricted in developing the law. If the **literal rule** is used the words of an Act are followed strictly. Although the **golden rule** applies if the literal rule leads to absurdity, this is still somewhat limited.

The **purposive approach** is an extension of the **mischief rule,** which asks what mischief an Act was passed to remedy. The purposive approach is wider, as it looks at the Act as a whole, and at the intentions of Parliament at the time the Act was passed. Why did it pass the Act, for what purpose? This approach was much favoured by Lord Denning, who led many judicial developments. It allows the law to develop to meet social and technological changes and can mitigate the harshness of the literal rule. In **R v R**, the HL interpreted the **Sexual Offences Act 1956** in a creative way, and held that a man could be guilty of raping his wife. Until this case, it was not rape as a wife was deemed to consent to sexual intercourse by marrying. Lord Keith said that the common law was *"capable of evolving in the light of changing social, economic and cultural developments"*. However, although the purposive approach allows for greater discretion, and thus development, it is arguable that judges are putting their own values on what they think Parliament intended, and so do not always reflect those intentions in their interpretation. How can a judge know what Members of Parliament were thinking when passing an Act? This is particularly true when interpreting an old Act, as what Members of Parliament intended some years previously may not be apparent in the light of changed circumstances and social values. It is difficult to know what the intention of Parliament was when the **Offences against the Person Act 1861** was passed for example.

It seems, though, that this approach is finding more favour than the more traditional literal approach. In **Pepper v Hart 1993**, Lord Griffiths said *"the days have long passed when the courts adopted a strict constructionist view of interpretation"*. This case was a development in itself, as judges are now allowed to consult Hansard, which reports the debates in Parliament during the passing of the Act. This aid to interpretation may help to ascertain the intentions of Parliament. The purposive approach was seen in **Clinton 2012**, where the CA interpreted the **Coroners and Justice Act** as excluding sexual infidelity if it was the only trigger relied on, but allowing it to be taken into account as one of the circumstances of D under **s 54(1)**. To do this they referred to various speeches in Parliament during the passing of the Act and looked at the Act as a whole when interpreting a section of it, a purposive approach to the legislation.

The various extrinsic and intrinsic aids can both assist in development and stifle it. Looking at other sections of the Act (intrinsic) would help to find its purpose, as would consulting Hansard (extrinsic), whereas the use of a dictionary (extrinsic) is likely to be favoured by judges using the literal approach, but this may not reflect the intentions of Parliament.

## Task

Choose a case from your area of study which is governed by an Act of Parliament. Apply the literal and purposive approaches and see whether you come to different results depending on the approach used. Consider which one you feel is best reflecting the intentions of Parliament.

Finally, under **s 3** of the **Human Rights Act,** judges must consider the **European Convention on Human Rights** when interpreting statutes. This could lead to development of the law, particularly in areas which appear to restrict a person's freedoms in some way. An example is **Murray v Express Newspapers** where JK Rowling won a case brought on behalf of her young son against a photographic agency for publishing secretly taken photographs of him. This was held to infringe his right to privacy under **Article 8 ECHR** although there is no specific right to privacy in English law.

## Examination pointer

When looking at an Act which is referred to in the source material, ask yourself what you think Parliament's intentions were when it was passed. Try to identify the purpose behind the Act, or the relevant section of the Act. You not only need to evaluate the law but also to focus on specific parts of it, so that you can apply it effectively. Look back at the Chapters which cover the particular area of law under discussion and make some notes on the relevant statutes.

### *Parliamentary development*

Although judicial developments are important, you may also need to discuss parliamentary (or statutory) reforms. Sometimes both judicial and statutory developments can be connected to the same area of law. It is quite usual for any major judicial developments to be followed by an Act of Parliament (as with **Holley** and loss of control above). This reasserts the position of Parliament as the supreme law-maker.

## Example

The case of **R v R 1991** was an important *judicial development*. The HL accepted that a man could be convicted of raping his wife. This had not previously been the law as, until this case, a wife was deemed to consent to intercourse by marrying. The decision led to *Parliament* reforming the **Sexual Offences Act**. This put the judicial development on a statutory footing. The case is also an example of *judicial precedent* set whilst *interpreting* this Act of Parliament.

Make sure you are aware of how the law has developed through Acts of Parliament or Regulations in the particular area covered in the Special Study booklet. When you read the source material, note any Acts that are mentioned and ensure you know what the law was before this – and after, if there have been further developments.

Some areas of law are a mix of common law and statute. Once an Act is passed it still has to be interpreted in court, so not only does Parliament sometimes follow up on a judicial development (as in **Holley**), but also the courts will follow up and develop statutes – as we saw with **Clinton** in statutory interpretation above. Another example is the law on attempt. Before the **Criminal Attempts Act 1981**, there was no offence if the crime was impossible to commit. In **Anderton 1985**, the HL held that a person was not guilty of handling stolen goods when the goods were not stolen, which did not seem to be in line with the **Act**. The following year the HL overturned this decision in **Shivpuri**, and found a person who smuggled vegetable matter believing it to be illegal drugs could be guilty of attempting to deal in drugs. More recently, in **Pace and Rogers 2014**, the CA held that the *mens rea* for attempt was intent to commit the offence and this meant all the elements of the offence, including that it is in fact criminal property.

## The Law Commission

Another major influence on parliamentary law reform is the Law Commission. The Law Commission's proposals for reform, in the form of a report, will often be attached to a Bill, which may later become an Act. Areas where the Commission is active have been highlighted in the chapters on the substantive law and in the summaries. Look back at these for the particular topic under discussion in the source material and check any recent developments on the Law Commission website. The home page is at http://lawcommission.justice.gov.uk/.

Links to specific pages sometimes change so look under the various headings, such as the A-Z of projects or consultations to find what you need.

## Task

Go to the Law Commission website and make a note of any proposals for reform relating to your area of study. Keep this for a discussion of the developments of the law and note down a few quotes to help with your critical analysis of it.

## Examination pointer

Don't forget that the Special Study unit has a focus on A02 and requires you to analyse and evaluate the law. Look for controversial cases as these will be good ones to use to support an argument for or against judicial developments. In particular, look out for the use of judicial discretion (overruling, distinguishing, purposive approach etc.). Consider both the failures and successes of any developments, or lack of development. You can discuss how application of the rules has led to the development of the law or stifled development, and comment on how far this has achieved:

> *justice*

> *certainty*

> *the intended purpose of any Act of Parliament*

You should also look at any statutory developments critically, and be able to discuss whether or not these have clarified the law.

## Task

As you read over the substantive law on the area covered in the source material, note the role of the Law Commission in any reforms, or proposals for reform. Add any case developments to your notes, including any cases where an Act of Parliament has been interpreted in a way which has developed the law. Keep this for reference.

## Examination pointer

You will need a good knowledge and understanding of the relevant area of law so make sure you are fully aware of developments and any problems. However, you must remember to focus on the specific points raised by the question. The ability to be selective will be rewarded.

A final point is that you should *use* the source material. You should not just repeat what is there but refer to it (a line reference is fine, don't write it out as you will only be credited with how you analyse or evaluate it, not for repeating it). When given a case to discuss you will see that the material includes other linked cases, so these should be brought into your analysis and evaluation, with reference to how one case may have developed another or been developed by an Act of Parliament (possibly after recommendations by the Law Commission).

**Summary: The examination**

There are three questions on this paper and you must answer all three.

**Question 1** is an essay question which requires an analysis of the contribution of one of the cases from the source material to the development of the law.

**Question 2** is an essay question based on a quote from the source material. This requires a critical discussion with a balanced argument and reasoned conclusion together with supporting law, all in the context of the development of the law.

**Question 3** is a problem question comprising three parts. You will be given three short scenarios and will need to identify the relevant law and apply it to the facts in order to reach a logical conclusion.

Time management is important as the questions carry different marks.

**Question 1** = 16 marks

**Question 2** = 34 marks

**Question 3** = 30 marks

Remember that there are three assessment objectives which the examiners will follow when marking – see the introduction to this book but note that the focus is on AO2 for this Unit.

**Summary: How the law may be developed**

**Self-test questions**

*If the main rule of precedent is to follow what went before how can precedent be said to aid development of the law?*

*How might use of the literal or purposive approach mean arriving at a different decision on the same facts?*

*How might the Human Rights Act lead to a development of the law?*

*How might use of the literal rule stifle development?*

*Explain two particular judicial developments in your area of study*

*Explain two particular statutory developments in your area of study*

For answers to the tasks and self-test questions, please go to my website at www.drsr.org and click the button 'Answers to tasks'. For a range of free interactive exercises, click on 'Free Exercises' and then the OCR book.

**Summaries of how the law may be developed using precedent and statutory interpretation**

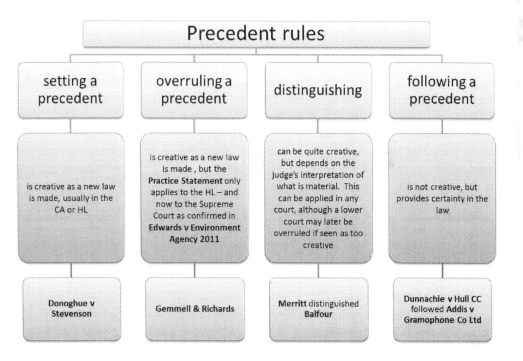

# Precedent rules

| setting a precedent | overruling a precedent | distinguishing | following a precedent |
|---|---|---|---|
| is creative as a new law is made, usually in the CA or HL | is creative as a new law is made, but the **Practice Statement** only applies to the HL – and now to the Supreme Court as confirmed in **Edwards v Environment Agency 2011** | can be quite creative, but depends on the judge's interpretation of what is material. This can be applied in any court, although a lower court may later be overruled if seen as too creative | is not creative, but provides certainty in the law |
| **Donoghue v Stevenson** | **Gemmell & Richards** | **Merritt** distinguished **Balfour** | **Dunnachie v Hull CC** followed **Addis v Gramophone Co Ltd** |

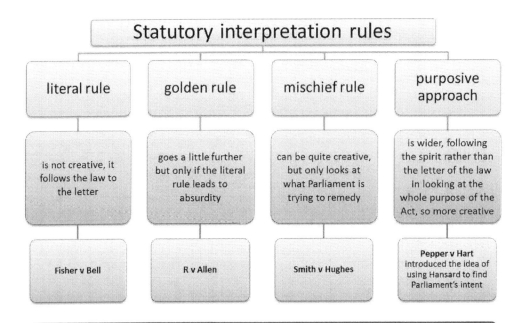

# Statutory interpretation rules

| literal rule | golden rule | mischief rule | purposive approach |
|---|---|---|---|
| is not creative, it follows the law to the letter | goes a little further but only if the literal rule leads to absurdity | can be quite creative, but only looks at what Parliament is trying to remedy | is wider, following the spirit rather than the letter of the law in looking at the whole purpose of the Act, so more creative |
| Fisher v Bell | R v Allen | Smith v Hughes | Pepper v Hart introduced the idea of using Hansard to find Parliament's intent |

Should judges make law? Balance the roles of the courts and Parliament.

## Unit G154: Special study examination practice

These questions are from the 2013 OCR papers. Note the marks: the second question earns more than double the first so you will need to plan your time accordingly, as discussed earlier.

For copyright reasons I cannot reproduce the source material here, but it contains quotes from judgments in the following cases

*Quick*

*Burgess*

*Bratty*

plus three extracts from academic texts.

As the source material is not here to look at, I have not made too many references to it in the sample answers. You are encouraged to use it however, and it can save you time. The judgments will include quotes from a particular judge in a case and I have included a few of these within this text book. The academic articles include an author's comments on the law and this type of thing is found in the 'Food for thought' sections here.

The three questions are followed by a guide on what you should include. For question 3, the short problems, these represent higher-level responses. For each of questions 1 and 2 (the essays) I have followed the guide with a middle-level response and then comments on how this could be improved to reach Level 5.

## Question 1

Discuss the relevance of the case of Bratty v Attorney General for Northern Ireland [Source 5 Page 6 Source Material] to the development of the law in relation to automatism

16 marks

*There is no A01 mark for this, so marks are all given for analysis and evaluation (A02) and whether this is logical and coherent (A03).*

The critical point (up to 3 marks) is the definition of automatism which developed the defence. Reference can be made to the source material for the definition, which is Lord Denning's judgment in **Bratty**. He said that 'the requirement that it should be a voluntary act is essential' and that 'no act is punishable if it is done involuntarily.' He then described an involuntary act as 'an act which is done by the muscles without any control by the mind such as a spasm, a reflex action or a convulsion; or an act done by a person who is not conscious of what he is doing such as an act done whilst suffering from concussion or whilst sleepwalking'. Thus, the act must be caused by an external factor, with no control by the mind.

Additional points (up to 6 marks) can include two or more of the following.

*Note that the additional points can be six single points, three points which are developed, two points which are well developed or a combination of these up to a maximum of 6 marks.*

The fact that Lord Denning said insanity is a mental disorder which has 'manifested itself in violence and is prone to recur' which suggests it does not apply to one-off occurrences which do not pose a continuing danger, unlike automatism.

That if the only cause of the involuntary act was a defect of reason caused by a disease of the mind this would be insanity and the alternative defence of automatism would not apply. A trial judge would be right in not leaving that defence to the jury.

That there here are two types of automatism, namely, insane and non-insane automatism. Whether automatism of either type should be left to the jury is a question of law for the judge to decide based on the evidence.

That an act will not be seen as involuntary only because D cannot control the impulse to do it.

That it does not amount to automatism if the lack of awareness was not total – **Attorney-General's Reference (No2 of 1992) 1994**

That the burden of proof with automatism is on the prosecution to prove it was a voluntary act. The standard of proof is beyond all reasonable doubt. This contrasts with insanity where the burden of proof is on D, on the balance of probabilities.

A discussion of the Law Commission's Scoping Paper of 2012, where it was noted that the defence had no clearly accepted definition, although the one in **Bratty** was the most often used.

Links to other cases (up to 3 marks) must be relevant and link to **Bratty**, e.g., to discuss the need for an external cause or one 'prone to recur'.

These could include any of the following:

    **Broome v Perkins (must be no control)**

    **Hill v Baxter (act must be involuntary/cause external)**

Sullivan (prone to recur)

Burgess (sleepwalking seen as internal despite Lord Denning's comment)

Quick (External cause but arguably prone to recur)

The remaining 4 marks are for A03 and this requires that you present the above in a logical and coherent way, use relevant material and communicate your points in a clear and effective manner using appropriate legal terminology.

### Question 2

Q2 refers to a quote from the source material as follows:

"Nevertheless, neither the 1991 Act nor the 2004 Act tackles the definition of insanity, and so the stigma of being labelled 'insane' remains".

Discuss the extent to which the law on insanity is unsatisfactory in the light of the above statement.

34 marks

The following guide is just that: a guide. You do not need to include everything but this gives you a range of material to choose from. You should pick out those points that make most sense to you so that you can discuss them confidently. The sample answer and comments should help you to see what you need.

### Assessment Objective 1 – Explanation (16 Marks)

Explain that insanity is defined by the M'Naghten Rules 1843 and that every person is presumed to be sane, unless proved otherwise.

Explain that a 'successful' plea of insanity results in the special verdict of 'guilty by reason of insanity'.

Note that insanity may be raised by the prosecution or judge as well as the defence.

Note that there is an overlap with diminished responsibility but that insanity is a general defence to all crimes, not just murder.

Define the essential elements of the defence of insanity from the M'Naghten Rules

Defect of reason – **Clarke**

Disease of the mind (prone to recur and manifest itself in violence) – **Bratty/Kemp**

Not knowing the nature and quality of the act – **Codere**

Not knowing the act was wrong – **Windle/Johnson**

Consider the role of judges and how the law has developed by reference to linked cases. There will be plenty in the source material and you are expected to *use* the material so be sure to pick out some relevant cases and criticisms from that. However, you should also use other sources too so look back at the chapter on insanity and note how the law has developed and how insanity has been interpreted by judges (refer to the quote in the question as regards the fact that the Acts have offered no definition so the defence is developed by the common law through precedent).

Refer to the relationship between insanity and automatism and the problem for people who suffer illnesses like diabetes and epilepsy, or who sleepwalk, using cases to support your discussion such as **Kemp/Quick/Hennessey/Sullivan/Burgess/Bilton**

Recognise the powers of the courts given under the **Criminal Procedure Insanity Act 1964** as amended by the **Criminal Procedure (Insanity and Unfitness to Plead) Act 1991** and the **Domestic Violence, Crime and Victims Act 2004**. Note that none of these Acts defines insanity, as noted in the quote.

*For Level 5 you need to include 8 relevant cases of which 6 must be developed by reference to the facts and/or the principal as appropriate. You should use material from within the source materials and from other sources.*

### Assessment Objective 2 – evaluation (14 Marks)

In your evaluation, you could discuss the Key criticisms from the study block summary, as far as they are relevant to the question.

> ***There is a problem with finding insanity in respect of people whose conditions are not normally associated with mental disorder, such as the 'diabetes' cases***

> ***The insanity defence originates from an 1843 case and should be updated because of medical advances***

> ***The stigma of an insanity verdict may also mean people who genuinely do have a mental problem do not plead the defence***

> ***The difference between not taking insulin, and taking it but not eating properly, are small but one leads to a defence of insanity and the other to automatism***

> ***The law on both insanity and automatism is unclear, as recognised by the Law Commission in their 2012 scoping paper***

You will need to provide an analytical evaluation of the area of law and with particular focus on the quote. You should develop the material above in A01:

Evaluate the definition of insanity (including the essential elements) and recognise the antiquity of the defence.

Note the 1991 and 2004 Acts amend the judge's role somewhat but do nothing to help explain or define the defence (refer to the quote in the question).

Evaluate the fact that the defence of insanity is not available to people who are aware of their actions but unable to control them, e.g., a psychopath such as Byrne. Note that such a person could use the defence of diminished responsibility (**Coroners and Justice Act 2009**) but only if the charge is murder.

Evaluate the need for medical evidence to establish the defence and the problems for jurors who have to try to understand complex and often conflicting evidence and technical psychiatric terms. (Also, although the final decision lies with the jury, the evidence of experts is likely to be persuasive and they are medical experts not experts in the law.)

Evaluate the reluctance of people to raise the defence because of the social stigma attached to it. (People may plead guilty to a minor offence rather than plead insanity, as in **Sullivan** and **Clarke**.)

Evaluate the problem for people who suffer illnesses like diabetes and epilepsy. Refer to cases such as **Kemp/Quick/Hennessey/Sullivan/Burgess/Bilton**.

Evaluate proposals for reform, e.g., The Butler Committee 1975 and the Law Commission's Draft Criminal Code.

Evaluate the most recent proposals for reform in the Law Commission's scoping paper in 2012.*

Reach a sensible conclusion drawing on your criticisms.

### Assessment Objective 3 – Communication and Presentation (4 Marks)

This requires that you present the above in a logical and coherent way, use relevant material and communicate your points in a clear and effective manner using appropriate legal terminology.

*You could include some of the following from the 'Food for thought' sections to develop these points. A sample conclusion follows these.*

### Food for thought 1

In its 'scoping paper' (a paper setting out what is within the scope of the project) on insanity in 2012, the Law Commission said

"... the law has not adopted a distinction between mental disorders and physical disorders, so that the latter are outside of the scope of the notion of "disease of the mind" in M'Naghten. Instead, it has adopted a distinction between internal and external factors which as we have seen leads to highly illogical results"

In cases like **Bratty** and **Kemp**, the defence of insanity may be appropriate. D's acts were to some extent purposeful and there is a danger to the public. The case of an epileptic thrashing out and hitting someone during a fit would be less easy to justify. There is a problem with finding insanity in respect of people whose conditions are not normally associated with mental disorder. Use the 'diabetes' cases to support a discussion of these problems. **Burgess** is also arguably too wide a definition. Should a sleepwalker be classed as insane? It leads to a second issue. Once insanity is raised – and remember this can be by the prosecution or the judge as well as D – D will often change the plea to guilty to avoid the insanity verdict. This is what happened in **Sullivan**. He pleaded guilty after the judge ruled the defence was insanity and was convicted of actual bodily harm. In **Quick**, on the other hand, the defect was held to be caused by the insulin itself. D's appeal succeeded because the defence of automatism should have been left to the jury.

A final point is that the stigma of an insanity verdict may also mean people who genuinely do have a mental problem do not plead the defence.

### Food for thought 2

The defence originates from an 1843 case and it is argued that because of medical advances it should be updated. Judges themselves have called for Parliament to look at the insanity defence.

There are arguments that the law could breach Article 5 of the European Convention on Human Rights which states that a person of unsound mind can only be detained where proper objective medical expertise has been sought.

The 1953 Royal Commission on Capital Punishment recommended the abolishment of the **M'Naghten Rules**. **The Homicide Act 1957** introduced diminished responsibility shortly after this which addressed some of the criticisms made. In 1975, the Butler Committee favoured replacing the rules with a new verdict of 'mental disorder'. This would arise where D was suffering from a 'severe mental illness' or 'severe mental handicap'. The burden of proof would also move to the prosecution.

The Law Commission's Draft Code adopted many of Butler's recommendations and specifically accepted that sleepwalking and spasms should come within automatism rather than insanity. The Commission made some further recommendations in 1995 but these were not acted on, and they identified insanity as an area in need of reform again in 2008. In their 2012 scoping paper, it was noted that the law lagged behind psychiatric understanding. The LC also said "English law has adopted an unusually, and arguably unjustifiably, narrow interpretation of the 'wrongfulness' limb" as interpreted in **Windle**. Another point made in the 2012 paper was that the defence was very rarely used, but it was accepted that this did not necessarily mean it did not need attention; on the contrary, it was noted that the complexity of the law and the out-of-date tests were part of the reason for the lack of use. A project has been set up to consider the responses to the scoping paper in order to identify "better and more up-to-date legal tests".

## Food for thought 3

As Lord Denning said in **Bratty**, a disease of the mind was *"any mental disorder which has manifested itself in violence and is prone to recur"*. If it is 'prone to recur' then D is a continuing danger to society. It is therefore right that insanity rather than automatism should be the defence, because automatism results in an acquittal. However, this does lead to inconsistency and arguably it would be better if automatism was a partial defence. The huge difference in the effect of the pleas of insanity and automatism is hard to justify.

## Food for thought 4

The CA in **Quick** implied that failing to eat makes automatism self-induced. It was not fully clear as they merely held that the defence of automatism should have been left to the jury. In **Bailey**, the same court suggested that whilst drink or drugs would mean the defect is self-induced, failing to eat would not. This leaves the law insufficiently clear.

The rules on insanity and automatism have led to sleepwalkers and diabetics being labelled insane – sometimes. The difference between not taking insulin, and taking it but not eating properly, is small but has a major consequence. The result is either that D is found insane or goes free.

In **Quick**, Lawton LJ said that the defence was a "quagmire of law seldom entered nowadays save by those in desperate need of some kind of defence". Not very reassuring!

## Sample conclusion

You could include a relevant quote from the source material or from the Law Commission. Here is a conclusion using the Law Commission's comment in its scoping paper and referring to the quote in the question.

"As the quote states, neither the 1991 Act nor the 2004 Act defines insanity, and so the stigma of being labelled insane is still a problem, as described above. Neither the Butler Committee recommendations nor the Law Commission Draft Code has been acted upon, so the law has developed by precedent alone. This does not seem to have produced a satisfactory result. In its scoping paper in 2012 the Law Commission said English law has adopted an "unusually, and arguably unjustifiably" narrow interpretation of the 'wrongfulness' limb" and also that it has adopted a distinction between internal and external factors which led to "highly illogical results". This is highlighted above in cases such as **Quick** and **Hennessey**. The development of the law by judges has therefore not led to a clear definition of insanity and it is to be hoped that Parliament will address the matter when the Law Commission finishes its new project and suggests further reforms".

## Question 3

*Note that you should use the source materials and your own knowledge when answering the questions. Remember you need to have a clear conclusion (more than 50% commitment).*

Consider whether a defence of insanity or automatism is most likely in each of the following situations:

(a) Samia sets off on a long journey to visit relatives. She has been driving her car on the motorway for several hours when she hits another car that has broken down on the side of the road. The driver of the other car, William, is injured in the crash, breaking his arm. Samia says she cannot remember crashing into the other car as she was in a 'trance-like' state. 10 marks

(b) Molly is sitting outside a café eating her lunch. She is disturbed by a wasp which flies around her making her panic. Quickly, in an attempt to get rid of the wasp, Molly tries to hit it with her hand. Instead she hits another customer, Pablo, in the face causing a bruise to his cheek. 10 marks

(c) Sylvia has been diagnosed with diabetes. She has been told by her doctor that she must inject herself twice a day with insulin to control her condition. One day she does not take her insulin. Later that afternoon she takes a purse and a mobile telephone belonging to her colleague, Davinder. Sylvia cannot remember anything about the events that occurred that afternoon. 10 marks

*For each part question there are 3 marks available for the critical point, 6 for other applied points and 1 for the conclusion. So you need a discussion of the critical point (the definition of the defence plus a brief explanation of it), application (two or three points) of the relevant law to the facts using a case in support and a sustainable conclusion (that is backed up by the supporting case). As mentioned, there is no sample answer for these short scenarios but inclusion of all the following points would put the answers in Level 5.*

### Assessment Objective 1 – Knowledge (10 marks)

Explain the defence of insanity using the **M'Naghten Rules**: D must show that at the time of the act 'he was labouring under such a defect of reason, from a disease of the mind, as to not know the nature and quality of the act or if he did, he didn't know what he was doing was wrong'.

Note the defence is proven on a balance of probabilities and results in a verdict of 'not guilty by reason of insanity'.

Explain automatism using the definition in **Bratty** as 'an act done by the muscles without any control by the mind, such as a spasm, a reflex action or a convulsion; or an act done by a person who is not conscious of what he is doing'.

Note that the cause of the act must be external and that the defence will not succeed where D still retains some control.

**Assessment Objective 2 – Application (20 marks)**

Note that there are twice as many marks for A02 so the focus is on your *use* of knowledge, i.e., whether you apply the law accurately and reach a logical and supported conclusion.

**(a)** There is no internal factor so the most likely defence is automatism.

Explain that automatism can only be used as a defence if Samia's action of crashing into William's car was involuntary. For Samia to plead automatism her act must be 'an act done by the muscles without any control by the mind, such as a spasm, a reflex action or a convulsion; or an act done by a person who is not conscious of what he is doing' (you can just refer to the Source material here – **Bratty**).

Explain that the cause of the actions must be external and that the external factor must be something that she had no control over – **Hill v Baxter**.

Explain that she may argue that the monotony of the road caused her trance-like state but that if she retained some control this argument will fail because there must be a 'total destruction of voluntary control' – **AG's Ref (No.2 of 1992)**.

Consider whether Samia's actions of continuing to drive for so long could mean that any loss of control was self-induced. A self-induced incapacity will not excuse – **Quick**.

Conclude that as the facts are similar to those of **AG's Ref (No.2 of 1992)** the defence will fail.

**(b)** Identify that the cause here is an external factor so automatism is the most likely defence. Explain that automatism can only be used as a defence if Molly's action of hitting Pablo was involuntary – **Hill v Baxter**.

Explain that for Molly to plead automatism her act must be 'an act done by the muscles without any control by the mind, such as a spasm, a reflex action or a convulsion; or an act done by a person who is not conscious of what he is doing' (again you can just refer to the Source material here – **Bratty**).

Explain that the cause of Molly's actions must be external in and that this could something like being attacked by a swarm of bees, the hypothetical example given in **Hill v Baxter**.

In Molly's case the *actus reus* was not voluntary, it was a reflex action to an external factor, the wasp.

Discuss whether Molly's actions were simply reduced and/or whether she retained some control of her actions. There must be a 'total destruction of voluntary control' – **AG's Ref (No.2 of 1992)**. If she had a choice, e.g., of taking evasive action by moving away (which would not be so easy in a car, the example used in **Hill v Baxter**) she could fail in this defence. Because she did not take evasive action, it is possible that her actions could be seen as self-induced.

Conclude that despite this, as the facts are close to the example given in **Hill v Baxter** and her hitting at the wasp seemed to be a reflex action, she is most likely to succeed. (*Note that this is sufficiently clear as it shows more than 50% commitment.*)

**(c)** Identify that Sylvia could use either defence depending on whether the factor causing her actions was internal or external.

Explain that the fact that Sylvia has been told by her doctor she must take the insulin twice a day means that even if automatism applied it is likely to be seen as self-induced – **Quick**.

Explain that as she did not take her insulin the cause was the diabetes and so internal – **Hennessey**. Insanity is therefore the appropriate defence.

Explain that she will be presumed sane so will have to prove all of the elements under the **M'Naghten Rules**, on a balance of probabilities.

Sylvia must be suffering from a 'defect of reason'. There has to be a complete deprivation of the powers of reason rather than simply a failure to exercise them. Temporary absentmindedness is not a defect of reason – **Clarke**. Explain that although the facts here appear similar **Clarke** may not be followed because in **Clarke** it was only absent-mindedness, whereas here she has not taken her insulin which caused a hyperglycaemic episode.

The 'defect of reason' must be caused by a 'disease of the mind'. This was defined in **Bratty** by Lord Denning as 'any mental disorder which has manifested itself in violence and is prone to recur'. Identify that this is possible if she fails to take her insulin again.

Explain that the physical state of the brain is irrelevant, it is whether her mental faculties of reasoning are impaired that is Important – **Kemp**.

The disease of the mind must prevent her from knowing the 'nature and quality' of her act or that it was 'wrong'. This means legally, and not just 'morally' wrong – **Windle/Johnson**. She does not remember anything so presumably did not know the 'nature and quality' of her act.

Conclude that, as in **Hennessey**, the cause was the diabetes itself, an internal factor and so a finding of insanity is likely.

### Middle level answers for Questions 1 and 2 and how to improve them

*As you read the answers consider how they could be improved in light of the above. There is a comment at the end of each on how to develop the answer to achieve the highest level.*

### Question 1

The definition of automatism comes from Lord Denning's judgment in that case (Source 5). He said that 'the requirement that it should be a voluntary act is essential' and that 'no act is punishable if it is done involuntarily' (line 4). He then described an involuntary act as an act which is done by the muscles without any control by the mind such as a spasm, a reflex action or a convulsion; or an act done by a person who is not conscious of what he is doing such as an act done whilst suffering from concussion or whilst sleepwalking' (lines 6-8). Thus the act must be caused by an external factor, as in Quick, but this may not include sleepwalking, as decided in Burgess. It must also be 'without any control'. This shows that it is not automatism if the lack of control was not total and this was followed in Attorney-General's Reference (No2 of 1992) 1994 where a driver failed in the defence.

There are two types of automatism, insane and non-insane automatism. The first is commonly just called insanity. Lord Denning said, also in Bratty, that insanity is a mental disorder which has 'manifested itself in violence and is prone to recur'. This suggests that insanity is the appropriate defence where there is a continuing danger, as in Hennessey.

In the Law Commission's Scoping Paper of 2012, it was noted that the definition in Bratty was the most often used showing it was indeed important to the development of the defence. However the Law Commission also noted that the defence had no clearly accepted definition, so Lord Denning's comment did not set a precedent which has then been followed consistently.

### Comment

*This is a middle-level answer including the critical point with some analysis in the first paragraph, and briefly developing two further points. It could be improved by better reference to the question (as in the last paragraph but not elsewhere) and greater development of the cases. A brief conclusion is also needed.*

*The following comments expand on the answer to reach Level 5.*

*Add the following to the beginning of paragraph one.*

The case of Bratty is relevant to the development of the law of automatism because ….

*Add the following in paragraph one after Burgess, this develops the point and links the cases to Bratty.*

In **Quick**, a diabetic took insulin but failed to eat and this caused him to attack someone. The insulin was said to be an external factor, unlike in **Hennessey** where he failed to take the insulin so the act was caused by the diabetes, an internal factor. However, in **Burgess**, a sleepwalker was deemed insane even though Lord Denning referred to sleepwalking as an external factor in **Bratty**. This indicates that the law can be inconsistent and **Bratty** has not sufficiently clarified it.

*Add the following to the end of paragraph two.*

This differentiates it from automatism which can be a one-off occurrence and is another reason the case is important to the development of the defence. If there is a continuing danger, or as Lord Denning put it the act is 'prone to recur' it will be insanity rather than automatism. This may seem unfair in cases of people with diabetes or epilepsy but if they cannot control what they do, they present a continuing danger to other people. In **Hennessey** he was partly at fault in not taking his insulin so arguably it is right that automatism failed as a defence. Even in **Burgess**, although it may seem unfair, sleepwalking is 'prone to recur' so there is a continuing danger as Lord Lane CJ pointed out in his judgment (Source 3 lines 19-20 and 33-36).

*Add the following to the end of paragraph three to improve the conclusion.*

This suggests that **Bratty** has not been as significant to the development of the law as Lord Denning might have hoped. Also, as noted above, the Law Commission said the distinction made in **Bratty** led to "highly illogical results". So although **Bratty** had an important role to play in the development of automatism, the defence should be further developed by Parliament to provide a clearer definition.

**Note**

*I have included the definitions from Source 5 but if you are short of time you can just refer to the line numbers as I did later with Source 3. This reference is to Lord Lane CJ's judgment in* **Burgess** *as follows:*

Source 3 lines 19-20 "if there is a danger of recurrence that may be an added reason for categorising the condition as a disease of the mind".

Source 3 lines 33-36 "It was a disorder or abnormality which might recur, though the possibility of it recurring in the form of serious violence was unlikely. Therefore since this was a legal problem to be decided on legal principles, it seems to us that on those principles the answer was as the judge found it to be".

**Question 2**

Insanity is defined by the M'Naghten Rules 1843. Every person is presumed to be sane, unless proved otherwise. To prove otherwise there are several factors to consider. Firstly, there must be a defect of reason – Clarke. This must be caused by a disease of the mind (prone to recur and manifest itself in violence) – Bratty/Kemp. Also D must not know the nature and quality of the act – Codere or that it was wrong – Windle/Johnson

As the quote in the question states, the 1991 and 2004 Acts do nothing to help explain or define the defence so it is left to judges to develop the law through precedent. Although Lord Denning offered a definition in Bratty (Source 5 lines 4-8) this has not always been consistently applied. There is a problem with finding insanity where the condition does not seem to be a mental disorder. The stigma of an insanity verdict may also mean people who genuinely do have a mental problem do not plead the defence or change their plea to guilty if the prosecution or judge bring up the defence. It is perhaps also unsatisfactory that insanity may be raised by the prosecution or judge as well as the defence.

The CA in Quick implied that failing to eat makes automatism self-induced. It was not fully clear as they merely held that the defence of automatism should have been left to the jury. In Bailey, the same court suggested that whilst drink or drugs would mean the defect is self-induced, failing to eat would not.

The insanity defence originates from an 1843 case and should be updated because medical knowledge has changed since then. If either the 1991 or the 2004 Act had provided a definition this could have taken into account medical advances since 1843. This should not be left to development by judges because they do not have the necessary medical knowledge. As pointed out in Source 2 line 17, the definition of insanity is a legal not a medical one. A project has been set up by the Law Commission to consider the responses to the 2012 scoping paper in order to identify "better and more up-to-date legal tests". If a test were to be suggested then Parliament should pass an Act that defines insanity, which it failed to do in the 1991 and 2004 Acts mentioned in the question. In Quick, Lawton LJ said that the defence was a "quagmire of law seldom entered nowadays save by those in desperate need of some kind of defence". The Law Commission also recognised the law was rarely used but said that this did not necessarily mean it did not need attention; on the contrary, it was noted that the complexity of the law and the out-of-date tests were part of the reason for the lack of use.

The defence of insanity is not available to people who are aware of their actions but unable to control them e.g., a psychopath such as Byrne. A person like Byrne seems to fit the label of insane far more than a diabetic or sleepwalker. Although Byrne could use the defence of diminished responsibility (Coroners and Justice Act 2009) this only applies if the charge is murder. In cases like Bratty and Kemp, the defence of insanity may be appropriate. D's acts were to some extent purposeful and there is a danger to the public because they are 'prone to recur'. If an act is 'prone to recur' then D is a continuing danger to society. It is therefore right that insanity rather than automatism should be the defence, because automatism results in an acquittal. As Lord Lane CJ said (Source 3 line 20), if there is a danger of recurrence that may be an added reason for categorising the condition as a disease of the mind, what Lord Denning called the 'continuing danger' theory. However there is still a problem in that the huge difference in the effect of the pleas of insanity and automatism is hard to justify.

## Comment

*Level 5 requires 8 relevant cases of which 6 must be developed by reference to the facts and/or the principal as appropriate. Here there are 8 cases but few are developed. The answer is excellent towards the end but the mark scheme sets clear limits on what can be achieved*

*without using additional relevant case. It is important to bear this in mind because an otherwise perfect answer without sufficient cases cannot reach Level 5.*

*There needs to be more evaluation of the definition of insanity and the essential elements. Add the following to the end of the first paragraph.*

In **Clarke**, it was held that temporary absent-mindedness did not amount to a defect of reason. It must be a defect caused by a disease of the mind and this usually requires that the act is 'prone to recur and manifest itself in violence' as Lord Denning said in **Bratty**.

*There is reference to the question but it could be a little better developed. Add a case example of plea – changing, e.g., **Sullivan** and then the following to the end of paragraph 2.*

It is unsatisfactory that people who suffer illnesses like diabetes and epilepsy, or who sleepwalk, are labelled as insane. As the quote says, the stigma remains. There seemed little difference in the cases of **Quick** and **Hennessey** but one was acquitted and the other found insane. Cases like this highlight the relationship between insanity and automatism. The difference between not taking insulin, and taking it but not eating properly, is small but one leads to being labelled as insane and the other to automatism and complete acquittal. Many people would see this as unjust.

*Paragraph 3 provides a glimpse of why the law is unsatisfactory but could use a little development, add the following.*

This leaves the law insufficiently clear which is not satisfactory. Similarly, in **Burgess** a sleepwalker was found insane but not in **Bilton**. The rules of precedent, especially stare decisis, should ensure consistency in the law but this is not the case. If the law is inconsistent justice cannot be achieved.

*Paragraph 4 contains a well-developed analysis of the problems with reference to the question, the source and to two relevant quotes, one from the Law Commission and one from a judge. This cannot be improved on.*

*Paragraph 5 is also well developed and just needs rounding off. Add the following (you can use the one given above in the guide instead; this amends that one so that it follows on from the candidate's mid-level answer).*

Despite the lapse of time, neither the Butler Committee nor the Law Commission recommendations have been acted upon, so the law has developed by precedent alone. This does not seem to have produced a satisfactory result. As the Law Commission noted in 2012, the tests are out of date and this is part of the reason for the lack of use of the defence. As the quote notes, neither the 1991 Act nor the 2004 Act tackles the definition of insanity. It is therefore time for Parliament to act and provide a legal test that also takes into account the views of the medical profession as to what amounts to insanity in the twenty-first century.

All these abbreviations are commonly used. You may use them in an examination answer, but should write them in full the first time e.g., write 'actual bodily harm (ABH)' and then after that you can just write 'ABH', similarly with the defendant (D) and the victim (V).

Case names should be in full the first time but can be shortened in later use if they are lengthy.

**General**

Draft Code – A Criminal Code for England and Wales (Law Commission No. 177), 1989

CCRC Criminal Cases Review Commission

ABH actual bodily harm

GBH grievous bodily harm

D defendant

C claimant

V Victim

CA Court of Appeal

HL House of Lords

SC Supreme Court

**Acts**

S – section (thus s1 Theft Act 1968 refers to section 1 of that Act)

s1 (2) means section 1 subsection 2 of an Act

OAPA – Offences against the Person Act 1861

OLA – Occupier's Liability Act

**In cases (these don't need to be written in full)**

CC (at beginning) chief constable

CC (at end) county council

BC borough council

DC district council

LBC London borough council

AHA Area Health Authority

**Judges and other legal personnel (these don't need to be written in full)**

J Justice

LJ Lord Justice

LCJ Lord Chief Justice

LC Lord Chancellor

VC Vice Chancellor

AG Attorney General

CPS Crown Prosecution Service

DPP Director of Public Prosecutions

AG Attorney General

## Acknowledgements

We are grateful to the Oxford, Cambridge and RSA Examinations (OCR) Board for examination questions

Note: Where worked solutions to, and/or commentaries on questions or possible answers are provided it is the author who is responsible for them. They have not been provided or approved by OCR and do not necessarily constitute the only possible solutions.

I am also grateful to my husband Dave for many hours of proof reading and for his hard work on the diagrams.

Printed in Great Britain
by Amazon